MW01028912

PRAISE FOR *THE FORENSIC*

"It's hard to believe that an accountant can write a book about accounting and have it be a page-turner, but that's exactly what Paul Regan's *The Forensic* is. It reads like a well-conceived mystery novel, but details a true story of intrigue, criminal activity and obfuscation of the law. When the facts of the fraudulent financial activity are augmented with the mystery of Howard Hughes' clandestine lifestyle, the story rises to the level of a thriller. Regan has taken what is usually a boring subject and turned it into a very exciting read."

—*BRIAN PETER BRINIG, JD, CPA, LAW PROFESSOR, FORENSIC ACCOUNTANT, AUTHOR*

"A fascinating, real-life tale of old Hollywood glamor and CIA intrigue. This period of US history has always fascinated me and learning about the details of Howard Hughes and his very own spy games drives home how influential Hughes was. A flawed, but charismatic man, Hughes has captured many people's imaginations, and the author uses that fact to weave an engaging retelling of events. Most importantly, Paul Regan bravely pursued justice and made it so money couldn't buy a billionaire out of his problems."

—*KATHERINE COOPER, ENGINEER, AUTHOR, AND NUCLEAR INDUSTRY ADVOCATE*

"*The Forensic* reminds financial enthusiasts the vital role that scrutiny, the process of checks and balances, must play, in opposition to the myopic worship of wealth."

—MARCIA ELIZABETH CHRISTIAN FAVALE,
RESTRUCTURING AND FINANCE EXPERT

"Every sentence has the reader asking herself 'what's next' as the details come to light of a virtuous CPA and his path that crossed Howard Hughes. Coupled with fascinating historical facts that paint a detailed picture for the reader, this story keeps you on the edge of your seat and constantly rooting for the success of Paul Regan, who knew little of what this mission would encompass when he first encountered the bombastic and greedy Hughes."

—KATHRYN BURMEISTER, ESQ,
AUTHOR OF OVERCOMING ADDICTION
TO THE STATUS QUO

"Just when you thought you knew everything about the extremely strange life of Howard Hughes. Thank you, Paul Regan, for this fascinating read!"

—TRACE J. SHERER, ESQ. MEDIATOR,
AUTHOR OF NERVES OF STEEL

"Paul brilliantly captures a moment in time when the forces of greed, corruption and power can no longer stand up, when facing the dogged work and tenacity of two honest and bright people. It's the moment we all swoon for and deserve."

—STEFANIE OLSEN,
CONTRIBUTING EDITOR, NARRATIVE MAGAZINE

"Paul captures the essence of John Clark, who had a strong sense of justice and was only emboldened by the type of bullying tactics that he and Paul both lived through during the case. John was a brilliant lawyer and a bulldog when it came to getting at the truth. He taught me as a young lawyer to let the facts tell the story and, in that regard, he was very similar to Paul. Together, they were a dynamic duo, able to cut through all the obstructions and coverups, and successfully unwind a very complex set of facts and circumstances to expose Hughes and his fraudulent enterprise."

—STEPHEN J. FOWLER, PROTÉGÉ,
FORMER LAW PARTNER AND FRIEND

"A great story and a primer on smart, creative lawyering and deep-dive forensic accounting. John Clark and Paul Regan school Howard Hughes on how to bring down even the wealthiest, most stubborn opponent."

—ROBERT B. THUM, PARTNER, PILLSBURY
WINTHROP SHAW PITTMAN LLP

THE
FORENSIC

THE
FORENSIC

How the CIA,
a Brilliant Attorney
and a Young CPA
Brought Down
Howard Hughes

PAUL REGAN

DEDICATION

To my mentor, John Bales Clark, Esq. It was John's guidance, integrity, and skills that inspired and guided my career in forensic accounting. And to Barbara, my wife of more than fifty years, who has provided me with the love and support to succeed in the extreme stress and high-stakes world of complex business litigation and related frauds. Without her love and support, my career would not have been possible.

TABLE OF CONTENTS

ACKNOWLEDGEMENTS

Writing a memoir that is entertaining is much more difficult than I ever dreamed. For this book, many lent their considerable effort and skills and I thank them for their attention and caring. Those friends, family and colleagues include: my wife, Barby; my sisters-in-law, Margaret and Pat; my daughter, Courtney; my nieces, Stephanie and Megan; as well as my friend, Stefanie Olsen. Finally, to Candi Cross of You Talk I Write. In this case, I wrote and Candi edited by adding life and "pop" to my words, and carving out parts that were not necessary to the heart of my story. I sincerely thank each of these wonderful people for their fine contributions to this story.

FOREWORD

Stories of the bad guys, their greed and corruption pervade our news: the CEOs with seven-figure salaries while their stocks collapse, the politicians whose sole motivation is maintaining their power. Still, there are the stories we hear less often, stories of altruistic present-day Davids, who, armed with little more than a slingshot, stand bravely before a towering Goliath. This is one such story of a young man armed with only a pencil and his accounting ledgers as he topples the billionaire, Howard Hughes, and his bulldog lawyer, Chester Davis.

Forensic accounting is the investigation of financial records to discover whether they have been manipulated for fraudulent purposes. In 1932, an IRS accountant was one of the first to use forensic accounting when he investigated the infamous gangster, Al Capone, and discovered that Capone owed the government over $200,000 in unpaid taxes. Al Capone was not sentenced to prison for his bootlegging syndicate nor for his multiple vicious murders, but for simple tax evasion. During the years that followed, forensic accounting was mainly used by lawyers to augment settlements in celebrity divorce cases. Today, it has a much broader use thanks to one of the leading experts in the field of forensic accounting in complex business litigation, Paul Regan. In his fifty-year career, Paul has testified in more than 125 trials and arbitrations and worked on more than 1,000 complex litigation matters.

I met Paul in 1963 on the evening of my older sister, Barbara's junior prom when he arrived as her blind date. After he brought her home that night, he drove off beeping the horn of his blue VW bug. From that day on, his VW and distinctive late-night honks were permanent fixtures in our family's life. My father, however, had his doubts about the young man who was captivating his family. Through high school, Paul had been more interested in having a good time than being a serious academic student. He had the Irish gift of storytelling and an exuberant laugh that was contagious, and his goal was to become a professional bowler. True, he was quite accomplished, having bowled several perfect games, but the bowling circuit was not my father's plan for his daughter's future. Not even my father's objections, however, could diminish Paul's enthusiasm.

In their junior year of college, while he and Barbara attended the University of San Francisco Paul found his vocation in accounting. From that time on, he excelled in all his classes. He found he could solve the puzzles within the numbers and then easily elucidate them for others. He could also apply his remarkable memory, unswerving focus, and a steadfast moral compass. On his graduation with honors from USF in 1968, Paul immediately began working at Peat, Marwick, and Mitchell, one of the "big eight" International CPA firms that had sought him out earlier in the fall. He and Barbara married within a week, and shortly thereafter, he was designated the "in-charge" for the Air West Airlines account. Little did anyone know that this account would lead him straight into the jaws of evil.

The audit by Paul and his team took place during a critical time in the life of the airline. In the spring of 1968, Air West was formed through the merger of West Coast, Pacific, and Bonanza Airlines. It was immediately courted by the billionaire, Howard Hughes, who wanted to acquire his own airline with a hub in Las Vegas, where he had invested millions in hotels, casinos, and real estate. In December 1968, after months of negotiations and pressure from Hughes, an agreement was reached. Hughes would take on all the airline's assets and liabilities and pay the share-holders an agreed-upon amount. The actual closing, however, did not occur until the end of March 1970. Because of the delay in the closing, in December 1969, Paul and his team returned to Air West's headquarters for the audit of its 1969 financial statements. Then early in 1971, Paul returned alone to audit Air West's 1970 records for the three months ending March 30, 1970. It was during this audit that Paul noticed massive irregularities, accounting entries by Hughes' accountants that violated the purchase agreement and cheated the Air West shareholders out of millions. He realized the shareholders needed legal counsel, which led him to John Clark, who had recently been named one of California's "super lawyers." Their partnership on the Air West case, pitting them against one of the most powerful, greedy, and unscrupulous men in the world, was just the beginning of a lifelong friendship in their efforts to bring down the bad guys.

During this pandemic year, while many of us were binging on food and old movies, Paul decided to delve into his first case and write a book about it in honor of his friend, John Clark, who died in the summer of 2019. Applying the same relentless research he used in his professional life, he uncovered a mine of information, including newly released CIA files. In so doing, he discovered that the case involved the CIA, the FBI, a Russian nuclear submarine, grand theft, assault with a deadly weapon, and much more. In this book, Paul recounts the most thrilling story of his life. Read on and enjoy!

Margaret Scott
Former Head of The Girls' Middle School, Palo Alto, CA
Former Upper School Head of The Spence School, NY, NY
July 2021

PORTRAIT OF A GENTLEMAN WHO WINS CASES

"Don't raise your voice. Improve your argument."

—*DESMOND TUTU*

J OHN B. CLARK, Esq. received an academic scholarship to Stanford Law School and earned his law degree in 1961. He joined the international law firm of Sullivan and Cromwell in New York upon graduation and began a successful and expansive international career as an attorney, mediator, and arbitrator. Most importantly, his colleagues described him as "a gentleman who wins cases." As a lawyer, he was a truth finder who practiced with integrity and passion. His clients and those working with him loved him for his caring, honesty, and fairness.

The truth finder was my friend, mentor, and fierce leader in the fight to take down Howard R. Hughes Jr. and his long-time and pugnacious attorney, Chester Davis. Together, we were unwavering in our dedication to restoring what was wrongfully taken from our clients.

This book mostly unfolds in the late 1960s and early 1970s. However, it does walk through portions of Hughes's amazing life experiences that resulted in his being one of the world's wealthiest and intriguing men, while also a man obsessed with greed, control, and selfishness. His Roy Cohn-like attorney, Chester Davis, was fixated on his loyalty to Hughes, and winning for him at all costs. Encountering him in court, I found him to be a loud, boisterous, rowdy man intent on destroying those standing between him and his success.

At the age of twenty-one, I was thrust into this story when I was too young to realize that I was to do battle with giants, at least two of whom breathed fire. I had just graduated, with honors, from college and married my high school sweetheart, Barbara. We now have three children, two daughters-in-law and a son-in-law, plus five grandchildren. We were married one week after we both graduated from the University of San Francisco and one week before I began my career in the San Francisco office of one of the then "Big 8" international CPA firms in the world.

My mother was a fantastic math teacher and instilled an affinity in me for how numbers are processed and how they can be used to find and present interconnected facts. My grandfather, Daniel Patrick Regan, was a California senator from the San Francisco Bay Area, while my father was an elected union official for the International Longshore and Warehouse Union. Grandpa was a Republican, Dad was Democratic. They were a study in contrasts. I helped put myself through college by working summers and holiday breaks with the longshoremen on the docks of San Francisco. With the confidence and support instilled in me by John and Barby, I, too, went on to hold elected office serving ten years on the town of Hillsborough's school board, twelve years on its town council, as well as its mayor. Then in 2002, I was elected to chair the then 30,000-member California Society of CPAs.

This story evolves into a battle fought by John and me as we unraveled an injustice perpetrated by Hughes and Davis on the shareholders of Air West, Inc. Along this journey, there was a parallel track involving the CIA, the Department of Justice and a Soviet submarine carrying nuclear missiles. The connection between mine and Clark's journey, the CIA, and the Soviet submarine was coincidental; however, without that connection, our careers may not have been as golden as they became. This secret connection, and our efforts to use it to sink Howard Hughes have been told to only a very few, until this book.

John married his high school sweetheart, Susanne, in 1964, and they raised six children. He had a wonderful combination of intellect, curiosity, sense of humor, street smarts, integrity, and wit, all with no apparent ego. He commanded the respect of friends, colleagues, and opponents alike. He died at age eighty-two. It was at the honoring of his life on July 20, 2019, at his ranch in Aspen, Colorado that I was inspired to write this book to honor the memory of this wonderful gentleman, friend, mentor, and colleague.

While this book is based upon historical events and persons, it is not always a precise history of the events and persons presented. The timing of events and some of the names of participants have been changed and portrayed to better suit the story's convenience and presentation. The opinions expressed within this book are based on my own understanding.

CHAPTER 1

A SHARK IN HOLLYWOOD

"Money is like love; it kills slowly and painfully
the one who withholds it and enlivens the
other who turns it on his fellow man."

—*KAHLIL GIBRAN*

I T'S EASY TO forget that Hollywood, California was once ranch land in the 1800s. By the time newly minted millionaire Howard Hughes arrived from Houston with stars in his eyes, he encountered a very different Hollywood; the epicenter of the silent film era and one that could surely benefit—or be swallowed whole—from his bankroll.

Hughes had no interest in running the day-to-day operations of Hughes Tool Company ("Toolco"), the wildly lucrative drilling and manufacturing company he had inherited from his father when he was eighteen. Instead, he wanted to bring in someone to run Toolco that he had personally picked and would control. While Hughes was visiting in Los Angeles, he began to interview candidates. After another morning round of golf, Hughes interviewed a brilliant 36-year-old certified public accountant named

Noah Dietrich. At the time, Dietrich was working for the international certified public accounting and consulting firm, Haskins & Sells ("H&S").

Hughes and Dietrich were a collection of contrasts. Dietrich craved to understand how companies operated and how he could make them more profitable. Hughes had no interest in solving operational issues, he wanted the money that the company made. Dietrich liked to solve problems, while Hughes wanted someone else to solve them so he could play golf or make movies. Dietrich was a stocky five-foot-seven, which meant that the lanky six-foot 4-inch Hughes towered over him physically and psychologically.

At one point during their interview, they spoke about Hughes's golf game. Hughes handed Dietrich his scorecard from the round he had completed just before the interview. Though the scorecard showed his score for each hole, it had not been totaled. Dietrich briefly reviewed the scores, then complemented Hughes on his score of 2-over par. Hughes was so impressed by Dietrich's quick math that the interview concluded. Although Dietrich had clinched the job, Hughes did not let on that he had made up his mind. He dismissed Dietrich from the interview after Dietrich initiated a brief discussion of Toolco's business and its history. Dietrich returned to his work at H&S thinking that his interview was a failure.

A few weeks later when Hughes called Dietrich at H&S, without any comments about his being hired, Howard told Dietrich he needed to prepare for and attend an important meeting at Toolco in Houston. With that, Dietrich assumed that he had been hired, and his strange journey with Hughes began.

It did not take Hughes long to be pleased with his hire. Dietrich was a quick study and made reliable, practical business decisions that were good for Toolco's profits and Hughes's growing fortune. In fact, after Hughes left Toolco with Dietrich in-charge, he and Dietrich generally only communicated on significant issues (or what issues were thought by Hughes to be important), in memos, or by telephone. Dietrich retired from Toolco in 1957 after serving as its CEO for thirty-two years. However, even after his retirement, Dietrich continued to oversee and make key decisions for Toolco, and Hughes, until 1970.

With Dietrich in place at Toolco, Hughes and his first wife, socialite Ella Rice of prestigious Rice University roots, promptly left Houston and moved to Los Angeles. Hughes wanted to pursue his desire to become a movie producer. He decided that the fastest route to that goal, was to spend more time with his uncle, Rupert Hughes, who was now a successful screenwriter in Hollywood.

Upon arrival in Los Angeles, the newlyweds moved into a bungalow at the Ambassador Hotel, a mecca for movie stars dripping with glamor and opulence. Not long after that, Hughes tasked Dietrich to find a suitable home for he and Ella, even though Dietrich was busy in Houston running Toolco. When it came to doing work that did not interest him, the Hughes motto became, "Noah can do it." Following an extensive search, a Spanish-style hacienda home with five bedrooms plus two maids' rooms was found. The home was located on S. Muirfield Road in Hancock Park. Importantly, it was located directly across from the ninth green of the Los Angeles Wilshire Country Club. Howard's needs had been met.

With Ella settled into the home on S. Muirfield Road, Howard started a movie production company. He had Dietrich amend the charter of a Toolco subsidiary so that it could make movies. It operated under the name Caddo. After producing successful movies using the name Caddo, Hughes changed its name to Hughes Productions. He enjoyed having his name within the name of companies he owned. He quickly became an infamous playboy. At this time, Hughes was consumed by golfing, producing successful movies, nightclubbing with actresses, driving expensive cars, and often "forgetting" to go home.

Besides making movies, playing golf, and playing the field with beautiful actresses, Hughes was fascinated by everything about airplanes. He had loved them since he was a child and learned to fly as a teenager after his father's death. In the late 1920s, he directed and flew a plane in the successful WWI thriller that he produced titled, "Hell's Angels," which starred sex symbol Jean Harlow. "Hell's Angels" boldly combined Hughes's passions at the time: women, movie making, and aviation. For more than two years, Hughes labored on "Hell's Angels," often working twenty-four- and sometimes thirty-six-hour stretches at a time. His constant absences from the house on Muirfield Road and rumors of his playboy lifestyle, proved too much for his wife. Ella left Hughes and returned to Houston, filing for divorce in 1929, after only four years of marriage.

YOUNG HOWARD HUGHES, PORTRAIT, CIRCA 1930. SOURCE: GLASSHOUSE IMAGES / ALAMY STOCK PHOTO.

During a flight over the set of "Hell's Angels," Hughes crashed his plane. The crash resulted in a piece of metal lodging in his skull. The metal piece, which was never removed, caused migraine headaches and erratic and bizarre behavior that continued throughout his life.

HOWARD HUGHES STANDING BY HIS H-1 SILVER BULLET HOLDING HIS PILOT'S HELMET CIRCA 1935. SOURCE: PICTURELUX / THE HOLLYWOOD ARCHIVE / ALAMY STOCK PHOTO.

Thousands of people gathered for the premiere of "Hell's Angels" in Hollywood in 1930. The enigmatic Houstonian now had fame and fortune in Hollywood. The movie received an Academy Award nomination for "Best Cinematography" and made Hughes a movie mogul. Hughes's life by the ripe age of twenty-five was glorious.

In all, Hughes produced or presented twenty-eight star-studded films, including:

- "Hell's Angels" (Jean Harlow)
- "Scarface" (George Raft, Boris Karloff)
- "The Outlaw" (Jane Russell)
- "The Conqueror" (John Wayne, Susan Hayward)
- "Jet Pilot" (John Wayne, Janet Leigh)
- "Macao" (Robert Mitchum, Jane Russell)
- "The Las Vegas Story" (Jane Russell, Victor Mature)
- "Sky Devils" (Spencer Tracy)
- "His Kind of Woman" (Jane Russell, William Bendix)
- "Two Tickets to Broadway" (Tony Martin, Janet Leigh)
- "One Minute to Zero" (Robert Mitchum, Ann Blyth).

YEAR: 1930 UNITED ARTISTS / ALBUM SOURCE: ALBUM / ALAMY STOCK PHOTO.

Over the course of thirty years helping to shape the modern movie industry, Hughes had many affairs with Hollywood starlets, including Jean Harlow, Jane Russell, Ginger Rogers, Katherine Hepburn, Bette Davis, Marlene Dietrich, and Ava Gardner.

One of the more controversial movies that Hughes produced and directed was The Outlaw. This was Jane Russell's first film. Russell had signed a seven-year contract with Hughes in 1940. Although the film was completed in 1941, its limited release was delayed until 1943, over a censorship dispute with the Motion Picture Production Code. The dispute focused on Howard's gratuitous display of Russell's cleavage. Hughes was quoted as saying, "there are two good reasons why men go to see her. Those are enough." Although Hughes had used his engineering skills to design a bra to showcase her breasts, Russell's autobiography confessed that the bra was so uncomfortable that she secretly removed it and wore her own padded bra with the straps pulled up to elevate her breasts. In 1946, after an extended battle of wills between Hughes and the Motion Picture Association of America, which went to federal court, the film gained a general release when Hughes agreed to cut about thirty seconds of screen time. This modest concession overcame the objections of the folks in charge of enforcing the Production Code folks at that time.

The Outlaw Poster. Source Pictorial Press Ltd / Alamy stock Photo.

While Hughes was busy making movies, he was also very much involved in aviation. As a pilot, he flew a plane that he and Richard Palmer designed. Hughes had lured Palmer away from Lockheed Aircraft Corp., where he was a project engineer. He was convinced to leave Lockheed when Hughes asked him the question, "Would you like to help design the fastest plane in the world?" They named it the H-1 Silver Bullet. While flying the bullet in 1935, Hughes shattered the world flying speed record. It flew at 352 miles per hour over Santa Ana, California, soaring past the previous record of 314 miles per hour.

In 1937, he set a record in his H-1 by flying from the West Coast to the East Coast in seven and a half hours. And in 1938, he set another record while radio listeners monitored him as he flew around the world. He did this in a new plane, the Lodestar, in less than four days. After flying around the world, he landed in New York as a national hero. More than a million people greeted him with a massive parade like the one for Charles Lindbergh, the first pilot to solo a nonstop trans-Atlantic flight, in 1927.

In the mid-1940s, aides to Hughes noticed that he was exhibiting obsessive-compulsive behaviors. These behaviors likely arose from injuries he suffered from the metal that remained in his skull from his plane crash while filming "Hell's Angels" and were exacerbated after crashing an amphibian Sikorsky S-43 aircraft into Lake Mead in 1943. Hughes had come in too steep and crashed the plane into the lake, killing two of the crew. Hughes had a severe gash in his head but was rescued from the lake's cold water as the aircraft sank.

Another aviation crash caused severe injuries to Howard in 1946, when his newest plane, the XF-11, developed engine trouble. While Howard was attempting an emergency landing on a fairway at the Los Angeles Country Club golf course, he crashed the plane into a North Linden Drive house in Beverly Hills, California. He was severely burned and suffered multiple fractures. Hughes survived but began taking painkillers, which resulted in his life-long dependence on prescription drugs.

The crash site, located at the corner of North Linden Drive and Whittier Drive, is now known as the "Bermuda Triangle of Beverly Hills." This designation is based on several eerie events that have taken place in the perimeter of this triangle:

- One year after the Hughes crash, "Bugsy" Siegel, a mobster who had developed the Flamingo Hotel in Las Vegas and was the leader of the organized crime group, Murder Inc., was reading a newspaper in the home across the street from where Hughes crashed his XF-11. Five bullets blasted through Bugsy, killing him in the house.

- Years later, Jan Berry of the popular music duo, Jan and Dean (known for the hit song "Dead Man's Curve"), smashed his speeding corvette into a parked truck, suffering partial paralysis of his right arm.

- Finally, in 2010, Roni Sue Chasen, a publicist who had represented many musicians and actors, including Michael Douglas, and directed a number of Academy Award campaigns for films, including "Driving Miss Daisy" and "The Hurt Locker," was shot and killed while driving home from the Hollywood premiere of the film "Burlesque." Her wrecked car came to rest in front of the now famous Siegel and Hughes homes and next to where Berry had hit the parked truck.

HUGHES XF-11. SOURCE: AVIATION ONE / ALAMY STOCK PHOTO.

Hughes did not just fly aircraft; he owned airlines. Trans World Airlines ("TWA") was born in 1930 when Transcontinental Air Transport merged with Western Air Express. Howard gained control of TWA in 1940 through a series of stock purchases both by him personally and by Toolco. By 1958, he had put all his

TWA stock into Toolco. After that transfer, Toolco owned 78 percent of TWA's stock.

Although Hughes led TWA's expansion to serve Europe, the Middle East, and Asia, he put TWA behind in the high-stakes jet aircraft race. United, American, and Pan Am had placed large orders for Douglas DC-8s and Boeing 707s in the mid-1950s, while TWA did not.

TWA fell behind these other carriers, in part because Howard interfered in TWA's strategic operating and financial decisions. Due to his interference, indecisiveness, and lack of transparency, no bank would give the airline funds while it was still in his control. During a protracted court battle, Hughes sold Toolco's entire TWA ownership through a public offering in April of 1966. In exchange for his shares, he received cash of $546.5 million, a fortune that would be worth more than $13.4 billion in 2020 dollars assuming a 6 percent growth!

At this point, Hughes was reported to be one of the richest men in the world. Without his beloved aviation and movie ventures, he thirsted for new diversions. With the massive amount of cash from the sale of his TWA stock, and the continuing millions flowing from the profits of Toolco, he looked to Las Vegas.

CHAPTER 2

DEVOURING LAS VEGAS

*"The insatiable need for heartless power and ruthless
control is the telltale sign of an uninitiated man—the most
irresponsible, incompetent and destructive force on earth."*

—MICHAEL LEUNIG

WITH THE SALE of his TWA stock, Hughes envisioned a new use for his wealth, one that rekindled his energy. He intended to become the largest property owner in the gambling capital of Las Vegas. That property would include casinos, hotels, and raw land. Then he would buy an airline that would make Las Vegas its hub to feed his casinos, hotels, and land. The land would enable more development and allow employees to buy homes that could be built on that land. Las Vegas would be his province.

Hughes understood that he needed to find a suitable "right-hand man" to help him dominate Las Vegas. Someone daring, creative, willing and well-connected to the Mob, with the right adversaries and allies. He found that man in Robert A. Maheu, a businessman and lawyer who had graduated from Georgetown

Law in Washington, D.C. With his fluency in French, he had served in counterintelligence after the United States entered World War II. While assigned in France, he had purposely spread misinformation about allied troop movements, including false information about the invasion at Normandy.

ROBERT MAHEU IN HIS NEVADA OFFICE IN LATE 1970. SOURCE: GETTY IMAGES / THE LIFE PICTURE COLLECTION.

After the war, Maheu worked for the FBI and the CIA. Since the mid-fifties, he also had experience working for Hughes on a project basis. During this time, Maheu and his Washington-based company worked on a monthly retainer with the CIA as a "cut-out" performing assignments in which the agency could not be officially involved, such as securing prostitutes for foreign government officials or hiring the Mob for even grislier tasks.

One of Maheu's most notorious cut-outs was to arrange for

the CIA to hire Mafia bosses to kill Fidel Castro (these activities were confirmed in 2017 when the National Archives released the JFK files). The CIA and Maheu knew that the Mafia had lucrative investments in Cuban casinos that had been seized by Castro, and they were eager to recover those assets. Maheu's go-to contact for this assignment was Johnny Roselli.

Roselli enlisted Sam Giancana and Santo Trafficante, Jr., a Florida Mob boss and one of the most powerful mobsters in pre-revolution Cuba. Giancana controlled a major Mafia empire based in Chicago that was bigger than the five families of New York's La Cosa Nostra. At the time, Roselli served as the Mob's man in Hollywood. Roselli and Giancana began their life in crime together, working for Al Capone. As long-time buddies, Roselli and Giancana reportedly shared the same girlfriend, Judith Campbell Exner. Exner was also reported to be President Kennedy's mistress.

Although the CIA had authorized Maheu to offer the mobsters $150,000 to "rub-out" Castro, they rejected the offer. Instead, they volunteered to take on the effort for free, citing their "patriotic duty." They also expected that their services would be rewarded with certain leniencies by the feds toward their "domestic operations." Efforts to assassinate Castro extended from 1960 until early 1963 when it was called off after several near misses, but failures, nevertheless.

Maheu's projects for Hughes were more mundane. They included dealing with a starlet attempting to blackmail Hughes and spying on Ava Gardner while she was dating Frank Sinatra and spying on other starlets of interest to Hughes.

Maheu's friendship and "projects" with Johnny Roselli would also come in handy in Las Vegas. Roselli not only had helped organized crime control Hollywood, but he also had extensive experience in Las Vegas. Maheu's collection of education, contacts, and experience was just what Howard needed to command Las Vegas.

Hughes offered Maheu a desirable position as chief of his Nevada operations. When people spoke with Robert, they were to feel that they were talking with Hughes in exchange for a very handsome compensation package of $500,000 (more than $12 million in today's dollars), an extraordinary expense account with access to a fleet of private aircraft, contacts at the highest level of government, industry, and Hollywood (including its celebrities), and other luxuries. This combination of money, luxury and access to power at all levels of government and celebrity dazzled Maheu. He readily accepted Hughes's offer.

Robert Maheu was a colorful character with a reputation for getting difficult (or nearly impossible) jobs done. It is widely believed that the "Mission Impossible" television show and movies are based on Maheu and his private investigative agency.

Hughes's need to find a surrogate was especially important for him because of his reclusive lifestyle. His crash in 1946 of the XF-11 resulted in severe burns and multiple fractures, causing some disfigurement and an addiction to painkillers. He also developed a phobia about germs and a maniacal passion for secrecy. This passion for secrecy was self-defeating since it fed the media's need to follow his every move both physically and of his business transactions. From 1950, until his death, he became the most famous recluse in the world.

Maheu moved to Las Vegas in 1966 to become Hughes's full-time surrogate. He was not only chief advisor in Las Vegas, but he also acted as Hughes's liaison with politicians, celebrities, and businessmen for all of Hughes's Nevada operations through 1970. Like Hughes's other aides and advisors, he communicated with him only by memo and telephone. During all his work with Hughes, Maheu never met Hughes in person. Business dealings were void of intimacy and emotional interactions. The master plan for Las Vegas did not require such pesky personal contact.

In 1966, Republican Paul Laxalt was running for governor of Nevada against Democrat, Grant Sawyer, who was seeking a third term. Laxalt was a decided underdog. Hughes telephoned Maheu and the call went something like this: "Robert, this guy Laxalt in Nevada is running for governor. He says Nevada's casino business is run by the mob and he would work with the feds to get them out. The guy he's running against disagrees. I want to send Laxalt $50,000 to his campaign. I also want you to meet with him and tell him that as soon as he's elected, I will start buying casinos and throw the mobsters out of town. But there is one condition. He needs to agree that I will not have to appear personally before the Nevada Gaming Control Board or the Nevada Gaming Commission to own and operate the casinos that I buy. Instead, you will be my Nevada guy and testify as my surrogate and Chief Executive of my Nevada operations. Also, Robert, make sure that you get cash into the hands of key state legislators and guys on these Boards and Commissions to help Laxalt make this plan work."

Before meeting with Maheu, Robert hobnobbed with his contacts at the FBI, including J. Edgar Hoover, director of the FBI, who was enthusiastic about Laxalt's plan to drive the mobsters out of Nevada, along with Hughes's plan to buy casinos and let his friend Maheu run them. Soon, Maheu delivered the cash and important message to Laxalt, who couldn't wait to elevate his campaign against Sawyer and the mob. Laxalt also advised Maheu of several men who would need to be convinced about Howard's need to avoid testifying in person by having Maheu testify as his surrogate.

The cost of this "convincing" service? Additional cash. The coordination of this cash distribution would largely fall to a Las Vegas lawyer, Thomas G. Bell, who possessed strong ties to many in Nevada politics. Maheu brought him in to help execute Hughes's plan to take over many of the hotels and casinos in Las Vegas. Substantial sums were funneled to Democrats and Republicans, always in cash, delivered by Bell at his office in Las Vegas.

On November 8, 1966, Paul Laxalt defeated Grant Sawyer with 52 percent of the vote. It was time for Hughes to pounce on Las Vegas. He contacted the chief of his LA office at 7000 Romaine Street, Frank William "Bill" Gay, an executive vice president and board member of Toolco.

"Bill, I am moving to Las Vegas. I will probably be there for a few years. I need you to select five guys to be my 'secretary-nurse' aides. They should be Mormon. I like Mormons since they don't smoke or drink and have an ethic of loyalty, hard work. And they keep their mouths shut. I need these guys in Vegas before the end of the month."

Bill Gay, himself a member of The Church of Jesus Christ of Latter-Day Saints, selected five men: three were Mormon, another was a Presbyterian who was married to a Mormon, and one was a Catholic. This team was later dubbed by many as the Mormon Mafia led by Howard Eckersley and Levar Myler, joined by George Francom, Roy Crawford, the Presbyterian, and John Holmes, the Catholic. The Mormon Mafia would soon become the only people to have daily contact with Hughes until he died in 1976.

After the election, one of Laxalt's first meetings was to fly to Washington to meet with J. Edgar Hoover with the broad objective of establishing a cooperative relationship between his office and the FBI. Mission: removal of the mob from Nevada's gaming industry, and to confirm that Hoover supported Howard Hughes's plan to buy several casinos quickly while having Robert Maheu be his surrogate in Nevada. Hoover assured him of his strong support of Laxalt's goals and objectives.

With allies, and the plan and cash in place, the casino collection began, starting with the Desert Inn and Casino whose owner, Moe Dalitz, was a liquor bootlegger that directed a gang of gambling racketeers out of Cleveland. The Desert Inn ("DI") had a great location (right on the strip, where the Wynn and Encore now stand). Plus, the DI played a major role as one of the casinos robbed in the original "Ocean's 11" movie, released in 1960, which starred Frank Sinatra (as Danny Ocean) and Peter Lawford, Dean Martin, Joey Bishop, Sammy Davis Jr., and many others. Hughes had watched this movie many times in his Bel Air home and had admired the way it showcased the glitz and glamour of Las Vegas.

In late November 1976, Maheu arranged for Hughes to leave his home in Bel Air, which he shared with his wife, Jean Peters, whom he had married in 1957. She and Hughes had dated for eleven years before they married. Bel Air is a beautiful community, even finer than its neighbor, Beverly Hills. The home was conveniently located on a secluded piece of land about half a mile from the swanky Bel Air Hotel and 1.5 miles from the Bel Air Country Club.

Peters herself had retired from a successful acting career in the movies. After co-starring with Marilyn Monroe, Joseph Cotton, Clifton Webb, and others in films like "Niagara," "Three Coins in the Fountain," "Zapata," "Apache," "Pickup on South Street," and "A Man Called Peter," she gave up her glamorous career when she married Hughes. After retiring from acting, she became involved in charitable work, arts and crafts, and studies at UCLA. She had also become something of a recluse. After Hughes moved to Las Vegas, she remained in Bel Air.

However, she grew tired of his absence, and they divorced in 1971. After fourteen years of marriage, Hughes agreed to pay Peters $70,000 a year in lifetime alimony. This payment included a provision that it was to be adjusted for inflation. Given the wealth earned and accumulated by Hughes during their marriage, this was an extremely favorable arrangement for Howard, but not so for Peters. She never wrote or spoke in public about her years with Howard Hughes. It is assumed this silence was the result of a condition of her continuing to receive her lifetime alimony.

Jean Peters. Source: Pictorial Press Ltd / Alamy Stock Photo.

Maheu arranged for Hughes to travel to Las Vegas in his infamous two-car private train. Upon his arrival on Thanksgiving Day, his aides quickly moved him into the Desert Inn's ninth floor penthouse whose suites were generally used by the casino's high rollers. The elevator to the ninth floor had an armed guard sitting in front of it around the clock as it opened to the penthouse. On a rotating basis, the nurse-aides occupied an office adjoining Hughes's bedroom. The only entrance to Hughes's bedroom was through the Mormon Mafia's office.

Maheu reserved the eighth floor of the Desert Inn for Hughes's Nevada operations offices. The reservations for both floors were for ten days at $26,000 per night. They overstayed the ten days. The Desert Inn's majority owner and general manager, Moe Dalitz, asked Hughes and his group to vacate the entire two floors to accommodate an influx of high rollers that had reservations for the holidays.

Hughes and his Mormon aides were not placing any bets in the Desert Inn's casino. This doubly motivated Dalitz to have Hughes and his group leave in order not to cause an inconvenience to his regular high roller customers who had reservations during the holidays, as well as to profit from their gambling losses.

In response to Moe's pressure, Maheu called his old friend, Johnny Rosselli (from the Fidel Castro assassination cut-out), the Las Vegas enforcer for the Chicago mob. Maheu called in a favor, and Rosselli had Dalitz hold off a few days while Hughes and his entourage stayed longer as non-gambling guests. In the mid-1960s, no one had more power in Las Vegas than Moe Dalitz, but Rosselli's power came from Chicago, and it trumped Dalitz's.

Still, Dalitz's patience wore thin again as the Holidays got closer, and Hughes remained in the penthouse. Maheu again tapped a higher power by calling his Teamsters Union friend, Jimmy Hoffa. Hoffa then called Moe Dalitz. He reminded Moe of the Teamsters Union's loan that funded Dalitz's purchase of the Desert Inn, and that Moe needed to give Hughes and his group more time.

In early 1967, it was time to reverse the tables on Moe Dalitz. Maheu told Dalitz that Hughes wanted to buy the Desert Inn.

This meant that Hughes intended to acquire control of its hotel, casino, land, and golf course. Hughes, Maheu, and Dalitz toggled back and forth over the price for nearly two months. Eventually, they decided on a price for 100 percent control of the Desert Inn and all its properties.

Moe Dalitz then needed to work with his minority owners to secure the deal, which was closed on March 27, 1967. The price was slightly more than $13 million (more than $300 million in today's dollars). Hughes needed to focus on swift legislative action and approval of his control and operation of the Desert Inn.

Hughes, Maheu, and Laxalt quickly came up with a scheme that would sway the politicians and gain the public's support. The Nevada legislators had been paralyzed over whether to establish a medical school. The argument focused on its cost and how to fund it, particularly the projected operating losses during its first several years. On the same day of the Desert Inn deal, March 27, 1967, Hughes penned a personal letter to Laxalt on his letterhead:

Dear Governor Laxalt:

Last Thursday, March 23, in the *Las Vegas Review-Journal*, there appeared large headlines covering five columns as follows: "Medical School to Die?" *The Las Vegas Sun*, on the same day, headlined: "Senate Action Could Be Kiss of Death for Medical School." In the *Review-Journal* this morning, Monday March 27, there was given the sum of money required each year to make possible the medical school—between two hundred thousand dollars and three hundred thousand dollars [to cover its operating losses].

If it meets with the approval of those responsible for this project, I would like to instruct my attorneys to prepare a document, in language and form satisfactory to the state's attorneys, which will be legally binding and enforceable upon me and upon my estate after my death. This document will consist of a written agreement to make a gift to the university of the sum mentioned above, each year for twenty years, commencing wherever the university requires the money. I attach no strings or conditions to this proposal. The medical school need not be located in Southern Nevada. The state is free to locate the school wherever it may desire.

Howard R. Hughes

Laxalt immediately broadcast the Hughes letter to the press. At the same time, Maheu successfully applied for a license to operate the Desert Inn casino in Clark County. The State Gaming Control Board met in Carson City on Thursday, March 30, and promptly recommended to the State Gaming Commission that it approve the Desert Inn's sale to Hughes.

The following day, the State Gaming Commission, in a 5 to 0 vote, concurred with the Gaming Control Board's decision and awarded a license to Hughes to operate the Desert Inn. District Attorney George Franklin said, "He received a gaming license without having to go through the normal background check or even appear in front of the Nevada Gaming Commission."

Because of Laxalt and other state officials' intervention, Hughes became the only licensee who was not required to appear personally before the Nevada Gaming Control Board or the Nevada Gaming Commission. Laxalt argued that Hughes was a special case and that Maheu was an acceptable surrogate. With his license to control and operate the Desert Inn, Hughes and Maheu were off to the races. With his beloved Hollywood a thing of the past, Hughes ground his ambitions into the glitz and glamor of Las Vegas.

When the Desert Inn deal closed, its eighth floor officially became the nerve center of Hughes's empire, and the ninth-floor penthouse became Hughes's personal residence, as well as a base of operations for his Mormon Mafia. The window drapes in his bedroom were closed on Thanksgiving Day 1966 and were not pulled opened again until Howard Hughes moved out on Thanksgiving Day, four years later.

In 1967 and 1968, Hughes bought several other hotels and casinos, including:

- The Desert Inn's neighbor, The Sands Hotel and Casino, also of "Ocean's 11" fame for $14.6 million. It had been owned by crime bosses, including Meyer Lansky, who was known as the "Mob's Accountant." At the time of its purchase, The Sand's hotel had 777 rooms and a huge gambling casino. Adjacent to it was 183 acres of prime real estate. Maheu now lived in a home on the edge of its golf course. Hughes quickly added a 500-room circular tower. The hotel and casino became a Las Vegas landmark. The casino was frequented by Frank Sinatra and the other members of the Rat Pack. In the late 1990s, The Sands was demolished to allow for the construction of The Venetian.

- The New Frontier Hotel and Casino's owners included Anthony Joseph Zerilli and Michael Polizzi, two high-ranking members of the Detroit Mafia family. Hughes purchased it for approximately $14 million. It was located at 3120 South Las Vegas Boulevard, across the street from what is now The Encore and what was the Desert Inn. It was an excellent addition to what had become Hughes's neighborhood.

- The Castaways Hotel and Casino was a 19-story hotel with 445 rooms and a casino. Its location was the major attraction to Hughes, on South Las Vegas Boulevard, across the street from The Sands. The Mirage now occupies that site.

- The Silver Slipper Hotel and Casino was the first Nevada casino to be shut down on cheating charges, for the use of rigged dice and other fixed games. Its landmark silver slipper rotated and faced the window of Hughes's bedroom in his Desert Inn penthouse. He was concerned that a photographer could climb into the slipper and take photographs of his bedroom window, even though he always kept the drapes closed. After unsuccessful attempts to have the rotating slipper turned off and sealed, Hughes purchased the property for $5.4 million. He then had the slipper sealed, it was turned away from his bedroom window, and he stopped its rotation.

- The Landmark Hotel and Casino was a few blocks away. It was a thirty-one-floor tower and casino whose construction began in 1961. It was scheduled for completion in early 1963, but the owner, Frank Caroll, ran out of funds, and construction halted in 1962. In 1966, the Teamsters Pension Fund provided a $5.5 million construction loan to complete the project, but Caroll again ran out of funding while the Teamsters' loan swelled to $8.9 million.

THE SILVER SLIPPER. SOURCE: MANUEL LITRAN/PARIS MATCH VIA GETTY IMAGES.

Who better to quickly eradicate the Teamsters' loan and take the project over than Hughes? The problem was that Hughes had gobbled up too many properties already, according to the Department of Justice (DOJ). The DOJ pointed to the Sherman Antitrust Act[1], and deemed that Hughes was attempting to

---

1 This act outlaws every contract, combination, monopolization, attempted monopolization, or conspiracy to monopolize for the purpose to restrain trade.

monopolize and restrain competition when, a few months earlier, he tried to purchase the Stardust Resort and Casino. This denial infuriated both Hughes and Maheu. However, for the Landmark Hotel deal, Maheu worked out an agreement that was viewed favorably by the DOJ. Hughes, following Teamsters' ally Jimmy Hoffa's suggestion, would pay off each of its three dozen creditors 100 percent of the amounts they were owed. This gained the strong support of the Las Vegas community and the Teamsters Union. Large donations to Nixon's presidential campaign coffers were also rumored.

Many of these creditors were local businesses at risk of substantial losses, some even going out of business, if the project declared bankruptcy. This economic hardship to local businesses, as well as pressure from Hoffa (and perhaps President-elect Nixon), convinced the feds to overlook the Sherman Antitrust issues posed by Hughes's acquisition of the Landmark Hotel. The sale to Hughes was approved on January 17, 1969. In all, Hughes paid $17.3 million to acquire the property and $3 million to finish the project. It opened on July 1, 1969, with 400 slot machines, 503 hotel rooms, and a 14,000 square foot casino on the ground floor and a smaller casino on its 29th floor.

Hughes also made several other Nevada-related acquisitions, including:

- A 25,000-acre parcel of land partly within the official city limits of Las Vegas and partly within unincorporated Clark County called Summerlin. It is named after Hughes's grandmother, Jean Amelia Summerlin. Although not developed during Hughes's lifetime, it now has a population of approximately 100,000 and is one of Nevada's most affluent communities. Its development includes more than 200 parks, twenty-four schools, fourteen churches, nine golf courses, three resort hotels, retail, and entertainment centers (including premier shopping, dining, and the Las Vegas Ballpark), and a state-of-the-art medical center.

- In 1967, he purchased George Crockett's business, which owned Alamo Airport on Las Vegas Boulevard South. Alamo Airport owned one of the terminals on the site of McCarran International Airport, as well as much of the land surrounding McCarran International Airport. Today, McCarran International airport is the fifth busiest in the United States and tenth throughout the world.

- During his stay at the Desert Inn, Hughes became frustrated that the local television stations stopped broadcasting at midnight. Hughes was an insomniac who liked to watch TV well into the night (and sometimes, all night). This led to another job for Maheu: Convince Hank [Herman M. Greenspun] to sell his station KLAS. Channel 8, a CBS affiliate with great local connections and the vehicle to run movies that he wanted to see, without interruption by those annoying ads after midnight.

Hank Greenspun supported Hughes's campaign to buy hotels and casinos from the mob and became an ally of his efforts to enhance the economic growth of Las Vegas and reduce the mob presence. Hughes was leveraging his new friendship with Greenspun by calling him during all hours of the day and night, telling him which movies to show or complaining about the movies that were being shown.

These vexatious calls to Greenspun likely broke down his nervous system. The man simply could not take anymore and turned his attention to the $3.6 million being offered for the TV station.

Following the deal, increasingly isolated Hughes could watch twenty-four hours of TV, including the movies he wanted to watch, after midnight, without ads. Amazingly, if he decided that he did not like the movie that was on, he would call the station, stop that movie, and start another. Never mind the needs of any other viewer. This is the level of power that Hughes wielded.

Because of the resistance of the DOJ and their threatened use of the Sherman Act, Hughes and Maheu knew they were finished with buying land, hotels, and casinos in Nevada. Hughes now craved a return to owning an airline. An airline would not only get Howard back into the aviation business, but he could cause it to build an expansive hub in Las Vegas to fill his hotels and casinos and sell his land for homes to be purchased to support the growth in population of Sin City. It would also make his terminal at McCarran International Airport and his land around it increase substantially in value.

CHAPTER 3

THE TRUTH ABOUT SWORDFISH

*"Ocean is more ancient than the mountains and
freighted with the memories and the dreams of Time."*

—H.P. LOVECRAFT

WHILE HOWARD HUGHES was building his empire in Las Vegas and enjoying his new television channel, there was an event transpiring in the Pacific Ocean that would ultimately impact his fortune. This event would eventually expose Hughes and reunite Maheu to the CIA. It would also result, in a vary circuitous path, to provide John Clark, a lawyer and me, a young CPA, with documents that were key to a five-year litigation effort against Hughes.

The K-129[2], a Soviet diesel-electric powered nuclear submarine, served in the Soviet Navy's Pacific Fleet. It was completed in 1960 at 330 feet in length with three diesel engines and three

---

2 Much of the information in this memoir about the K-129, the Hughes Glomar Explorer, the related Project AZORIAN and Project MATADOR was described in CIA documents that had been classified as "Secret." These sources were declassified and approved for release on January 4, 2010 and January 9, 2014.

shafts. When it was submerged, its top speed was 16.25 miles per hour. It was based out of the Rybachiy Naval Base in Kamchatka, Russia, which is on the southeast side of Russia's Kamchatka peninsula, about 1,000 miles northeast of Japan.

Soviet submarine K-129 (carrying hull number 722). Source: CIA Legacy Museum, The Exposing of Project AZORIAN, March 17, 2020.

On February 24, 1968, K-129 left its base on a mission captained by V. I. Kobzar, with 97 sailors aboard the 1,750-ton submarine. Surprisingly, approximately 40 of these men were new to sub-deployment. The sub carried three R-21 nuclear missiles with a range of 700 nautical miles and two nuclear torpedoes. Shortly after leaving its Rybicki base, Captain Kobzar took the sub down into a deep-water test dive.

The year of 1968 was the time of the Cold War when U.S. Navy attack submarines often tailed Soviet missile submarines. U.S. submarines would follow these submarines as they deployed from their home ports. Not far outside of the bay that provided natural protection for the Soviet's pacific submarine fleet, the USS Swordfish (SSN-579), a Skate-class submarine, waited. It was quieter and faster than the K-129 and could easily keep up with it on its path toward Hawaii.

U.S. Skate-class submarines trailed Soviet submarines by using a passive sonar system that had several advantages over active sonar. Passive sonar's most important advantage is its silence, which eliminates the return ping of active sonar. A return ping would alert the target submarine that it was being followed and provide the signal's source location. Passive sonar also informs the sender of the target's range, course, and speed—perfect for following a submarine. Using passive sonar, a sub can find a target submarine from many miles away and in any direction. In the 1960s, the Soviet fleet did not yet have passive sonar.

After its deep-water dive, Captain Kobzar returned to the surface to report by radio that everything had gone as planned. The K-129 proceeded on patrol. Although it crossed the International Dateline (the 180th meridian), it failed to make its radio report after this crossing. Its next radio report would not be until it reached its patrol area. However, the sub significantly diverted from its planned course, and it never reached its intended patrol area, near the Hawaiian Islands. As a result, the only radio report that it made followed its deep dive test.

The K-129 proceeded on a course that took it hundreds of miles away from its scheduled route. On March 8, 1968, the Swordfish followed K-129 until they both reached their maximum depth of approximately 800 feet. Neither of these submarines was capable of safely diving deeper than 800 feet. But the K-129 continued going deeper. It disappeared from the Swordfish's sonar, well beyond its maximum depth. It came to rest at the bottom of the Pacific Ocean in 16,440 feet of water, 1,560 miles northwest of Hawaii. All ninety-eight aboard perished.

By mid-March, Soviet naval authorities became very concerned after Captain Kobzar's two missed radio check-ins. It was standard procedure at that time for subs to break radio silence and contact headquarters if an emergency arose, but there had been no such calls. Urgent communications from Kamchatka went unanswered. By late-March, Soviet naval authorities declared that the K-129 was missing.

During the third week of March, a Soviet-organized air, surface, and sub-surface search-and-rescue effort was in place. These efforts by the Soviets were closely scrutinized by U.S. intelligence. They were consistent with the loss of the K-129 as if it had proceeded on its expected patrol pattern. However, the U.S. Navy had acoustic records from four Air Force Technical Applications Centers in the Pacific, and acoustic data from its sound surveillance system array in Adak, Alaska, data which confirmed the location, date, and time of what appeared to be a small explosion within K-129. These systems confirmed what the Swordfish had witnessed. The site of the sunken K-129 was known by the U.S. Navy, and it was a site that was hundreds of miles away from where the Soviet Navy had been searching.

Soviet search efforts lacked the equivalent of the U.S. data and intelligence. They were unable to locate the K-129, and eventually Soviet naval activity in the North Pacific returned to normal. The K-129 was declared lost with its 98 crew members, and the Soviet Navy believed it was hundreds of miles from where it had come to rest.

In essence, what caused the loss of K-129?

The "official" Soviet Navy's theory surmised that while operating in snorkel mode (very near the surface), due to a mechanical failure or improper reaction from its inexperienced crew, the sub flooded, causing it to sink. The unofficial opinion of many Soviet Navy officers, which the U.S. Navy denied, was that it was struck from underneath by the Swordfish while the K-129 had surfaced. This impact by the Swordfish exposed it to flooding, causing it to sink.

Although the U.S. Navy denied that the Swordfish was responsible, it did receive emergency repairs to a damaged periscope and sail section in Yokosuka, Japan, beginning on March

17. This damage may have been consistent with the Swordfish having struck an object above it.

Detailed photographs were taken months later of the sunken submarine by the USS Halibut, a specially equipped submarine that operated secret underwater espionage missions using a "fish" equipped with cameras, strobe lights and sonar. Photographs from this device revealed that the K-129 was relatively intact at the bottom of the Pacific.

The K-129 was principally in two large pieces. The sub's forward section and the section past its sail were separated by 100 yards. The fact that the K-129 was in two pieces confirmed that the K-129 had suffered an explosion, as reported by U.S. Navy and Air Force acoustic records and sound surveillance systems at the time the submarine was sinking to the bottom of the Pacific Ocean.

CHAPTER 4

AIR WORST

*"The greater the difficulty the more glory
in surmounting it. Skillful pilots gain their
reputation from storms and tempests."*

—*EPICTETUS*

JUST OVER A month after the loss of the K-129, on April 17, 1968, the U.S. Civil Aeronautics Board approved the merger of West Coast Airlines, Pacific Air Lines, and Bonanza Air Lines to form Air West, Inc. The three airlines officially merged on July 1, 1968. Air West provided service to more than eighty cities in the western portion of the United States, as well as to airports in Canada and Mexico.

Air West began its operations on Monday, July 1, 1968. This turned out to be a disastrous choice of timing since that Thursday was July 4 and the beginning of a hectic four-day travel period. Faced with this challenge, Air West's untested new computer system for scheduling departures and arrivals failed miserably. Numerous flights were delayed for hours or canceled. All over the western states, Canada and Mexico, newspapers, and television stations chronicled the airline's humiliating debut.

Newspapers, television and radio outlets throughout the western United States attacked the airline for its botched debut, but the media in Las Vegas was particularly unmerciful. Sin City relies heavily on airlines to bring in guests to stay at its hotels, gamble in its casinos, attend shows, and eat in its restaurants. City officials complained to the Civil Aeronautics Board, arguing that the airline's poor service was a threat to the economy of Las Vegas.

Hughes preyed on this fiasco as an excellent opportunity for him to swoop in to acquire the airline and restore public confidence in the safety of Air West and provide reliable service to its various destinations, particularly to its Las Vegas hub. Howard devised a multiprong scheme.

He turned off the television. Barefoot and in his pajamas, he sat down at the desk in his bedroom in the penthouse of the Desert Inn. He outlined a detailed attack plan in a memorandum to Maheu for him to execute:

Bob, this Air West debacle is a golden opportunity for me. I have a plan to exploit this fiasco. This is how I see what we need to do, as soon as possible.

We need to orchestrate a campaign of fear, uncertainty, and disruption ("FUD") through newspapers, radio, and television. We need to get this FUD in the minds of travelers, shareholders, and the Air West board of directors. The campaign will instill fear of flying this unreliable and unsafe airline. We will push stories that it cannot support its destinations without cancellations and delays. Finally, we'll disrupt its ability to bring its three airlines into one efficient and successful operation. All of this will bring about sharp revenue declines and losses to the airline; its shareholders and directors will beg for someone to bail them out of an economic disaster.

Bob, I want you to begin working with members of the Air West board of directors to sell the airline to me at a price equivalent to its current trading price per share, plus a small control premium.

We can get our friends to buy significant amounts of Air West stock, then sell them in large trades at critical times, depressing the stock price when we need to pressure the directors. We will protect our friends from these losses by covering the difference between their selling price and the attractive price per share that we will offer to Air West's shareholders to accept our deal.

Finally, the purchase contract will contain a provision where I can back out of the deal if Air West's net worth (its assets less its liabilities) is less than 75 percent of its net worth as of July 31, 1968. I don't intend to back out of this deal, but I can use this provision to reduce the agreed purchase price through: (a) the FUD campaign described above (which will cause losses that will reduce the airlines net worth), (b) cause pressure on the stock price by selling large blocks of stock at perilous times for the company and its shareholders, and (c) we're going to get Haskins & Sells into Air West to find assets that I don't want to pay for and cause them to be written off, and recording additional liabilities, both of these actions will be recorded before the closing, reducing the purchase price.

So, Bob, I want you to get on these actions right away. It will be essential to increase Air West's operating losses, reduce its assets, and increase its liabilities. Each of these will reduce Air West's net worth. Taken together, these impacts will push Air West's shareholders to eventually agree to sell the airline to me at a lower price than the price agreed to when we strike a deal.

Call me ASAP to discuss this further if you have any questions.

HRH

Maheu's first task was to review the list of Air West's directors, looking for anyone he knew. He settled on Patrick J. Hillings, a former Republican congressman from California who succeeded Richard Nixon in Congress when Nixon ran successfully for the U.S Senate in 1950. Hillings did Maheu a favor by contacting Nick Bez, an Air West board member, executive vice president and one of its largest shareholders. Bez had founded West Coast Airlines in 1941.

Maheu called Bez, and they agreed to meet on July 30, 1968, at the Century Plaza Hotel in Century City. This hotel is located on the Avenue of the Stars, only six miles from 7000 Romaine Street, Hughes's records and communications center.

Maheu called Hughes shortly after his meeting with Bez. He relayed that Bez was interested in striking a deal and was pleased that Mr. Hughes was attracted to a purchase of Air West. Hughes was excited and insisted that the campaign of fear, uncertainty, and disruption ("FUD") proceed while Maheu continued his efforts to meet Bez and others on the Air West board. The FUD campaign would put pressure on the board to accept Hughes's offer.

Now, Maheu had marching orders to not only continue working with Nick Bez but to expand that effort to Air West's other board members. He also began working with Hank Greenspun to help with the FUD campaign to denigrate "Air Worst" with a humongous net. Finally, efforts were set in motion with the Civil Aeronautics Board to approve Hughes's acquisition of the airline.

On August 8, 1968, Maheu met with Bez and others on the Air West board that had been on the board of West Coast Airlines. The meeting was in Seattle at the Olympic Hotel, an elegant hotel in downtown Seattle on a hill overlooking Pike Place Market and Elliott Bay.

At that time, shares of Air West were trading on the American Stock Exchange at $16 per share. Since this trading price was for only a small portion (say, 100 shares) of the Air West's 3.9 million shares and Hughes wanted to control 100 percent of the airline's stock, Maheu knew that he needed to offer a "control premium" for acquiring 100 percent control of the airline. Control premiums often range from 20 percent to 40 percent above the stock market trading price for non-controlling blocks of shares. This normal range of premium would dictate a price to Hughes ranging from $19.20 to $22.40. The Bez group insisted on $25 per share. Maheu expressed shock and surprise. He informed them that he was only authorized to offer $20 per share and that the $25 demand was not reasonable. The meeting ended without agreement.

Maheu called Hughes, telling him that they should back off for six months to a year. By then, the FUD campaign would weaken the Air West Board, and they would seize a better price. Hughes, however, was anxious to get back into the airline business and bring more customers into a new expanded Las Vegas hub. He sent Maheu back to the negotiating table immediately. On August 11, the Bez group and Maheu signed an agreement whereby Bez would use his best efforts to close the deal with the rest of the board consistent with the following terms:

- The purchase price would be $22 per share (a control premium of 37.5 percent).

- The books and related records would be examined by Haskins & Sells, before the closing, and their analyses could be provided to Hughes.

A press release announcing the Hughes Air West agreement was dated August 11, 1968.

The Bez group had kept their meeting with Maheu secret, without notice to the Bonanza and Pacific board members. After reading the press release, opposition to the sale was firm. Maheu, however, pressed forward with a substantive meeting in Phoenix (Bonanza's old headquarters city). A persuasive person and past captain of his college debate team, Maheu presented the endless benefits of having the financial and political resources of Toolco and Hughes himself.

The opposition group eventually agreed that if the stockholders (13,000 stockholders holding 3.9 million shares) voted to accept the agreement, they would support the Hughes agreement and present it to the Civil Aeronautics Board for approval.

Meanwhile, the FUD campaign continued, hammering away about Air West's dreadful service, declining revenues, economic losses, and safety concerns. The bad publicity frightened customers and shareholders alike. Maheu hired Jimmy ("The Greek") Snyder, the renowned oddsmaker and public-relations man, to draft a series of press releases praising the Hughes offer and criticizing those who opposed it. Snyder did not disclose that he was receiving a large monthly retainer from Hughes. Instead, he represented that he was hired and supported by a group of Air West shareholders.

Snyder also enlisted the support of Nevada's popular senator, Alan Bible, who publicly criticized Air West's service and preached that a Hughes takeover would solve the "deplorable situation" created by "Air Worst's" pitiful service.

In his *Las Vegas Sun*, Hank Greenspun wrote that "Air Worst" was discouraging people from coming to Las Vegas (both Pacific Air Lines and Bonanza Air Lines had routes serving Las Vegas). Greenspun also touted that Howard Hughes was willing to buy the airline just to improve its service to Las Vegas. This ruckus not only sold more *Las Vegas Sun* newspapers (owned, edited and published by Greenspun), but he was also a prominent real estate developer in Las Vegas, which benefited from Hughes development of Las Vegas and by his building a fortuitous hub at its airport.

During Air West's board meeting, Maheu and Hughes arranged for his ever-present lawyer, Chester Davis, to speak to the entire board. Davis had represented Hughes for many years in the TWA litigation. He was a tall, heavyset, energetic man with a pit bull approach to representing Hughes, acting as his personal attorney and general counsel to his vast business interests.

CHESTER DAVIS, FRONT CENTER AND WILLIAM GAY, RIGHT REAR, LEAVING THE COURTHOUSE IN THEIR LITIGATION WITH ROBERT MAHEU. SOURCE: BETTMAN VIA GETTY IMAGES.

Davis carried a massive ego and an abusive personality. He stressed that Hughes would acquire Air West's assets, assume all its liabilities, and pay its shareholders $22 for each share held. But there was concern by some of the directors that this offer was not in the stockholder's best interests for the following reasons:

- Although the Airline had gotten off to a rough start, its long-term prospects were strong, and the $22 per share offer would soon be surpassed once the startup's hiccups were overcome and the economies of scale and other benefits of the merger of the three carriers were realized.

- The Purchase Contract allowed Hughes to back out of the deal if Air West's net worth fell below 75 percent of its July 31, 1968 net worth. With its operating losses incurred to date, and likely losses continuing through the closing of the purchase, there was concern that Hughes would use this provision to leverage a substantial reduction of the $22 per share purchase price to the shareholders.

After considerable discussion, the board voted 13 to 11 to recommend to Air West's shareholders that they accept Hughes's offer. However, it was provided that the recommendation could be withdrawn if a better offer was presented before the closing of the sale to Hughes. The stockholders' meeting was set for December 27, 1968.

A proxy statement was prepared with significant input from Chester Davis's team. It stressed that shareholders would receive $22 for each of their shares of Air West. Buried in its voluminous disclosures was a statement that stockholders might receive less than $22 per share if its net worth at the closing was less than 75 percent of the airline's net worth on July 31, 1968. There was no disclosure that its losses since July 31 were substantial and continuing, and, as a result, the net worth condition might not be met on the closing date.

The stockholders held their meeting at the Thunderbolt Hotel (now an Aloft Hotel) adjacent to the southern runway of San Francisco International Airport. The vote resulted in 52 percent of the shares being cast for the approval of the sale to Hughes. All that remained was for the Air West board of directors to approve the transaction the next day, a Saturday. Such was not to be. The board voted 13 to 11 against the Hughes offer in favor of a last-minute offer from Northwest Airlines.

With only Sunday, Monday, and Tuesday remaining before the Hughes offer expired, Davis immediately launched a crushing plan. With Hughes's approval, Davis immediately marshaled forces to sue, on behalf of Air West's shareholders, each of the individual directors who voted against the Hughes offer. The complaint sought damages equal to stockholders' losses due to the directors' refusal to honor the stockholders' vote to sell to Hughes. The complaint would also ask the court to seize dissident directors' stock until the case was resolved, which would likely be for a very long time. This seizure would cause financial distress to many of the directors since, for many, much of their wealth was tied up in Air West stock.

In addition to this litigation strategy, Maheu, Hughes, and Davis triggered a stock sell-off to occur on Monday morning. Hughes called long-time business associates Hank Greenspun, David Charnay[3], and George Crockett[4], who owned large blocks

---

3 Hughes had numerous business partnerships with this industrialist and film and television producer.

4 Crockett owned Alamo Airport which he sold to Hughes in 1967, which became part of McCarran International Airport and one of its terminals. Alamo also owned, and Hughes acquired, much of the land surrounding McCarran airport.

of Air West stock. The deal struck was for each of them to put sell orders in for their stock on Monday morning. To the extent that the selling price they received was less than $22 per share, Hughes promised to make up the difference.

On Monday morning, the complaint was filed in Wilmington, Delaware, and another lawsuit was filed in New York. Hughes's public relations team sent press releases to the major news media. Calls to the dissenting directors were made and telegrams were sent to them personally with threats and encouragement to change their vote in favor of Hughes's offer.

Immediately following the 13 to 11 vote against the Hughes offer, the dissenting directors sent Edmund Converse (forthcoming chairman of the board and CEO of Air West) and Joseph Martin, Jr. (a director and an attorney in the San Francisco law firm of Miller, Groezinger, Petit, Evers & Martin) to New York to meet with Northwest officials. Their meeting on Monday morning was making substantial progress until the participants received news about the Delaware complaint. The news of this complaint caused the Air West directors to seek assurances and protection from Northwest against the Hughes litigation.

Following lunch, both word of the New York complaint and the news of selling pressure on Air West's stock were received. This selling pressure had caused its share price to decline by 16 percent. This collection of bad news caused the folks from Northwest to lose all interest in its acquisition of Air West. As a result, by the end of the day on Tuesday, six Air West directors changed their vote from no to yes to sell to Hughes. The deal was completed when Maheu and Davis flew to Seattle that afternoon to secure Nick Bez's signature on the Purchase Contract.

In order for the deal to close, all that remained was approval by the Civil Aeronautics Board ("CAB"), which included, as part of its ruling, an agreement on which Hughes entity would control the airline. Generally, this process went as planned, but progress toward approval was slow. In the end, the CAB ruled that the acquisition was "consistent with the public interest" and concurred with the hearing examiner that the purchase price to Hughes of $22 per share was "fair and reasonable to all stockholders of Air West."

It wasn't until October 23, 1969, that it was determined that Hughes Air Corporation ("HAC" also known as Hughes Air West), would be named to own and operate Air West's assets. HAC would have two stockholders, Toolco would own 78 percent of the stock, while Howard Hughes would own the remaining 22 percent. The delays encountered during the CAB approval process and the tardy establishment of Hughes Air Corporation pushed the Closing until March 31, 1970.

The slow pace of progress from the December 31, 1968 approval by the Air West board of directors to the March 31, 1970 completion of the Hughes purchase fit right into Hughes and Chester Davis's playbook. The FUD campaign wreaked havoc on Air West's revenues and accelerated its losses, which totaled $20.8 million. These losses caused Air West's net worth to plunge significantly below the requirement that, at closing, the airline's net worth would be at least 75 percent of its net worth as of July 31, 1968.

Hughes and Davis had plans to use this failure of the "net worth" provision of the Purchase Contract to reduce the net purchase price received by Air West's shareholders by millions of dollars. This purchase price reduction resulted from the losses caused by the FUD campaign, and by Hughes and Davis insisting that improper accounting adjustments be recorded by Air West before the closing as of the March 31, 1970. This sleight of hand would be accomplished by changing the way Air West accounted for its assets and liabilities at the closing from the accounting principles it had used as of July 31, 1968.

The 75 percent net worth provision specifically called for Air

West's assets and liabilities to be presented in accordance with generally accepted accounting principles ("GAAP"), and that it would use the same generally accepted accounting principles at the closing of the sale as Air West used as of July 31, 1968. But Hughes and Davis had other ideas. In late 1969, they hatched a plan to implement changes in Air West's accounting methods that would save Hughes millions.

CHAPTER 5

CUTTING MY TEETH ON A BILLIONAIRE

"Character cannot be developed in ease and quiet. Only through experience of trial and suffering can the soul be strengthened, ambition inspired, and success achieved."

—*HELEN KELLER*

MY EARLY SUMMER of 1968 was a whirlwind. I graduated with honors from the University of San Francisco ("USF") on June 1, married to my high school sweetheart, Barbara ("Barby"), on June 8, and began working at PMM on Monday, June 17.

While at USF, my major was as an accounting specialist. The accounting specialist track was designed for students who wanted to work for a public accounting firm after graduation, hoping to become a Certified Public Accountant ("CPA"). The accounting specialist track offered few electives because of its heavy focus on taking every accounting-oriented course offered at USF.

I had an attraction to accounting. I even looked forward to

doing the homework and going to class to solve the puzzles that accounting presented. Because I was ranked in the top ten in my class, I was fortunate to be recruited by the Big 8 accounting firms very early in my senior year. The routine was for the accounting firms to select students to be interviewed on campus. Then, if the interview went well, an office visit would take place. At the accounting firms' office, the candidates visited with several staff accountants, managers, and partners. Then the candidate would be taken to a nice restaurant near the office. After lunch, the candidate would meet a few more of the firm's accountants before returning to campus.

My office visit with PMM was in late September of 1967. In the morning, I met with several partners, managers, and staff. I was taken on a tour of the office and then had a wonderful lunch with two staff accountants, at Orsi's, a fine Italian restaurant in San Francisco's Financial District. It was the rare occasion that PMM staff would have a cocktail at lunch. However, since I had not yet reached my twenty-first birthday (October 6), I declined and chose my drink of choice, a Coca Cola on ice.

Following lunch, while I was meeting with a few others in the firm's office, the partner, who was in charge of recruiting, gathered feedback from those that had met with me during the morning and at lunch. He decided to make me an attractive offer immediately. However, although PMM was my first choice, I did not accept the offer right away because I had other offers to consider, and I had other office visits to make. Nevertheless, in November of 1967, I chose to join PMM shortly after my scheduled graduation from the University of San Francisco in June of 1968.

In the spring semester of 1968, I took a tax class taught by Mike Raddie, a partner in PMM's San Francisco office. At the end of the first day of the tax class, Raddie called me to meet with him at the front of the classroom. He was standing next to the teacher's desk when he looked sternly at me with his most serious face and stance with his hands on his hips.

He warned me in no uncertain terms: "I understand that you accepted an offer to join PMM in our San Francisco office."

"Yes sir, I like the firm very much and enjoyed meeting the people during my office visit in September."

"Well, I want you to know that if you don't get an A in my class, the offer is void, and you'll have to find a job somewhere else."

Harsh news to hear! I had many other offers that I had turned down. I considered going back to my second choice, but I decided to work especially hard in Raddie's tax class, making sure to arrive on time at 8:00 am, do all the homework, speak up in class, and studying extra hard. My focus paid off. I earned an A and joined PMM two weeks after graduation.

My assignment on the Air West engagement commenced only two months after joining PMM.

The merger of West Coast Airlines, Inc. and Bonanza Air Lines, Inc. into Pacific Air Lines, Inc., to form Air West, Inc., was accounted for on a pooling of interest basis of accounting. Simply put, this method of accounting combined the existing assets, liabilities, and net worth of the three airlines using the same amounts recorded on the books of the three individual airlines.

For example, the engines and airframes recorded on the books of each of the three airlines was simply added up, and that total became the amount shown for its engines and aircraft on the financial statements of Air West. This method was appropriate given the nature of the transaction. Each airline's accounting principles were in accordance with generally accepted accounting principles and were the same accounting principles used by each of the separate airlines.

The new board of directors of Air West selected as its outside independent auditor, the international accounting firm of Peat, Marwick, Mitchell & Co. ("PMM"), now known as KPMG. PMM was one of the world's Big 8 international accounting firms. PMM had been the auditor of Bonanza Airlines out of its Phoenix office.

As the new auditor of the combined airline, PMM needed to understand the accounting methods used by each of the separate airlines prior to July 1, 1968. In the late summer of 1968, a PMM manager and I were assigned that task. I was thrilled to get in on the ground floor of this interesting new client. I had always harbored a fascination with airplanes, and this gave me an opportunity to gain a deep understanding of how the airline industry worked. This was only my third assignment at PMM since I joined the firm. I viewed it as a plum assignment at my young age of 21.

The manager and I visited with the auditors for West Coast Airlines in Seattle and Pacific Airlines in San Francisco. The manager on the Bonanza Airlines audit for PMM came to San Francisco to meet with us for several days to review Bonanza's accounting practices.

Having met with the auditors in charge of the three predecessor airlines' audits, and studied their work papers, we became thoroughly knowledgeable of all three airlines' accounting practices. We determined that those methods complied with generally accepted accounting principles and fortunately, they were consistent with each other.

My next assignment came in the form of an audit of a large international bank, but I hoped to return to the Air West audit when it resumed later in 1968.

My hope was fulfilled when, along with several other PMM staff, I returned to Air West in late 1968 and early in 1969 to resume the audit of the airlines' financial statements for the year ended December 31, 1968. The manager with whom I had worked on the Air West matter in late summer had left PMM by the time the year-end audit began. Because of my "seniority" on Air West audit, I was tasked with supervising the PMM team at Air West in San Mateo. My two principal assistants were Tom Adler and Mary Kay Griffin.

In contrast with his Oklahoma Sooner background, Adler was a bit of a hippie. His hair was long, especially for a conservative CPA firm in downtown San Francisco. In contrast to the hippie movement in the western portion of San Francisco, the Financial District reeked of conservatism. Adler's father was a lawyer in Oklahoma and he had inherited his father's skills in presenting his views, while remaining friendly, even when there were disagreements.

Mary Kay Griffin was a transplant from Utah and a Mormon. She was a newlywed, extremely personable, and easygoing. She and her husband, Griff, lived in Silicon Valley on a street appropriately named Easy Street. Both Adler and Mary Griffin were tireless in their work effort, extremely talented, and committed to doing their very best. Their work was terrific, and they were wonderful colleagues in support of me and the PMM team on the Air West engagement.

Over the next two years, our core team of three young accountants would work together over long and demanding hours. We became trusted colleagues and good friends. The new PMM audit manager was a bit of a loner, and strangely, both he and the partner on the audit rarely visited the job site at Air West. Neither the PMM manager nor the partner had any significant presence during the firm's work at Air West.

Air West's accounting department was in two buildings in downtown San Mateo, California. A City of San Mateo fire station stood between the two buildings. San Mateo is a suburb of San Francisco, about 6.5 miles south of San Francisco International Airport.

Air West's revenue accounting department was located on the entire third floor of the office building at 181 2nd Avenue in a massive, mostly open space. The executive offices were on the fourth floor. Revenue accounting for an airline is very tricky since when a flight is booked by or for a passenger, the amount collected represents a liability until the passenger takes the flight. It is even more complicated when another airline sells a ticket to a passenger where a leg of the flight is taken on one airline, and another leg is taken on another airline.

For example, assume in December 1968, a passenger purchased from United Airlines a flight from New York to San Francisco, which then connected to an Air West flight from San Francisco to Santa Barbara. United would then clear the transaction that night using the airline clearinghouse in New York, giving Air West the agreed amount of cash for the flight from San Francisco to Santa Barbara. Air West would increase its cash and record a liability until the passenger's flight from San Francisco to Santa Barbara was taken. After the passenger took the flight to Santa Barbara, Air West would reduce the liability and increase its revenue.

Air West's other location in downtown San Mateo was a short walk from 181 Second Avenue to the Mills Square building, past the firehouse to 100 South Ellsworth Ave. All the non-revenue accounting functions of Air West occupied the eighth floor of the Mills Square building. The PMM auditors had offices in both buildings, each located in the southwest corners of the respective buildings. When we had a full staff of ten, the quarters were tight but not uncomfortable.

The 1968 audit was handled with great care by the PMM staff for several reasons. First, we were young and trying very hard to do the best audit possible. In addition, most of the audit took place from December 1968 through March 1969, right after the approval of the sale of the airline to Hughes by the shareholders and the board, but before the closing of the sale to Hughes. The final reason that the staff took such great care in performing the audit was their knowledge that Howard Hughes was going to purchase Air West's assets and assume its liabilities. As a result, they considered this audit a high-risk engagement, particularly with the litigious Howard Hughes as the buyer.

The team's new manager and partner believed this audit was just a one-time engagement, soon to be taken over by Hughes's long-time audit firm Haskins & Sell ("H&S" is now known as Deloitte). As a result, neither the manager nor the partner took an active role in the audit of Air West's 1968 financial statements. This combination of factors motivated the young PMM team to work harder, and make sure that the shareholders of Air West received the top-notch work that they deserved.

After months of effort by a staff working thousands of hours, the PMM team determined that Air West's December 31, 1968, financial statements were prepared in accordance with GAAP, consistently applied. The PMM auditors were all smart, dedicated young accountants who had toiled without the leadership of the manager (or the partner) assigned to the audit. The entire audit team recognized that the manager felt that he was "too good" to waste his time on a client that would soon be acquired by Howard Hughes who would immediately switch to his long-time audit firm, H&S. This was a dead-end assignment of which the manager and the partner wanted no part.

But my staff and I bonded as a team and made sure that we did our job thoroughly.

On the evening that the financial statements were ready to go to the printer, the manager showed up around 5:00 pm to visit with me in the PMM office in the Mills Square building of Air West. He thumbed through the thousands of audit work papers for around fifteen minutes, then he asked me: "Are you sure that your audit work on these financial statements is up to snuff and that the annual report is ready to go? I don't have time to review these work papers tonight before the printer's deadline. So, tell me, is it okay for the partner to sign the audit report tonight at the printer's office in San Francisco on his way home?"

I wanted to tell him that it was more than a little late for him to ask that question and if there were any issues with the financial statements, that was likely the result of his failure to show up and do his job. Instead, not wanting to risk his wrath, I said, "Not to worry, these financials were mighty fine and ready to go public." Just as important, I added that Air West's accounting principles used on December 31, 1968, were consistent with those used by it as of July 31, 1968. The manager left without further review of the audit work papers.

He later informed me that he met with the partner at the printer's office, which was decked out with fine wines, liquor and snacks for attorneys, accountants and clients waiting for other annual reports, prospectuses, and proxy statements to be proof-read. I suspected that the manager and the partner, true to form, sampled the available wine, liquor, and snacks without even reading the financial statements before giving their approval for print.

As the closing of the purchase agreement with Hughes dragged on until March of 1970, PMM was surprised to find itself back again to audit Air West's December 1969 financial statements. In November of 1969, I was assigned to the same large office on the eighth floor of the Mills Square building to plan and perform PMM's audit of Air West's December 31, 1969, financial statements.

In December, I insisted that Adler and Griffin rejoin the team, along with several others. A new manager replaced the manager from the 1968 audit; however, the partner from the 1968 audit continued for the 1969 audit. As it turned out, the new manager's home was only seven blocks from Air West's offices in San Mateo. Occasionally, he would stop by the PMM auditors' office at 100 South Ellsworth in the morning on his way to PMM's San Francisco office, or on his way home. Generally, his visits were less than thirty minutes. I soon learned that the new manager had the same lack of attention to the engagement as the prior manager, for the same reasons.

Although the acquisition had been agreed to by the parties as of December 31, 1968, the closing had yet to occur. It was particularly important to me that each member of the PMM team was keenly aware that, to comply with the purchase agreement, Air West's assets and liabilities on December 31, 1969, had to be accounted for using the same accounting methods that were used by Air West on July 31, 1968.

For example, aircraft had to be depreciated using the same methods and over the same time periods. Prepaid expenses had to be recorded consistently, including costs incurred to obtain the rights to serve cities on its route system, a costly process in the era of the Civil Aeronautics Board, the body that controlled which airlines flew to which cities.

Another example was the accounting method for engine overhauls. An engine overhaul in 1968 on a Boeing 727 or DC 9 Aircraft cost more than $1 million, and it provided the airline thousands of flight hours into the future. It was Air West's accounting practice to record its overhaul cost as an asset and amortize (expense) that cost over each hour flown in the future until the total time on that engine (as called for by regulations) required a new overhaul.

A new feature of the 1969 audit by PMM was the review of its work by a team from H&S. Part of the purchase agreement, inserted by Chester Davis, was that H&S would have access to and could copy any audit work paper created or obtained by the PMM auditors. The H&S team was also given an office in the corner opposite the PMM team on the eighth floor of the Mills Square building.

The H&S team members were frequent visitors to the PMM office. The protocol was for H&S to request the PMM work papers from me. I would then log out the documents, noting the work paper letter and number, the subject, and the date H&S borrowed the working paper. When H&S returned the work papers, I would update the log with the date the document was returned. H&S also had frequent questions of PMM, which were discussed with the appropriate PMM auditor, which usually meant that I was part of the discussion.

PMM's audit of Air West's December 31, 1969, financial statements was completed on March 17, 1970. PMM's opinion, in which it had invested thousands of hours of analysis, was that these financial statements had been prepared in accordance with GAAP, and applied consistently with Air West's December 31, 1968, financial statements. These 1969 financial statements showed that Air West's net worth was below the Purchase Contract's required $16.2 million. This shortfall resulted from the losses sustained during the period from July 1968 to December 31, 1969, in large part because of the adverse impact of the FUD campaign.

I knew that H&S made copies of the PMM work papers that it had borrowed, but I did not know that it provided copies of key PMM work papers to Chester Davis, or that Davis would then send another copy of these documents to Howard Hughes for his comments. Hughes's comments often included instructions to Davis with demands and questions about the assets or liabilities that were the subject of the PMM work papers. Hughes instructed Davis in a telephone call about accounting entries that he, barefoot and in his pajama bottoms, demanded be made from his bedroom in the penthouse at the Desert Inn—including massive write-offs.

Davis had concerns about this path and responded from his office in New York that the Purchase Contract requires that the assets be recorded consistent with the accounting methods in place by Air West as of July 31, 1968. He repeatedly told Hughes that insisting on writing off millions in assets that were recorded in accordance with GAAP would be a violation of the Purchase Contract.

Hughes impatiently responded that he didn't give a damn about accounting niceties. Besides, in a month, the Air West employees would all be working for him, he warned, so they needed to accommodate the dollar signs in his eyes rather than follow accounting protocol. He vowed to make notes directly on the papers and return them to Davis.

After a few days, Chester received the copies of the PMM work papers with comments clearly written on them in blue. They had comments like, "Chester, I'm not paying for this; get it written off, HRH." Or "Chester, be sure that they write this stuff off, HRH." The initials HRH had a distinctive circle wrapped around it from the bottom right of the last H, over the top, and returning under the back to the last H again. It looked like an eye-catching seal from His Royal Highness as shown below.

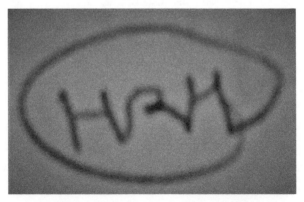

THE INFAMOUS SIGNATURE, OR SEAL, OF HOWARD HUGHES.

Chester knew that he needed to list and detail Hughes's demands, then arrange to meet with the key H&S and Air West accounting personnel as soon as possible. In mid-March of 1970,

Davis, H&S, and members of the Air West accounting management team met at H&S's offices in the Financial District in San Francisco at 44 Montgomery street in a large conference room decorated with antique Asian art.

The agenda was clear. Although Davis did not disclose that the accounting adjustments came from Hughes, he listed the assets to be written off and liabilities to be created. The liabilities would provide Hughes with a large "cookie-jar" of reserves to absorb the costs of transitioning from Air West to Hughes Air West and boost its profitability immediately after closing of the Purchase Contract.

During this meeting, Davis hammered the Air West accounting team with the fact that Air West's losses resulted in a violation of the purchase contract's net worth requirement (although most of these losses resulted from Hughes's own FUD campaign). As a result, Davis proclaimed that Hughes could walk away from the purchase agreement.

Davis stressed that if Hughes did walk, Air West would go bankrupt, and Air West's management team, including those in the meeting, would be out of a job. Davis also emphasized that if Hughes did go through with the closing on March 31, 1970, they would soon be working for Mr. Hughes. Then Davis informed the group that he wanted a host of specifically identified assets written off and certain additional liabilities recorded before the closing. Otherwise, they would all soon be unemployed.

Although the assets to be written off and liabilities to be recorded would mean that the closing net worth would no longer be determined in accordance with generally accepted accounting principles and would not be prepared on a basis consistent with the accounting methods used to determine Air West's net worth as of July 31, 1968, that was of no concern to Davis or Hughes. What was important to them was that Air West's net worth at the closing was less than the 75 percent net worth provision of

Section 9.1 of the purchase agreement and, in his mind, that gave Hughes carte blanche as to how its assets and liabilities were recorded.

Davis also knew that Hughes had told him which assets to write off and which liabilities to increase, and he was going to make sure that each of those accounting entries would be recorded on Air West's books before the closing. He did not tell the Air West and H&S employees that Hughes directed the specific adjustments since he wanted those details to be protected by the attorney-client privilege.

At the end of the meeting, Davis again made it clear to the Air West folks that "you are going to write off the assets that I don't want Hughes to pay for, and book those liabilities that I want you to record and you're going to make these accounting entries before March 31, 1970." Finally, Davis instructed the H&S representatives to be sure that the accounting entries were made and to confirm with him that they were recorded as of the closing date.

CHAPTER 6

FORBIDDEN ROMANCE IN THE VAULT

"Lust's passion will be served; it demands,
it militates, it tyrannizes."

—MARQUIS DE SADE

THE CLOSING DOCUMENTS included a provision for a Deposit Agreement, calling for Air West to put $2,250,000 (almost $44 million in today's dollars) of the sales proceeds it received from Hughes into an escrow account. Then, if Air West's total cash, accounts receivables, prepaid expenses, and other current assets, net of its accounts payable and accrued liabilities (such as payroll due but not yet paid) were determined to be less than their recorded amounts as of March 31, 1970, that reduced amount would be disbursed back to Hughes Air Corp. ("HAC") from the funds held in escrow. Air West would then be entitled to keep any amounts not paid to HAC from the $2,250,000.

The Deposit Agreement resulted in a long series of significant accounting disputes. In April of 1970, the PMM team started again with its key core of Griffin, Alder, and me. H&S arrived with a team of ten auditors, led by partner, Rob McComb and Prentiss Block as the person in charge of the staff at Air West's offices. Soon thereafter, I called PMM's San Francisco office for reinforcements as the two teams' daily disagreements mounted.

The friendly cooperative relationship that existed between the PMM and H&S teams during the 1969 audit now vanished. It was replaced by an adversarial relationship at every turn. The PMM team also totaled ten by June of 1970.

The items in dispute at one time totaled more than 100. They included adjustments to most of the accounts included in the Deposit Agreement. Although the two teams' debates were often heated, the relationships were kept at a professional level—except for one case, a little too amorous.

One member of the PMM team was an attractive young woman named Jennifer, or Jen. She tended to wear clothing that stretched the business dress code, particularly with very short skirts. Betty, a middle-aged woman in charge of Air West's accounts payable department, maintained a forceful presence on the eighth floor. She viewed herself as a protector of Air West.

Prior to the closing by Hughes, Air West was usually short of cash. Its accounting system cranked out its checks to vendors five days before their due date. Instead of putting these checks in the mail, to conserve cash, Betty would hold many of them in a filing cabinet behind her desk.

She then held the checks unless the vendor had great leverage against Air West such as, "If we don't receive payment by Friday there will be no more fuel in your aircraft in Seattle."

Others without strong leverage would have to wait. Betty had grown to be a hardened protector of Air West never to be taken lightly. Betty complained about Jen's miniskirts to her boss, George Scotch.

George told me that Jen was causing an uproar among the women in the Accounts Payable Department and Betty in particular (not to mention the distraction to the few guys in that department) and that I needed to stop this disruption. This led to an awkward conversation that I had with Jen about the distraction and disruption her skirts were causing in the client's office and that she needed to wear longer skirts to Air West's office. Needless to say, women at the Big 8 CPA firms were not yet "permitted" to wear pants to a client's office.

Jennifer protested her innocence. I had to persist. After all, Betty was a force that I did not want to challenge. And Jen's skirts were a distraction!

Jen was also a very friendly young woman. She was not a part of the tension between the PMM and the H&S teams. Plus, she had taken a liking to Richard, an H&S auditor about her age. Members of both the PMM and H&S teams noticed that Jen and Richard often had extended conversations and sometimes went to lunch together. This fraternization was unusual because the PMM team was very close and generally went to lunch as a group. It was now even more unusual given that the two audit teams were on the opposite end of more than 100 accounting disputes.

In June of 1970, Jennifer walked into the vault on the eighth floor of the Mills Square building. The vault was a large room that took up about a third of the southside of the eighth floor. It contained shelves on each wall and a large table that filled the center of the room. The shelves had ledgers, computer printouts, and boxes of accounting documents, while the table generally had several ledgers and other records scattered across its surface. Shortly after Jennifer walked into the vault, Richard followed.

He locked the door from the inside.

There was no time for extended conversations during this encounter. Jennifer and Richard threw their arms around each other and kissed passionately. Jennifer's shoes fell to the floor as she edged her way onto the center table. Richard and his hands transformed into an octopus around her body.

Betty, the middle-aged protector of decency and Air West, burned with suspicion. She had watched Jennifer walk from the PMM room to the vault, measuring Jennifer's skirt length with her leery eyes. Then Betty noticed that Richard followed her into the vault. She wondered what these two were up to, especially when Richard closed the door and she suspected, locked it.

While Jennifer was splayed on the table without her shoes and embracing Richard in their noisy passions, she and Richard did not notice that Betty, armed with her key to the vault, had quietly inserted the key into the lock. Then in one swift and silent action, Betty opened the door to witness the half-dressed Jennifer with Richard's hands up her blouse. Still, they were oblivious to Betty while in their passionate embrace. Betty's scream immediately turned passion into embarrassment as the rest of the eighth-floor occupants rushed to the vault to gawk at the cause of the commotion.

This immediately set off a scandal and spread throughout the entire Air West community in San Mateo. George Scotch hurriedly gathered me and my H&S counterpart, Prentiss Block, into his office to go over the reported details growing more scandalous by the minute. It was agreed that Jennifer and Richard would leave Air West's offices straight away and return to their respective offices in San Francisco.

I called Judy, PMM's HR manager to discuss this incident and warned that Jen was driving to the San Francisco office to visit with her, and that Jen should arrive in around thirty minutes. Upon arrival, she was told that she would leave the firm immediately due to her behavior and poor judgment. Likewise, Richard never returned to the Air West engagement.

Jen's departure was not unexpected. In the sixties and early seventies, the Big 8 international accounting firms ruled their employees with strict codes of conduct that were often brutally enforced.

Some of the rules were written. Many were not. I had seen a first-year staff accountant escorted to the elevator and ordered never to return for the "crime" of having the poor judgment of wearing "penny" loafers (rather than tied leather shoes) to the office. On another occasion, when a senior accountant appeared on Monday morning during "busy season" (generally from January through April) wearing a cast on his foot, the partner asked him what happened. The senior accountant told him about the major tumble he suffered while skiing in Lake Tahoe. The partner fired him on the spot for being so foolish as to go skiing during the busy season, risking an injury that would slow down his ability to perform for his clients during that time of year.

Particularly for staff accountants, life was demanding in the Big 8 accounting firms during this time. The environment resembled a boot camp. In those days, to become a CPA, accountants had to work for two years at a CPA firm, and pass a two-and-a-half-day exam, (passed by less than 40 percent of those taking the exam) to become a CPA. These requirements gave CPA firms the upper hand when dealing with their staff accountants during those first two years. But Jennifer and Richard's escapade in the Air West vault was a clear violation of both firms' written code of conduct. The vault romance became a legend in both the H&S and PMM San Francisco offices.

Interaction between PMM, H&S, and Air West personnel was strictly by the book after these shenanigans in the vault. All interaction was 100 percent professional. As the Deposit Agreement debates over accounting adjustments continued into the fall of 1970, the number of adjustments in dispute was negotiated down to forty-four. Individual adjustments ranged from a high of $299,416 for what H&S called "a needed increase to

Air West's Reserve for Uncollectible Accounts Receivable" to an adjustment of $3,961 for "amounts due from McDonnell Douglas for an aircraft part." In total, H&S, and Chester Davis, argued that the Working Capital deficiency was more than $3.1 million. If this held, HAC would take back the entire $2,250,000 escrow balance, plus interest.

In mid-November of 1970, the attorneys for Air West and Hughes met, without accountants from PMM or H&S, to resolve the forty-four accounting entries that remained in dispute. Chester Davis was his usual self: forceful, arrogant, blunt, and irrepressibly obdurate. The Air West counsel presented their academic arguments against this blunt force as best they could while remaining civil and rational. Air West gave up $1.5 million of the $2,250,000 sale proceeds to HAC from the escrow account. The approach used by Air West's attorneys proved no match against the brutal hurricane-force winds of Chester Davis.

CHAPTER 7
MONEY HORROR SHOW

*"You don't learn from successes; you don't learn
from awards; you don't learn from celebrity;
you only learn from wounds and scars and
mistakes and failures. And that's the truth."*

—*JANE FONDA*

WHILE THE ACCOUNTING issues raged over the Deposit Agreement, the world of Howard Hughes endured new tensions. Besides paying as little in taxes as he could get away with, Hughes's other number one rule was not to suffer losses. His number two rule: follow the number one rule. However, during this time, Hughes realized, to his horror, that John H. Meier, who was hired by Maheu at the urging of Bill Gay, had invested millions of Howard's money from 1968-1970, in nearly worthless mining claims all over the state of Nevada.

Although these mining ventures gained Howard notoriety and added to his adventurous reputation, the losses tore at his mind. He forgot that it was Gay that got him into these mining fiascoes, and falsely blamed Maheu. As much as Maheu tried to explain to Hughes that Meier's mining ventures were Bill Gay's idea, Howard pushed back at Maheu. In his mind, Maheu's carelessness and lack of supervision caused him to lose millions in these mining ventures.

In May of 1970, Hughes also found out that Maheu had planned, without his approval, to purchase Los Angeles Airways. He found this out when one of the Mormon Mafia handed him a press release that stated:

Clarence M. Belinn, president of Los Angeles Airways, Inc., and pioneer of southland helicopter operations, disclosed today that an agreement in principle has been reached whereby the Howard Hughes interests will purchase the company. Tentative plans provide for Hughes to acquire Los Angeles Airways for $3,116,640, which is estimated to net $8.00 per share to the stockholders.

Hughes's attention to the Air West acquisition had clouded his memory that he and Maheu had discussed this acquisition in early 1968. However, since that time, Los Angeles Airways had been involved in two horrible crashes of its Sikorsky helicopters. The first occurred on May 22, 1968, in Paramount, California. At the time, it was the worst helicopter-related accident in U.S. aviation history, killing all twenty-three passengers and three crew members during a regularly scheduled flight from the Disneyland Heliport in Anaheim, California, to Los Angeles International Airport.

Incredibly, on August 14, 1968, another of its Sikorsky helicopters crashed in Compton, California, killing eighteen passengers and its three crew members. This flight was from Los Angeles International Airport on its way to the Disneyland Heliport. These two accidents had crippled the company, and its financial circumstances deteriorated significantly as a result.

Hughes was furious that he would be associated with this aviation nightmare and its risk of financial loss to him. His anger was directed at Maheu, and he demanded that the deal be called off immediately. Hughes then ordered Chester Davis to orchestrate an exit from this atrocious deal.

Hughes was also stewing about Maheu's tendency to leave in place the management of the acquired casinos. He worried about their skimming cash from the cages and taking money from his pockets. He was convinced that the mining losses, the Los Angeles Airways incident, and the lack of adequate profits from the casino operations were Maheu's fault.

Hughes pounded into Davis that he wanted him to hammer Maheu, not just about the Los Angeles Airways problems, but the massive mining losses and the unsatisfactory profits from the casinos, all of which were, he claimed, Maheu's fault. These concerns culminated in Hughes's later stating in a telephone news conference in January 1972, that Maheu was a "no-good, dishonest son-of-a-bitch and he stole me blind."

Davis rented the Presidential Suite on the Century Plaza Hotel's top floor in Century City on the Avenue of the Stars (next to Beverly Hills) and adjacent to the Twentieth Century Fox Studio facilities. He gathered Maheu, Robert Gay, Raymond Holliday, and several other executives from Toolco. There were heated exchanges in the large living room, after which the group moved into the dining room, to take advantage of its well-stocked bar.

The bar did not help calm the combatants' nerves as the arguments, shouting, and insults continued. Maheu also revealed that in addition to the purchase price of Los Angeles Airways stock, he had also agreed that Hughes would guarantee loans amounting to several million dollars. Although the discussion continued, it was clear to all but Maheu that he and Los Angeles Airways were soon to be out of the Hughes orbit, ending a relationship that began in 1955, although incredibly, he never met Hughes face to face. Again, all exchanges had been by memo or the telephone.

Upon Hughes's fourth anniversary of his stay at the Desert Inn, he decided to leave Las Vegas for good. On Thanksgiving Day of 1970, Howard left the Desert Inn and Las Vegas on a private jet to the Britannia Beach Hotel on Paradise Island in the Bahamas.

He was leaving behind a Las Vegas transformed from a crime-based, mob-owned casinos and hotels, to the new large corporate organizations building massive billion-dollar complexes. These complexes included hotels, casinos, five-star restaurants and their celebrity chefs, shops, and vast entertainment venues that show-cased the world's biggest stars.

Las Vegas would never be the same, and neither would Howard Hughes.

Unbeknownst to Hughes, people at the CIA were brain-storming ways to exploit their knowledge of where the K-129 had come to rest and equally important, the fact that Soviets thought that it rested hundreds of miles away from its deathbed. It would result in one of the most expensive and elaborate projects ever undertaken by the CIA.

Hughes didn't know it yet, but he would play a key role in those plans and it would eventually catapult my career into forensic accounting.

CHAPTER 8

GIANT CLAWS

"If you are not willing to risk the unusual,
you will have to settle for the ordinary."

—*Jim Rohn*

JOHN PARANGOSKY HAD established a reputation as
one of the finest team builders and managers in the CIA. He
joined the CIA in 1948. By the early 1950s, he had participated in all aspects of the development of the U-2, a spy plane
used by the CIA to provide both day and night, high-altitude
photo reconnaissance from 70,000 feet in all-weather to spy on
the Soviet Union and its military capacity and activities.

On May 1, 1960, Parangosky's beloved U-2 was shot down
by a surface-to-air missile of the Soviet Air Defense Forces while
performing photographic reconnaissance deep into Soviet terri-
tory. The pilot, Francis Gary Powers, flying the single-seat aircraft,
failed to use his CIA-provided suicide injection. Instead. he
parachuted to safety and was captured by the Soviets. The event
caused great embarrassment to the United States and resulted in
a major decline in its relations with the Soviet Union. The angry

response of its premier Nikita Khrushchev brought this event to the level of an international crisis. Powers was convicted on espionage charges and sentenced to ten years in a Soviet prison. His release was negotiated in February 1962 in a "spy swap" involving Soviet spy Rudolf Abel.

In the 1960s, John Parangosky served as executive officer and program manager for the CIA's OXCART program, which developed and produced the A-12 aircraft. The A-12 was the predecessor to the Blackbird SR-71, the fastest air-breathing manned aircraft in the world. The A-12 was a reconnaissance aircraft of unprecedented capability for its speed, range, and altitude. In recognition of his performance and contributions to the A-12 Program, in 1967, Parangosky received one of the CIA's highest awards, the Distinguished Intelligence Medal. In 1968, he became the mastermind of Project AZORIAN.

Parangosky (also known as Mr. P) was obsessed with ideas about how the United States could recover the K-129 from its watery grave, 16,440 feet below the Pacific Ocean's surface and 1,500 miles northwest of Hawaii. Driving his obsession was the knowledge that this submarine, with its three R-21 nuclear missiles, two nuclear torpedoes and incredible intelligence value, was resting hundreds of miles from where the Soviets thought it was located.

From the photographs taken by the Halibut, the first 136 feet of the K-129 (the forward torpedo area through the sail and one R-21 missile section) had broken away from the other two missiles, as well as the engine room through the stern. Since the forward portion contained the most important intelligence value, including one missile, the recovery would only need to retrieve this portion of the sub, rather than its entire 330-foot length.

In Mr. P's mind, this meant that the sub was "ours" for the taking. Even given the immense size, scope, technological issues, engineering challenges, cover problems, political risks, military concerns, and costs of such a recovery, Mr. P told himself that the intelligence value was well worth these immense stakes.

He developed a preliminary recovery plan and brought it to his boss, Carl E. Duckett, deputy director of the CIA and leader of its Directorate of Science and Technology. Duckett was an accepted leader of scientists and engineers and was widely known for his ability to turn technical information into "laymanese." He was also believed to be the agency's best marketer in selling its programs to higher-ups. Duckett took a personal interest in challenging and complex projects, and Mr. P. would serve him up one.

Mr. P. and Duckett had many meetings to review and refine his original concepts to recover the first 136 feet of the K-129. After a few weeks, they expanded their group to include others who were selected because of their ability to think creatively and overcome complex and unconventional problems. In early 1969, they were ready to meet with CIA Director Richard Helms to get his buy-in and advice on how to move from concept to reality with what was soon to be known within the CIA as Project AZORIAN.

To secure the meeting with Director Helms, Carl Duckett provided him with a general understanding of the Project. Helms was intrigued and agreed to have his assistant arrange for an in-depth meeting. Consistent with his role at the CIA, Director Helms possessed a great passion for the gathering and use of intelligence. The three men brainstormed the complexities of the Project for nearly two hours. Enthusiasm grew within the team, and their commitment to continue was firm.

However, Helms admitted that the political and military risks were daunting. Since this Project would also require Presidential approval, Helms was concerned that his relationship with the newly elected President Richard Nixon was not strong. He suspected that this was likely the result of the well-known exceptional relationship he had with President Johnson, a Democrat. He suggested the need for another team member to propose the Project to Nixon.

Helms told Parangosky and Duckett that the route to approval would be through David Packard and then Dr. Henry Kissinger, national security advisor to President Nixon. Helms explained that Nixon had pushed him out of the direct channel to the President that Helms had enjoyed with President Johnson. Currently, Nixon had assigned Helms to report to Kissinger. Helms felt that the best shot of getting buy-in from Kissinger was for the CIA and the Department of Defense to make the presentation together. They decided to meet with Nixon's friend from California, David Packard, the newly appointed deputy secretary of defense.

Packard was an innovator and an electrical engineer who, along with William Hewlett, founded the Silicon Valley giant, Hewlett-Packard, in Packard's garage. Shortly after Nixon was inaugurated on January 20, 1969, he named his friend Packard to his post at the Pentagon. Nixon looked to Packard to bring new ideas and bold action to reform the military's staid ways. Helms, Duckett, and Mr. P. were eager to circulate their recovery plan to Packard.

It was not easy to arrange a meeting with the new deputy secretary of defense. Many at the Pentagon were eager to capture the new guy's attention and time for their projects, but Helms and Carl Duckett persisted. Helms, Parangosky, and Duckett were to meet with Packard and his assistant in the secretary's office on Tuesday, February 4, 1969. In preparation, Carl and John gathered their team and refined every slide in their presentation, adding drawings of the proposed giant ship, the claw for grabbing the submarine, and a barge hiding the assembly of the claw and delivery to the ship.

The meeting's opening pleasantries were kept short. Just a few greetings and compliments to Packard on his new role with the department. His office was impressive with its wood paneling and many awards and mementos from his days at Hewlett-Packard ("HP") placed around the room. Packard had helped build HP into the world's largest producer of electronic testing and measurement devices. His gray pinstriped suit and personal stature displayed a clear reflection of wealth and success.

It was decided that Duckett would present the project to Packard. Duckett described how shortly after the K-129's initial deep-water test dive, the USS Swordfish noticed that K-129 proceeded on an unexpected course that took it hundreds of miles from its usual patrol, before sinking to the bottom of the Pacific Ocean on the morning of March 8, 1968. He stressed that the Soviets waited until the third week of March to organize its search-and-rescue efforts and that those efforts took place hundreds of miles away from where the K-129 had sunk.

The Soviets had no idea where their sub was, but the U.S. knew exactly where it rested on the ocean floor. The USS Halibut had photographed the submarine and confirmed reports of the sinking from the USS Swordfish. The K-129 lay largely intact on the ocean floor in two sections. The forward 136-foot portion of the sub with high intelligence (torpedoes through at least the first missile section) waited to be taken.

Duckett explained that this situation offered the United States an extraordinary intelligence opportunity, but it would be a challenge to marshal the immense engineering, financial and other resources necessary to recover the sub. The Project was incredibly complex and would likely become one of the CIA's most expensive ventures in its history. Helms stressed that the CIA fully supported the Project. Still, given the political and military risks of seizing a Soviet sub and bringing its contents to the United States, he wanted the Department of Defense and the President's support, which meant getting approval from Dr. Kissinger.

Packard was cautious about the military risks if the Soviets were to learn about this project, but he was enthusiastic about not only the intelligence value of the Project, but also, the challenge presented by the recovery effort itself. It was apparent that the recovery plan would take years to complete. The concept needed to be finalized, the equipment needed to be designed, constructed, and tested, and the related technology needed to be developed to turn this plan into a reality. In addition, the plan needed extreme secrecy throughout and a cover that would get buy-in from the public, the media, and, most of all, the Soviets, because they would be watching and could not know the goal of the project.

Now, the group needed to meet with Dr. Kissinger. David Packard made the arrangements to meet at the Pentagon. The focus was on the value of the intelligence to be gained versus the political and military risks, weighing one against the other. The intelligence included the nuclear missile and torpedoes, the code tables, and coding equipment. Dr. Kissinger was most interested in the value of the likely intelligence and the cover plan to keep the true purpose of the mission an absolute secret. He decided that Packard and Helms would form an executive committee. He also wanted Dr. Lee DuBridge, the President's science advisor, to join the committee. They would meet periodically and report on crucial progress and any concerns to Dr. Kissinger. He reiterated that it was essential to establish a solid cover for the Project.

On August 8, 1969, a high-level executive committee ("ExCom") formally convened. It consisted of Packard as chairman, joined by Helms and Dr. Lee DuBridge. Dr. DuBridge was president of the California Institute of Technology and had been approved by the Senate in February of 1969 in his role as the President's science advisor. The ExCom's assignment was to organize the team necessary for the submarine recovery effort, including developing its structure, management, assets, personnel assignments, and intelligence objectives. It was also agreed that a priority of the ExCom was developing the concept and implementation of a cover for the Project.

If these plans led to a realistic expectation of success, and the cover was air-tight, Dr. Kissinger would take it to President Nixon for approval.

Both John Paranogsky and Carl Duckett had been giving the cover scheme considerable thought. They presented the concept of a deep-ocean mining operation for manganese nodules, which are known to reside on the ocean floor at depths between fourteen thousand to seventeen thousand feet. Carl explained that these nodules are likely to carpet the area where the submarine sank, and they are of significant value.

The value of these potato-sized chunks of manganese is derived from their being mixed with iron, nickel, cobalt, and other useful metals. But its most immediate value in the United States is in its steelmaking qualities. Manganese is essential and irreplaceable for the making of steel. Its mining is dominated by just a few foreign nations and is considered one of the most essential commodities for the United States.

Duckett suggested that the eccentric Howard Hughes, known for undertaking alluring projects related to mining and exploration, be approached to provide cover for Project AZORIAN. Although Hughes would not be paying for this Project, the public would not know that. Still, the media and the Soviets would believe that he had the motivation and ability to afford the enormous expense of such an undertaking.

Duckett further suggested that Hughes have his name on the platform ship and the barge because that was an easy way to stroke Hughes's ego, given that he seemed to enjoy having the Hughes name on his ventures. Finally, he could be given a hefty contract to supply the expensive piping system that would link the claw to the ship.

The ExCom swooned. Its Project had a workable engineering design and a viable cover. Now, they needed to figure out a way to obtain Hughes's buy-in. Assuming they could get Hughes to join the scheme, Packard and DuBridge would update Dr. Kissinger, and he would present the Project to Nixon. Hopefully, the President would then approve this extravagant undertaking.

Extensive security measures were undertaken from the very beginning. Security clearances were severely limited to only those with an absolute need-to-know. A leak-proof environment was essential to provide the project with an ability to conduct its operations without tipping off the Soviets about its true goal. There could also be no evidence of U.S. military or CIA involvement in the Project. If the Soviets found out that any attempt was being made to recover their submarine and its weapons, there would be massive diplomatic issues and probable military intervention. This cover needed to be maintained with the utmost confidentiality. And it needed to be maintained for a an estimated four- to five-year period for the massive equipment to be designed, developed, constructed, tested, deployed to the site, and returned.

AZORIAN called for the construction of a platform ship, 619 feet long and 116 feet wide. The capture vehicle (the claw, also known as the Clementine), and a submersible barge to hide the construction and transport of the capture vehicle to the ship.

John Paranogsky led heated discussions and analyses of how the sub would be lifted from the ocean floor and it was not until July 1970 that the design team developed a clear favorite on how to lift the sub from the floor. It was termed the "Brute Force Direct Lift" method (or "Brute Force"). This method proposed using a string of connecting pipe that would descend as each 60-foot pipe section (two 30-foot "doubles") was added to the string.

This was expected to be repeated over 550 times as the giant claw was lowered to the ocean floor. Once the claw hovered over the 136-foot target portion of the submarine, the claw's fingers would wrap around the submarine and lift its 2,200,000-pound mass into the waiting platform ship, three miles above the ocean floor.

A well-publicized drawing, which can be viewed in the CIA Legacy Museum, depicts the four stages of this operation. The top left portion of the drawing shows the Clementine (including the Claw) emerging from the bottom of the Glomar Explorer's "Moon Pool." This was a space in the middle of the Hughes Glomar Explorer, ("HGE") which was a 199-foot long by 74-foot wide and 65-foot-high cavern directly underneath the HGE's 228-foot-tall derrick. Moving down the drawing, the bottom left scene shows the Clementine being placed directly over the K-129. Then moving to the bottom right portion of the drawing, it illustrates the Clementine detaching the bottom portion of itself, which is left on the ocean floor, then raising the remainder of the Clementine and the target portion of the submarine toward the Glomar Explorer. The final scene, on the top right of the drawing, shows the top of the Clementine and the recovered portion of the submarine about to be pulled into the HGE's Moon Pool. During this entire operation, the Glomar Explorer is connected by a 16,500-foot-long (more than three-mile) string of pipe that is lengthened or shortened using the 228-foot-tall derrick (seen in the center of the HGE in the photograph below) to add or remove sections of the pipe string. The forward and aft towers, also seen in the photograph of the ship, are called "docking legs." These legs were used to lower and raise the ship's bottom gates which allowed the Clementine to be lowered on its mission to retrieve the K-129, and to be returned to the ship with the sub, then closed to allow the HGE to return home.

ILLUSTRATION OF THE FOUR STAGES OF THE RECOVERY EFFORT. SOURCE: THE CIA LEGACY MUSEUM, THE EXPOSING OF PROJECT AZORIAN, MARCH 17, 2020.

HUGHES GLOMAR EXPLORER. SOURCE: BETTMANN / CONTRIBUTOR VIA GETTY IMAGES.

HMB-1 ON ITS WAY FROM REDWOOD CITY TO MEET THE HGE NEAR SANTA CATALINA. SOURCE: BETTMANN / CONTRIBUTOR VIA GETTY IMAGES.

On October 30, 1970, the design team presented the Brute Force method to the ExCom, together with the conceptual plan for the K-129's recovery. The team described two other alternatives for lifting the sub from the ocean floor that had been considered but were discarded as less reliable. The ExCom approved the Brute Force method and then moved its attention to the project's cover story. Everyone agreed that the cover story would be riveting enough to approach the Hughes organization.

The Clementine was equipped with television cameras that provided vision to the crew of the HGE, as well as lights and propulsion units to guide it to the landing site over the target portion of the K-129. Its claws were individually controlled from the Glomar Explorer.

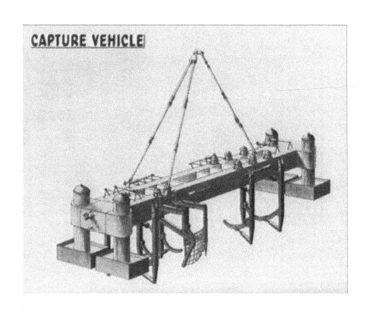

THE CLEMENTINE (THE CLAW): SOURCE, THE CIA LEGACY MUSEUM, THE EXPOSING OF PROJECT AZORIAN, MARCH 17, 2020.

CHAPTER 9

SIGNING THE BLACK CONTRACT

"Empires implode from within due to their own excesses."

—*GAD SAAD*

THE AGENCY KNEW that Robert Maheu had a long history of working with both the FBI and the CIA. It was decided that Packard would call Maheu. He and Maheu had met on several occasions, and they could meet as CEO to CEO. Packard called Maheu. They exchanged past stories and mutual acquaintances, then Packard stated he had a sensitive project to discuss. In fact, the project was so sensitive, Packard suggested that they meet in person in Las Vegas, in early November of 1970.

Maheu was cautious since this timeframe was not long after the meeting at the Century Plaza about Hughes's disastrous mining losses and the Los Angeles Airways debacle. Packard urged Maheu not to tell anyone about the meeting, and to be alone. Although Maheu was still wary, he agreed to meet Packard on November 4 at the Department of Defense office on Las Vegas Boulevard, just a few miles from Maheu's home on the Desert Inn's golf course.

Maheu arrived in time for the noon meeting that included

a catered lunch. Not long into their discussion, Packard told Maheu that he needed to sign a non-disclosure agreement ("NDA") to discuss the Project with him. Maheu was used to this type of secrecy from his days of cut-out projects with the CIA. After taking care of the NDA formalities, Packard gave Maheu a brief outline of Project AZORIAN. Maheu was now excited and flattered about the prospect of being involved in such a challenging effort that was so important to the country.

However, having been burned at the Century City meeting, and knowing that this was not a Nevada project (one of the issues with the Los Angeles Airways transaction was the perception that Maheu had overstepped his jurisdiction by extending his role outside of Nevada), he knew that what Packard proposed stepped far outside of the scope of his authority with Hughes. He refused to pull Howard into another "mining" project.

Maheu suggested that they call Raymond Holliday, who was then the head of Hughes Tool Company. Maheu and Packard both agreed that Hughes would more likely agree to the mining cover story, if it were tied to with a lucrative piping contract for Hughes Tool, and, since Toolco was not a public company, the real purpose of the project would not need to be disclosed to any outsider or to the United States Securities and Exchange Commission ("SEC"). Also, Hughes was famous for extravagant adventures and secrecy. In contrast, a public company involved in such a massive project would have to make disclosures in its 8-Ks, 10-Qs and 10-Ks to the SEC about its scope and cost. This would risk blowing the project's cover since these documents are carefully reviewed by the public who own, or are considering owning, its stock, as well as the press. Also, given that there would be little investment made by Toolco in the project, that absence and its related non-disclosures would be suspicious.

A conference call ensued between Maheu, Packard, and Holliday. Although the conversation was kept at a very high level with very few details and limited disclosure, Holliday was eager to meet with the new Nixon appointee. As it happened, Holliday was in Los Angeles meeting with Chester Davis on another matter. It was agreed that Packard, Maheu, Holliday, and Davis would meet the next day at the Century Plaza Hotel.

Once again, the presidential suite on the nineteenth floor, Davis's sanctuary, was the venue of choice to impress the deputy secretary of defense. Its sizeable living area was perfect for their meeting, and the conference room, just south of the living area, would enable Davis and Holliday to call Hughes in private to get his questions and ultimate buy-in on the concept and details of Toolco's involvement. They also needed the approval of Hughes to use his name.

There was a sitting room and a bedroom on the northern side beyond the living room where Packard could call Helms to go over any issues or areas where Packard wanted Helms' input as the meeting progressed. There was no shortage of privacy with multiple rooms and thirteen secure telephones scattered around the Presidential Suite.

Again, NDAs were signed (Howard's was faxed to him, signed, and returned). The meeting went exceptionally well. Hughes was on the telephone in the conference room for most of the meeting, waiting for updates from Davis, Gay, or Holliday and asking questions and delivering comments to be discussed with Packard. It made him feel good to be needed after the rough treatment that he had received over the "Spruce Goose" affair and the grilling that he had to endure during his testimony before Congress over that project.[5]

---

5 During World War II, Hughes had a contract with the U.S. War Department to build a "flying boat" capable of crossing the Atlantic with 750 fully equipped troops. Due to the shortage of aluminum it had to be built mostly of wood (hence the nickname the Spruce Goose). It had eight wing-mounted engines which lifted the largest aircraft ever build. Because of production issues, Hughes did not deliver the aircraft until after the war ended and was publicly criticized during his testimony before the Senate War Investigating Committee in 1947.

THE SPRUCE GOOSE. SOURCE: EUROSTYLE GRAPHICS / ALAMY STOCK PHOTO.

Although Hughes jumped at his name being involved in Project AZORIAN and the profits that the piping system would provide Toolco, he insisted that Chester Davis protect his interests. He would agree to a very generalized "black contract"[6] that would enable the parties to move forward in their respective roles. CIA contracts are not public, and there is an added veil of secrecy and lack of transparency to its "black" contracts. However, Hughes insisted that this black contract would be followed up with a more detailed agreement to be structured by Davis and agreed to by Helms.

Hughes made it clear to Davis that both contracts would spell out that Toolco was not on the hook for any of the costs and any of the liabilities that might arise to Toolco as a result of its performance under the contract. It would also not be called out in any way for the failure of the project. Howard wanted protection for any property taxes on the equipment, the ship, or the barge. And he wanted the piping system, the pipe, and any services that were

---

6 A highly secret CIA contract with vague terms and limited detail.

to be provided by Toolco to come with ample overhead recovery and a healthy profit for Toolco. Hughes knew that he was bestowing his very valuable name on this project, and that name was priceless to the United States for the cover he was providing. His name would not be provided for free; rather, it would command a handsome price within the overhead and profit included in the price of the piping system.

Packard and Helms agreed with Hughes's demands as relayed by Chester Davis. The terms of the black contract contained the provisions requested by Hughes. It was further agreed that Chester Davis would provide a more detailed agreement soon. The parties shook hands, enjoyed celebratory drinks from the bar and sealed the deal.

With the Air West deal closed and its Deposit Agreement skirmish put to bed (or so he thought), and this development with the CIA providing new interests for Hughes, he decided that it was time to show Maheu the door. On December 5, 1970, Hughes had Chester Davis fire Robert Maheu. Maheu immediately filed suit in Nevada state court to retain his position. He claimed that Hughes was coerced into firing him or that someone other than Hughes had ordered the firing. As was customary for Hughes and Davis, this lawsuit would also become a long and tortuous battle between Maheu, Hughes, and Davis.

The "black" contract was finalized and dated December 13, 1970. The contract #S-HU-0900 provided for the following:

- Hughes Tool Co. was the agent.
- Global Marine would be the undisclosed agent of the sponsor.
- The U.S. government was the sponsor.
- Global Marine and Hughes Tool were parties to a "Deep Sea Mining Project," and they would keep the sponsor from being identified as the true party in interest.

- Global Marine and Hughes Tool would be paid "for their services" and they would not reveal "any information whatsoever with respect to the Government's sponsorship of this contract, the department involved, or the work thereunder."

The public has never been provided further details about contract #S-HU-0900. However, the contract provided that Toolco would recover all its costs, with provision to cover its overhead, and an ample profit. The ship was to be named the Hughes Glomar (short for Global Marine) Explorer, and the barge would be called the Hughes Mining Barge or HMB-1.

Davis and Packard had many stressful conversations over the next several months, working out the relationship's details. Packard felt that Davis did not share any feelings for the fact that this project was of great value to the nation's interest. Instead, he believed that Davis was looking out only for Hughes and, therefore, Chester Davis. He was annoyed that Davis had no respect for the interests of the United States.

Now, with its cover in place, an ExCom meeting was called to summarize the progress to date. Dr. Kissinger was invited to assess the recent events and get the thoughts of Dr. DuBridge. The debate about the value of the intelligence versus the risks breathed fire into the project. Kissinger was also eager to discuss the details about the Hughes cover. At the conclusion of the meeting, both Dr. DuBridge and Dr. Kissinger agreed that they would support the project and pitch it to President Nixon.

Dr. Kissinger met with the President in the White House and reviewed the projects key issues and risks. Nixon asked about his friends Packard and Dr. DuBridge but not Richard Helms. Although President Nixon was concerned about the risks involved, he was convinced by his faith in the engineering and management skills of Packard and the enthusiasm of

Dr. Kissinger that the intelligence value to be gained from the nuclear missile and torpedoes outweighed the political and military risks. After all, there was no other source in the world where this information could be obtained. Nixon was convinced that this intelligence was of great importance to the nation's defense.

Nixon was also impressed by the cover story provided by the eccentric old miner named Hughes, still one of the world's richest men and its most famous recluse. The President approved the project, which became the most ambitious and challenging ocean engineering effort ever undertaken by the CIA.

The CIA has never released the total cost of Project AZORIAN. Estimates in books and on various sources on the Internet range from $500 million to $800 million in 1974 dollars which, assuming a cost of $600 million, amounts to more than $8 billion in today's dollars.

CHAPTER 10

BEST LAWYER IN AMERICA

*"There is no greatness where there is no
simplicity, goodness and truth."*

—*LEO TOLSTOY*

AFTER AIR WEST, Inc. sold its assets and transferred
its liabilities to Howard Hughes and Toolco on March
31, 1970, it needed to file a tax return for its year ended
December 31, 1970. The directors of Air West's successor entity,
A.W. Liquidating Company, determined that PMM would prepare this tax return. This tax return's critical time was the three
months ending March 31, 1970. During this three-month
period was when the company operated as an airline and transferred its assets and liabilities to Hughes. During the remainder
of 1970, the assets were held by A.W. Liquidating Company and
it had little activity during that nine months ended December
31, 1970.

I returned to the Mills Square building in San Mateo in
early1971 to prepare Air West's tax return for the year ended
1970. This time I was alone. I met with the assistant controller,

Marty Rollins, who had been with Air West since the merger of Bonanza, Pacific, and West Coast Airlines in 1968. Now, Marty was employed by Hughes Air West.

Rollins was a quiet, thoughtful man who was at ease with his responsibilities and the employees that he supervised. The eighth floor of the Mills Square building looked the same as when I left after completing the audit of Air West's financial statements for the year ended December 31, 1969, and my work on the Deposit Agreement that ended in November 1970.

Rollins showed me the desk where I would do my work on the airline's tax return. My old office was now reserved for the H&S auditors. No longer in an office, I would do my work in an open area surrounded by Rollins' staff, including the observant Betty in Accounts Payable. Her job now included keeping her eyes on me. Although the Hughes Air West employees dressed in an informal business attire, I was always dressed in a conservative business style. Every day it was a business suit and tie, a long-sleeve white or blue shirt, and black wingtip shoes.

Rollins informed me that the people, records, and files were still in the same locations that they had been during my prior work. After Rollins returned to his office, I walked around the floor to refresh my recollection of the where people and records were located. I also stopped to chat with a few folks with whom I had become friends over the past two years, particularly George Scotch. All seemed well, but now Betty's eyes pierced me most of this time. She was in her fifties and overweight with plump cheeks, making her eyes seem piercing, squeezed between her eyebrows and her cheeks. I sensed that she was now Marty's spy.

Of great importance to me was the contents of the now-infamous "vault." The vault contained many of the records that I needed to prepare the tax return. These records included the general ledger of Air West and the journal entries that revealed the adjustments to each of the account balances of the airline.

Notably, the vault also contained the supporting documentation for those journal entries. I did not have a key to the vault, but it was unlocked during the workday. Anything removed from the vault during the day, however, had to be returned before it was locked during the night. To my knowledge, no other romance had heated up in the vault since Jen and Robert.

Essential to my preparation of the tax return were the accounting entries that reflected events during the three months before the airline's sale to Hughes on April 1, 1970. I prepared a listing of the accounts and their balances at the closing date. I compared these balances to their balances as of December 31, 1969. Astoundingly, it became clear to me that millions of dollars of assets had been written off and expensed. In addition, more millions in liabilities had also been established just before the sale to Hughes. After further digging into the asset and liability balances containing the largest suspicious entries, I determined that all the unusual accounting entries had been recorded "as of" March 31, 1970.

For decades, Howard Hughes had been an international celebrity. His every move from hotel to hotel was on the front page of newspapers around the United States and in many countries. Until my involvement in the purchase of Air West, I had not been a careful watcher of his activities, but after working on the Air West audits, I, like so many others in the world, watched when stories about Hughes appeared on television or were written in the press. I noted with interest when it was reported that Hughes had to deal with the reality that his wife of thirteen years, the beautiful actress, Jean Peters, had filed for divorce on January 15, 1970. But most importantly, I determined that Hughes and his cohorts were not to be trusted.

During this work at Air West, I created work papers documenting and summarizing my findings. I also began to copy selected documents supporting my work. I did not want to leave the work papers I created at Air West or copies of particularly essential documents when I left the office at night, so I packed them into a large audit bag and took them to my apartment. I also did not want to leave the audit bag in the trunk of my red 1964 Mustang, so I lugged it up the stairs to the third-floor apartment that I shared with my wife, Barby. I carefully placed the briefcase in a corner of our living room where I could keep a close eye on it as if it contained the Hope Diamond!

I stored the remaining copies of Air West documents in a trunk, with a large padlock on it to secure it at the Air West office. During the workday, when I finished working with copies of key documents, I put them into my audit bag which had a combination lock on both ends of the case. I hoped this process would keep any prying eyes from snooping through the copies and any notes that I had made.

Auditors are trained to look carefully at accounting entries that are recorded at or near the end of the accounting period being audited or analyzed. In this case, the supporting documents in the files that I was analyzing contained notations indicating that, although the closing entries were dated Tuesday, March 31, 1970, many of the supporting documents had dates showing that the analyses and support was produced after March.

As I traced through the supporting documents, it also became clear to me that these papers were supporting accounting entries that were not in accordance with GAAP, and they were not consistent with the accounting principles used by the airline on July 1, 1968. To me, these entries were clear violations of the Purchase Contract between the Air West shareholders and Hughes.

In addition, these entries benefited Hughes, at great cost to Air West's shareholders.

I knew that these findings represented weapons that could be used against Hughes to recover millions of dollars that he had taken from my clients' pockets.

I decided that I needed to share these findings with the right attorney. My first choice was to speak with Joseph Martin, an Air West director and one of the named partners in the law firm of Miller, Groezinger, Petit, Evers & Martin. He was now also general counsel to the liquidating company that held the cash received from Hughes from the sale of Air West's net assets. He was my clients' counsel.

As it happened, my office at PMM in San Francisco was at 601 California Street, and Martin's firm was just across the street at 650 California. This part of California Street is one of the beautiful streets in San Francisco's Financial District. It is often seen in films and photographs, with cable cars climbing "halfway to the stars" from the Financial District to the top of California Street, where the Fairmont Hotel and other famous hotels are found. On the day that I decided to call Joe Martin, I was working in my office, which looked out at the Bank of America building, the tallest building in San Francisco at that time.

I took a long breath before calling Martin. Showtime. He picked up on the first ring as if he saw me dialing his number. "Joe, this is Paul Regan. I'm with Peat Marwick. I was in charge of the audit of Air West's 1969 financial statements. Now I'm working on its 1970 tax return."

Without hesitation, he replied, "Sure, Paul, I heard all about how you and your staff did such a great job on the Deposit Agreement. Those Hughes jerks wanted every last dime out of the escrow account, but your work enabled us to salvage some of the shareholders' money. What's on your mind?"

"Well, Joe, while doing my work at Air West on its final tax return, I've come across documents that make it clear to me that as of the day before the closing with Hughes, Air West's accountants recorded millions of dollars of accounting entries which violated the Purchase Contract. These entries reduced the amount that you and the other shareholders of Air West received from Hughes from the sale of the airline. I want to meet with a few of your best litigators to discuss what I'm finding, then lay out a plan for how I finish the tax return and what should be done about Hughes having cheated the shareholders out of millions from the sale of Air West's assets." There, the cat was out of the bag. No turning back.

I emphasized, "Joe, you know Chester Davis, *he eats people alive*. I'm looking for your smartest, toughest litigator to stand up to Chester and bring him and Hughes down for their bad acts. I also need to get help soon. I don't know how long the folks at Air West will put up with my copying their documents."

Martin assured me he would get back to me with his best picks for the job. And he certainly did. Later that day, Joe Martin called me with two partners' names and suggested that they meet me for lunch the next day at Sam's Grill & Seafood Restaurant. Sam's has a section that is designed for privacy. Martin told me that he would send a messenger over with detail of the backgrounds of the two attorneys so that I could review them before the lunch. It was agreed that I would stop by Joe's office at noon the next day, and we would make the three-block walk to Sam's for lunch.

When the messenger arrived at PMM later that afternoon, I poured over the backgrounds of the two litigators that I would meet with the next day. The first attorney's background was fine, the usual good schools, both undergraduate and law school, a listing of articles he had written, plus a list of important cases he had worked on over his career. Then I turned to the second litigator, John Bales Clark. His credentials jumped off the page in a flash of light.

From this background, my heart kind of raced at the prospect of working with John. Being an engineering undergraduate at Stanford told me that John was brainy, disciplined, and probably good with numbers. John's academic scholarship from Stanford Law School confirmed his keen intellect, and his role as editor of the *Law Review* spoke to his being near the top of his class at the law school. The fact that John had been a player on both the offensive and defensive lines on the Stanford football team was also consistent with the passion needed to both block Chester Davis and run around and over him when necessary.

I also knew that only the best candidates from the top law schools were recruited to join Sullivan & Cromwell's New York office, where he first worked out of law school. After he left New York for California, John was selected as a "California Super Lawyer" and as one of the best lawyers in America. Taken together, these qualifications told me that it was likely that John had trained his intellect, toughness, and desire to work hard. It also showed that he had applied these traits in law to become highly successful.

I was looking forward to meeting John to see if my perceptions about him on paper would be confirmed in person.

The next day, I left my office a few minutes before noon. I dodged a cable car while walking across California Street and stepped into the Hartford Building at 650 California Street, about halfway up the hill toward Grant Avenue and Chinatown. The receptionist greeted me and stated that the two attorneys would be with me shortly. Soon after, they joined me, and the three of us proceeded to Sam's for lunch.

Once in Sam's and seated in one of the private dining areas, with walls on three sides and a curtain for an entrance, I told the attorneys what I knew about how Hughes used his Fear, Uncertainty, and Disruption campaign, plus the accounting adjustments at the closing to shortchange the shareholders of Air West by millions of dollars.

Both attorneys had already gone through the background material they had received from their partner, Joe Martin. They were eager to hear about what I was "mining" from Air West's accounting records about the millions of dollars in backdated accounting entries that had further lined Hughes's pockets at Air West's shareholders' expense.

As I dug deeper into the details, John Clark became extremely interested, focused, and animated. He also asked great questions and made comments, which showed me that he was following the key issues and was excited about the stories that came along with the accounting details. John Clark clearly saw the makings of a compelling civil lawsuit against Howard Hughes and his corporations involved in the acquisition and wrongdoing. I confirmed in my mind that John Clark was the right man for the job. He was engaged, smart, tough, and had a passion to right the wrongs that he was hearing.

I believed that John was likely to be the type of person who would master the materials and bring sustained effort and energy to block and tackle both Howard Hughes and Chester Davis. He was ten years older than me, but at 35, he had enough experience to be effective and plenty of stamina to deal with the long effort that this hair-raising journey would require. In addition, John was still young enough that we could share our enjoyment of stories about: sports, music, politics, our wives and children, and a desire to fight for the "little guy" against the goliaths such as Howard Hughes and Chester Davis.

JOHN CLARK, CIRCA 1970, COURTESY OF SUSANNE CLARK

It was decided during the lunch that I would go back to Air West and not only continue working on its tax return but also, use that as an opportunity to gather copies of as many relevant documents as possible. These documents would be needed, not only as a basis for John to prepare a complaint in federal court in San Francisco, but to begin the subpoenas for even more documents and exhibits to the depositions that would follow.

I returned to San Mateo the next day with my audit bag and trunk to store additional document copies. I already had nearly everything I needed to prepare the Air West tax return. Now, I needed to copy as many additional documents as possible to prove that the millions of dollars in accounting entries made "as of" the day before the closing violated the Purchase Contract.

While most of these documents were in the vault, some were in other filing cabinets on the eighth floor of the Mills Square building, and some were on the third floor of 181 Second Street. I even asked some of the department heads for copies of relevant spreadsheets and supporting documents to gather as much evidence as he could before I left the Air West offices. Much of these activities were under the watchful eye of Betty, the fierce protector in accounts payable.

After two days of this effort, it occurred. While I was working at my desk, I saw Marty Rollins strolling toward me in his usual casual, but deliberate, manner. Stopping in front of me, he stated: "Paul, you've been working hard on that tax return and gathering lots of records. I believe it's time that you wrapped up things here at Air West. Tom (the Controller at Air West, who was with Bonanza Airlines) and I have decided that we need your desk the day after tomorrow for someone else. So, get what you need today and tomorrow, but then you need to be out of here."

I had expected that this time would come. Rollins' request was not unreasonable. I was determined to get what documents that I needed at Air West before Rollins' deadline. But now I noticed that I was being watched by both Betty and everyone around her. Rollins must have called a staff meeting suggesting that my activities be carefully surveilled. Now, it had come down to me against these Hughes's Air West employees who needed their future pay checks from Hughes.

I skipped lunch that day, not wanting to leave my documents behind in case the surveillance became more aggressive. To test out this concern, before I left my desk to go into the vault and make copies of documents at the copy machine just outside the vault, I put several harmless documents on my desk, carefully noting exactly where they were placed and in the order of a small number that I put lightly in pencil in the lower left corner of each document.

After being in the vault for fifteen minutes and at the copy machine for another five minutes, I returned to my desk.

Sure enough, the documents had been moved and one document that had been the third document in order was now the last. I now knew that, in the future, before I left my desk, I would lock up any important documents to keep them from the prying eyes of folks that were no longer on my side.

On my last day at Air West, I brought my lunch to the office to avoid being away from the documents for an extended period. Although I had made many friends in the office, those folks now worked for the almighty Howard Hughes. I had become an adversary in their eyes. There had been good times and hard times on the eighth floor of 100 South Ellsworth, but it was time to lug my stuffed audit bag to the garage under the building, bring the folding hand truck from my Mustang up to the eighth floor of the Mills Square building, and wheel the trunk full of treasured document copies back to the car.

I left Air West for the final time after spending a good part of the previous two and a half years at its San Mateo offices.

I was sad to leave that part of my life behind.

CHAPTER 11

ENDING FEAR, UNCERTAINTY, AND DISRUPTION

*"Tyrants have always some slight shade of virtue;
they support the laws before destroying them."*

—*VOLTAIRE*

I N LATE 1971 and early 1972, John Clark and I spent many days identifying key events and their related documents. We also identified persons who were involved in those events and the actions they had taken. We poured over Air West's 8-K's filed with the U. S. Securities & Exchange Commission, which reported significant events to its operations and financial status (generally within four business days from the event) that could be important to the issues to be included in the litigation. I also gathered pertinent press releases issued by Air West.

The San Francisco Public Library became our premier source of newspaper articles from Phoenix, Los Angeles, Las Vegas, San Francisco, and Seattle. We studied each of these publications for evidence reflecting the adverse impact on Air West of Hughes's FUD campaign.

I prepared charts of Air West's stock prices and the volume of shares traded by day. The stock prices and volumes were plotted on a timeline and referenced to key events and documents gathered in relation to Air West's stock price movements. The chart clearly showed a relationship between particularly harmful comments about Air West's service issues or stories about its maintenance or flight delays with resulting revenue declines and its falling stock prices. The FUD campaign had worked for Hughes.

The goal of the meetings between John and I was to determine what to include in the complaint to be filed in Federal Court in San Francisco on behalf of Air West's shareholders against Howard Hughes and any other persons or entities. A.W. Liquidating Company would bring this complaint. This new entity was formed to receive the sales proceeds from Hughes in exchange for his purchase of Air West's assets, net of the liabilities that he assumed. This company was then to distribute the proceeds to the shareholders of Air West, Inc. Its offices were located at the law firm of Miller, Groezinger, Petit, Evers & Martin.

During this period, John brought a new lawyer from Miller, Groezinger, to the team. Theodore ("Ted") Russell was a native Californian who had graduated from the University of California at Berkeley. Then, in 1969, he earned his law degree from its law school, Boalt Hall. He was bright and eager to prove to John that he could grasp the challenges of a complicated case against one of the world's most powerful men. He also had to demonstrate an understanding of complex accounting principles.

Ted's physical resemblance to Clark Kent (or Superman) was a topic of friendly joking among the team. He was someone with a bright future at the Pettit firm.

I led the lawyers through the critical accounting principles used by Air West in its July 1968, financial statements and showed how the backdated closing entries recorded "as of" March 31, 1970, violated the Purchase Contract. These were violations because the adjustments were not prepared in accordance with GAAP and the accounting principles used were not consistent with those used in the July 1968 financial statements. It was clear that every one of these closing-related accounting adjustments violated the Purchase Contract requirements.

With the help of my timeline charts, I also explained how the Hughes team's FUD (fear, uncertainty, and disruption) campaign started shortly after Air West's disastrously long 4th of July weekend, its first as a combined airline. The FUD campaign hurt Air West's revenue, which caused significant operating losses to the airline. These losses damaged its net worth and were another way that Hughes and his cronies improperly enabled Hughes to reduce the airline's purchase price received by the Air West shareholders.

During these weeks, the work was tedious but essential to understanding the main issues to be explained and laid out in a complaint that would stand the scrutiny of not only the Hughes organization, and Chester Davis and his associates, but also the federal District Court.

The documents were carefully analyzed and understood by the team. They also had to weave in the information from the 8-K's, press releases, and the relevant newspaper and magazine articles for evidence of the existence and adverse impacts of the FUD campaign. To gather and verify this evidence, Ted Russell travelled to San Diego, Los Angeles, Seattle, Phoenix, Las Vegas, and other cities to interview authors of these articles, as well as the people referenced in them. This process added substance to the extent, nature, and effectiveness of the FUD campaign for inclusion into the complaint.

On the east side of the law firm's twenty-first floor, we

converted a large conference into our war room, a gathering place for the people and the documents key to the issues of the case. Copies of essential pages of documents were taped to the walls; poster boards were used to display and discuss critical issues through elaborate charts, timelines, and bullet points.

After months of work, from this assortment of evidence, the complaint materialized. The civil lawsuit against Howard R. Hughes, Hughes Tool, and Hughes Air West emerged.

It was now time for John Clark and the team to gather and meet with the board of A. W. Liquidating Company. For their part, the directors debated the cost and difficulties of suing Howard Hughes. They had already funded the significant legal and accounting fees to date, and they knew from experience and reputation that Hughes was litigious and would be aggressively defended by his bulldog of an attorney, Chester Davis.

Some directors wanted to cut their losses and move on. Others were angered by the words "Air Worst" and other FUD actions, together with the "phony accounting entries" backdated to the closing date. A. W. Liquidating Company had retained a large portion of the sales proceeds from the sale of the airline to Hughes, so it had the money to fund the litigation.

With strong evidence and a fiery passion for justice, John convinced the directors that he and his team had the tools to win against Hughes and his comrades. When it came time to vote, the directors, by a large majority, authorized John to file the civil securities lawsuit.

CHAPTER 12
NIXON'S DILEMMA

"Nothing makes us so lonely as our secrets."

—PAUL TOURNIER

I N EARLY 1971, with its cover story in place, the executive committee of Project AZORIAN met to review the technical risk areas and the projected costs of the Project. The recovery's feasibility received a boost when another Global Marine ship, the Glomar Challenger, drilled a hole deep in the ocean floor, then withdrew the drill bit. It returned later and was able to place a new bit into the same hole. Initially, the Project had been given a 10 percent chance of success; now, its probability of success skyrocketed.

CIA Director Helms received a detailed review of the risks of the project and the value of the AZORIAN's target. He continued to give it the highest priority and concurred that the value of the intelligence far exceeded the project's cost and risks. Packard summed up the proceedings by stating that it was a clear consensus to proceed with Project AZORIAN.

However, by this time, the Hughes organization and

President Nixon had competing and growing concerns. The Hughes folks were worried about former right-hand man Robert Maheu and the scope of the lawsuit he was pursuing against Hughes. Simultaneously, President Nixon had become obsessed with Lawrence O'Brien, the Democratic National Committee chairman, who continued to be on a large retainer with the Hughes organization.

Nixon and his chief of staff, H. R. Haldeman, wanted John W. Dean III, the president's counsel, to investigate what O'Brien was doing for Hughes. Nixon's principal concern was that Maheu, through O'Brien, had learned of wrongdoing by Nixon and his campaign, and he was going to use it in his war with Hughes.

On January 26, 1971, John Dean prepared a memo to Haldeman. He relayed information that he had obtained from Bob Bennett, son of Senator Wallace Bennett of Utah and a spirited lobbyist for Hughes. He agreed to meet in Los Angeles with Bill Gay at Hughes's communication and document center at 7000 Romaine Street in Los Angeles.

When Bennett met with Bill Gay, he was advised by Gay that he could not provide any information relating to the O'Brien contract—even if asked by the White House. He did not elaborate, but it was clear that John Dean's assessment was correct when he stated that Gay would not give any information that might embarrass Hughes, such as nefarious campaign contributions. Bennett described to Dean that the litigation between Maheu and Hughes was a broad and bitter struggle, and it was clear that the two sides were trying to *destroy* each other.

Bennett did, however, reveal that Maheu had handled all of Hughes's political activity for the last fifteen years. Since O'Brien was close to Maheu, he believed O'Brien knew a great deal, including the $100,000 slush fund in Rebozo's safe that Hughes had given him.

It was clear to Nixon that Hughes, through Maheu, had

made O'Brien dangerous to him, and that the Maheu litigation was a war that could be trouble ahead. Although Hughes wanted a federal investigation of Maheu, his money would not buy it. Nixon was afraid of O'Brien and Maheu's retaliation. Bottom line, there was now clear tensions between Nixon and Hughes.

CHAPTER 13

LITERARY HOAX

"The universe is made of stories, not of atoms."

—MURIEL RUKEYSER

THROUGH MY OWN research to date, I suspect that the peculiar, filthy rich man famously portrayed and dramatized in "The Aviator" starring Leonardo DiCaprio is one of the most popular subjects of news media in history. Fact or fiction? That's always the question. Sometimes the lines blur in the quest to tell a good tale, which grossed over $200 million at the box office.

On January 7, 1972, a conference call and television interview were set up for Howard Hughes to denounce Clifford Irving's alleged autobiography of Hughes. McGraw-Hill had paid Irving an extraordinary advance of $765,000 for the book, *Howard Hughes: Confessions of an Unhappy Billionaire*. The Irving autobiography of Hughes had become a highly anticipated sensation. Now, Hughes's comments about the forthcoming book turned into a major event in itself—broadcast by television and radio around the world and listened to by millions.

During the interview, Hughes reviled Irving's book as a "hoax," stating that he had never met or spoken with him and no one in his circle had done so either. He announced that he was suing both Irving and McGraw-Hill.[7]

Straying from the autobiography topic, a reporter asked Hughes why he fired Robert Maheu.

Hughes responded: "Because he's a no-good, dishonest son of a bitch, and he stole me blind. You wouldn't think it could be possible with modern methods of bookkeeping and accounting and so forth for a thing like the Maheu theft to have occurred, but believe me, it did, because the money's gone and he's got it."

When asked how he felt about Maheu, Howard unloaded again: "*Bitterly* is a mild way of putting it… everything [Maheu] has done, everything short of murder, as a result of being discharged. I don't suppose any disgruntled employee who was discharged has even come close to Mr. Maheu's conduct…. In light of that litigation [the Nevada State Court case filed by Maheu in December 1970] and the struggle and harassment he has embarked upon, it's very, very difficult for me to tell you precisely the motives that led to [my leaving Las Vegas] without having some effect on the devastating, horrifying program of harassment that Maheu and his associates have launched against me."

These comments led Maheu to amend his previously filed lawsuit to sue Hughes for defamation of character. He claimed that Hughes's statement, broadcast to millions of television viewers and radio listeners, had libeled him. In the litigation, Maheu asked for $17.3 million in damages ($320 million in today's dollars).

After a lengthy trial with thousands of exhibits and 15,472

---

7 A criminal investigation of Irving led to his conviction and thirty-month jail sentence, of which he served seventeen months.

pages of testimony, the jury ruled in Maheu's favor on December 4, 1974. As if this volume of testimony and evidence was not enough to reflect Hughes's scorched-earth defense mentality and tenacity, this verdict was appealed, with Chester Davis also handling the appeal. It was not until 1978 that the US Court of Appeals for the Ninth Circuit upheld much of the jury's verdict.

And it was not until May 1979, after Hughes had died, that this litigation was finally settled under an agreement, the terms of which demanded that the details of the settlement remain confidential.

CHAPTER 14

THE SEDUCTION OF SUMMA

*"Business, numbers, negotiations, all
that stuff I wouldn't go near."*

—*Donna Karan*

IN THE SUMMER of 1972, Bill Gay, Raymond Holliday,
and Chester Davis decided that Hughes should sell his ownership in Toolco in a public offering. Holliday, the chief
executive officer of Hughes Tool Company, would become
Toolco's first chairman and chief executive officer. He looked
forward to running his own show. Bill Gay, head of Hughes operations at Romaine Street in Los Angeles, would become president
and chief executive officer of Summa Corporation, Hughes's new
entity. This would result in Gay running Hughes Air West and
the rest of Hughes's Nevada holdings. Davis would be a director
and general counsel of Summa Corporation.

Hughes was staying on the top floor of the twenty-story
Bayshore Inn in Vancouver BC at the time, alongside six male
attendants looking after him around the clock. At that time,

Howard was experiencing a mental and physical decline from a long history of injury and drug excesses.

Although Holliday and Davis submitted a mailed request to his aides requesting a discussion of the plan to take Toolco public, Hughes refused to discuss the issue. Davis moved forward anyway, hiring Merrill Lynch, Pierce, Fenner & Smith to underwrite the stock offering.

During this period, Hughes objected to selling his interest in Toolco, but Gay, Holliday, and Davis pressed forward for the sale. They hounded Hughes with the argument that Toolco had lost market share and that there was a weakening in the prospects for the drilling market. According to them, these vexing conditions led to a selling opportunity for Howard.

Although affection was out of character for Hughes, he still had some for the company founded by his father whose invention changed the world of oil exploration and provided him hundreds of millions of dollars.

Hughes and his aides left Vancouver BC and returned to Managua, Nicaragua, by private plane. Hughes had left there in March after staying only twenty-five days. He and his entourage had been treated well by Anastasio ("Tachito") Somoza DeBayle, the country's strongman ruler. Upon his return, Hughes met with Tachito, who announced, "I am very pleased that Mr. Hughes has accepted my personal invitation to once again visit with us here in Nicaragua. I know that all Nicaraguans will join in extending to him our traditional hospitality."

Raymond Holliday flew to Managua to meet with Hughes regarding the Toolco offering but was turned away again. Hughes reminded Holliday that his feelings for Toolco were strong. He regarded it as a living monument to his father and did not want to part with his legacy. Still, the legal and financial mechanisms had been set in place by Holliday, Gay, and Davis. It seems that Hughes, at the time, was not strong enough to stop them, and the opportunity for massive profits from the sale of his stock, which were likely to decline, was too hard to pass up.

The plan was to form a new Hughes Tool Company. Howard Hughes would contribute the assets and liabilities of the Toolco division to the new Hughes Tool Company and in return, Hughes would receive 5,000,000 shares of its stock, which he would then sell to the public. Toolco had been losing market share in the drill bit business as several of its patents had expired or were about to expire. The number of wells drilled in the United States had fallen by approximately 50 percent while the number of working drilling rigs had fallen by 40 percent. All of this led to a 75 percent decline in Toolco's profitability.

In early September, attorneys and financial consultants filed documents with the Securities and Exchange Commission and responded to its many questions. Soon, Raymond Holliday signed papers in Houston that established the new Hughes Tool Company. A Certificate of Incorporation was filed with the Delaware Secretary of State in Dover.

However, before the transfer could take place, and because of rumors about Hughes's health and the accusations by many, including Robert Maheu, that Chester Davis, Raymond Holliday, and Bill Gay now controlled the Hughes organization, the SEC required evidence that: (1) Howard was alive, (2) capable of deciding to sell, and (3) wanted to sell his interest in Toolco.

The SEC proposed that a group vice president or higher from Merrill Lynch and a partner from the law firm of Brown, Wood, Fuller, Caldwell & Ivey (representing Merrill Lynch) would meet with Hughes to discuss the SEC's concerns. Only if that meeting confirmed to their satisfaction that Hughes understood the transaction and wanted to sell the oil-tool division of his empire to the public, would the transaction move forward.

Julius H. Sedlmayr, a group vice president of Merrill Lynch, and J. Courtney Ivey, a partner in the law firm of Brown, Wood flew to Managua for a meeting with Hughes.

Their meeting with him was pushed back again and again.

Finally, days later, as Hughes was being given medication, a shower, a haircut, and shave by his aides, Sedlmayr's frustration reached its limit. He demanded that the meeting with Hughes take place in time for he and Ivey to catch their 6:45 am flight back to New York, or he would cancel the public offering.

Although Raymond Holliday and a Hughes tax lawyer had accompanied Sedlmayr and Ivey to Hughes's suite, he did not invite them to the meeting in his bedroom. Hughes only wanted to meet with Sedlmayr and Ivey. They found Hughes to be alert, reasonable, and well-informed. He even gave them a lively account of the history of Toolco and his father. He also argued that $30 per share for the Tool Oil Division was too low and should be increased to $32.

Further, Hughes made it clear that only the Tool Oil Division of Hughes Tool Company would be taken public and that his remaining assets would be moved into his Summa Corporation. They concluded that Hughes was witty and able to comprehend the documents. They asked him to sign the contract, then they left for the airport.

Shortly after returning to New York, they met with the SEC and presented its representatives with a copy of the contract to sell Hughes's interest in Toolco's Oil Division in exchange for 5 million shares of its common stock and resolved their questions about Hughes's competence and desire to sell his interest in Toolco.

Hughes's lawyers also arranged for Hughes to transfer Project AZORIAN'S so-called "mining arrangements" to Summa Corporation. Summa would then contract with Toolco for the piping and related systems needed to recover the K-129. This arrangement would be consistent with the protection of the project's cover.

Summa is Latin for "highest," an aspirational goal for this umbrella company that would hold the following companies under its wing:

- KLAS-TV (a CBS affiliate in Las Vegas)
- Hughes Airwest
- Hughes Sports Network
- Hughes Helicopters
- Sands Hotel and Casino
- Frontier Hotel and Casino
- Landmark Hotel and Casino
- Castaways Hotel and Casino
- Desert Inn
- Silver Slipper Casino
- Xanadu Princess Resort (Bahamas)
- Hughes Nevada Mining
- General American Oil Company
- Various land and land development entities
- The McCarran Airport terminal and land adjacent to the airport

Davis told the CIA about the plans to form a new Hughes Tool Company and the need to establish new contracts to move Project AZORIAN's Hughes related contract to Summa. Summa would then contract with Toolco for the piping systems arrangements.

The CIA was not happy about any changes to the existing arrangement, which had been working very well. But the new Hughes Tool Company would soon become subject to the disclosure requirements of the U.S. Securities & Exchange Commission. The folks at the CIA recognized the need for contract changes to be made. However, as long as Project AZORIAN still had the Hughes name associated with it, and the new Toolco would still be involved with providing the piping and related systems, the cover would hold, and the CIA accepted the transfer of the contract to Summa.

To the public, the eccentric and wealthy Howard Hughes would still be leading the charge in his deep-sea mining venture. However, the negotiations over the new contracts were tense, and Davis extracted additional "overhead coverage" for Summa. And since Howard Hughes would no longer profit from the delivery of the pipe itself, Davis demanded that the CIA explicitly pay Summa for the right to use the Hughes name to be used on the Hughes Glomar Explorer, the Hughes Mining Barge, and the project itself.

This was particularly disturbing to the CIA because the value of the Hughes name was already included in the pricing of the piping system. But Davis ignored that logic and insisted that for Hughes's continued involvement, a "fair" amount needed to be paid to Summa for the use of the Hughes name.

Although this sum has never been disclosed, it was likely in the millions. Director Richard Helms was extremely upset about this "blackmail" and greed. Like David Packard, he, too, was annoyed by Chester Davis' tactics and his constant loyalty to Hughes first, while the government and people of the United States were a distant second.

Davis sent a six-page memorandum to Helms that clearly outlined the new arrangement, including a presentation of the key terms of the relationship between the CIA and Hughes's new holding company, Summa Corporation, plus the large fee for the use of Hughes's name. Davis insisted that it be signed by Helms and returned by courier to Davis at Hughes's so-called fortress at

7000 Romaine Avenue in Los Angeles, Hughes's operations and record center.

Helms remained unhappy about this memorandum, particularly about his having to put his name on a document that showed the CIA paying millions for the use of Hughes's name. The memorandum was dated November 1, 1972 and signed by Helms on November 3. Its clarity and transparency were against his best judgment, and to make it worse for him, it had his name on it.

Hughes was the sole shareholder of Summa Corporation. Its officers were Bill Gay, EVP, Nadine Henley, SVP, and Chester Davis, its general counsel.

In early December 1972, Howard sold all 5,000,000 of his new Hughes Tool Company shares for $30 per share totaling $150,000,000 ($2.6 billion in today's dollars).

Merrill Lynch, Pierce, Fenner & Smith, Inc., handled the five million-share sale, which was quickly oversubscribed by a wide range of investors.

At the same time, Sun Shipbuilding and Drydock Co. had fabricated the ship's docking well and bottom structure and launched the keel of the Hughes Glomar Explorer in the usual champagne christening ceremony. The new Secretary of Defense, who succeeded David Packard, was Kenneth Rush. He attended the ceremony and was fully supportive of Project AZORIAN.

Sun Shipbuilding expected to deliver the remaining portion of the ship in late April 1973. The construction of the Hughes Mining Barge (HMB-1) had been launched in San Diego and was now in Redwood City, California, about ten miles south of San Mateo providing cover for the assembly of the Clementine. Toolco was pouring the piping string, and all 590 pieces were scheduled for delivery in June 1973.

CHAPTER 15

SCREAMING RED BLUR

"Speed provides the one genuinely modern pleasure."

—*ALDOUS HUXLEY*

IN JUNE OF 1972, I spent several weeks in John Clark's new office in the recently opened Transamerica Pyramid. The law firm had changed its name and was now known as Pettit Evers & Martin. It had moved a few blocks east and north from 650 California Street to this new San Francisco landmark at 600 Montgomery Street. John had an elegant office that looked out toward one of San Francisco's older landmarks, the 210-foot-tall Coit Tower, on Telegraph Hill. The Tower is a tribute to the firefighters who died fighting San Francisco's five major fires, including the great fire that followed the San Francisco earthquake in 1906. It is supposedly a coincidence that the Tower itself looks like a giant fire-hose nozzle.

After filing A.W. Liquidating Company's securities litigation complaint against Hughes, the next key step: document discovery.

Since Clark and Russell believed that they had the Air West

documents they needed, they focused on communications between Hughes and his management team. This avenue hit a brick wall as Hughes funneled all memoranda regarding Air West through his lawyer, Chester Davis. Davis successfully stonewalled these document requests as being subject to attorney-client privilege. Since virtually everything went through him, John concluded it was fruitless to pursue this path for additional documents. The court would not permit the penetration of this attorney-client privilege defense, including any communications between Howard Hughes and Davis.

An alternative approach called for the subpoena of documents from the accounting firm, Haskins & Sells. I worked with the Pettit team to prepare a detailed document request to be served on the custodian of records at the accounting firm's San Francisco office at 44 Montgomery Street. This request included all documents gathered and produced by H&S during its due diligence work done in connection with its review of PMM's audit work papers that it had prepared or gathered in connection with its audit of Air West's December 31, 1969, financial statements.

It also called for H&S's documents gathered or prepared in connection with the Deposit Agreement and the determination of Air West's closing financial balances as of March 31, 1970. The subpoena also called for any "desk files" of the individual H&S team members who worked on these assignments and any external correspondence and internal memorandum retained within H&S.

A blizzard of objections and legal battles and delays ensued.

Counsel for H&S, Brad Elgin at the Brobeck, Phleger & Harrison law firm, claimed that the requests were vague, overly broad, and burdensome. But after months of back and forth and arguments before the judge, five bankers' boxes of H&S documents landed in John's office in the fall of 1972. I soon began digging through and analyzing the thousands of documents in these boxes.

During my review, I kept the documents in the number order that had been consecutively stamped on each page's bottom right-hand corner. Attorneys call this number identification a "Bates number," courtesy of Edwin G. Bates of New York, who patented the machine in 1891 that stamped documents, advancing one number each time the device's handle was pressed onto a document. When a document was particularly important, I made a copy of that page so that it could be used to compare it to other documents, or to reference it to other materials, and for discussion with counsel.

Many of the documents were familiar to me, including copies of the PMM teams' working papers that H&S had reviewed during their due diligence work while PMM performed its audit of Air West's December 31, 1969, financial statements. Several of these copies now had handwritten comments on them from the H&S accountants. These comments by H&S were often notes for further analysis and for tracing to closing Adjustments, after adjusting for any events impacting the amounts during the three months concluding on March 31, 1970.

I noticed, however, a few issues that would slow down my analysis of these and the other H&S documents. First, many of the documents were copies of wide 10-column and 14-column spreadsheets that were copied as two and three separate pages. For key documents, I had members of my staff carefully tape these pages together, making sure that they read across the rows correctly. Then I also noticed that some documents were missing from the production.

I noticed that documents were missing by the way auditors organize their work papers. For example, Air West's prepaid expenses were listed on a 4-column spreadsheet labeled as work paper G in the top right-hand corner of the page. The auditor would then prepare a separate analysis of each type of prepaid expense listed on work paper G. For example, prepaid landing fees would be analyzed on work paper G-1 while the details of those prepaid landing fees were found on work paper G-1-1 and G-1-2 etc.

When the work paper references were placed above or to the left of a number or a comment, it meant that the source for that information was contained on the referenced document. So, for prepaid landing fees, a reference to a work paper letter and number (G-1 for example) on work paper G to the left or above an amount told me that the referenced work paper G-1 provides the details of prepaid landing fees. When the reference was placed to the right of a number or below it, it meant that amount or information was being brought forward to, and used in, the referenced document. So, on G-1 the total of the various landing fees would have the handwritten letter G below the total or to the right of it. And the total of prepaids on work paper G would have a handwritten A-1 on it, telling me that this amount was used on work paper A-1.

Yes, auditors are an organized bunch! But this system helps to "tie-out" the work papers. It also told me when referenced documents were "missing." This process makes auditors' work papers a tightly referenced web of self-contained documents. If some documents are "inadvertently" or intentionally not copied, this referencing technique will identify when referenced documents have not been produced. For example, if work papers G-1 and G-2 were referenced in H&S's work papers, but were not produced, the cross-referencing will shine a light on their absence.

To make matters even more time consuming, the documents had been shuffled so, for example, work paper B-5 (document number 007392) would be followed by an unrelated work paper, say U-7 (document number 007393) that was followed by unrelated work paper E-6 (document 007394). Therefore, my team spent many hours taping together pages of multi-column documents, then copying and putting the documents into their order by the letter designation given to them when they were prepared.

They would review the documents for any handwritten cross-references to documents that were missing. Then one of the staff created a listing of those work papers that had not been produced by H&S (or its counsel). This listing would show the document number and a brief description of what the missing document was likely to contain. This analysis took another two months of work.

John was furious with the "shenanigans" involving the H&S document production. He and his associates presented another document request, which contained the list prepared by my team, detailing each referenced document that had not been produced and which document contained the telltale reference to that document. Without the specificity of this chronicle, there would have been endless arguments about missing documents and denials about the production of every document requested.

Such is the nature of large-scale corporate "civil" litigation.

After another appearance before the judge and another month later, the "missing" documents were received by Pettit, Evers & Martin, and the work by my team of organizing and analyzing key documents continued. Several of the new documents focused on updating various asset and liability balances as of December 31, 1969, to their balances as of March 31, 1970. I then traced these balances into the March 31, 1970 closing entries, which eliminated or greatly reduced the recorded amounts of these assets in Air West's closing balance sheet. In addition, several of these working papers focused on increases to liabilities.

These adjustments resulted in larger liabilities at the closing. Both the reduction in assets and the increases to Air West's liabilities reduced Hughes's purchase price and therefore the amount received by Air West's shareholders.

Finally, several "Memoranda to the File" summarized these adjustments. Many of these memoranda had been referenced in the original production but had not been produced.

After months of analyzing the H&S working papers, it was decided that John Clark would notice the deposition of the H&S person most knowledgeable about the H&S working papers that had been produced in this dispute. But before this deposition could take place, John had to master the accounting issues behind each adjustment. Such mastery is needed for an attorney asking well-prepared deponents about their area of expertise and the work they had performed.

This level of preparedness is particularly important for questions to be asked of the well-prepared deponent that is intent on avoiding certain admissions or sensitive topics. Such deponents will often answer that they "do not recall" the issue or event that is the subject of the question. Or the deponent will give a non-answer or a misleading answer that avoids the purpose of the question.

The "I don't recall" response is often overcome by showing the witness that their name is on a document. This increases the likelihood that the deponent will recall the issue or event that is the subject of the question. Better yet, if the work paper shows that it was prepared by, or a comment was made on the work paper by the witness, the "I don't recall" response would call into question the honesty of the witness, making his or her recall more likely.

Many witnesses, when confronted with these circumstances, must "have their recollection refreshed." Like the referencing discussed above, audit work papers are helpful for "refreshing the witnesses' recollection" because they identify the name of the preparer, the reviewer, and the initials of anyone else that contributed to its preparation or review.

Suppose counsel questioning the witness has not mastered

the documents' subject matter and the documents that form the basis for the questions. In that case, counsel will not realize that an answer provided by the witness was a non-answer or a misleading answer. In depositions of reluctant or uncooperative witnesses (which many highly coached witnesses are), it is often not the first question of a deponent about an issue within a document that gets a meaningful answer. It is the second, third, or fourth follow-up questions that drive a responsive and meaningful answer.

John and I prepared a detailed outline of the questions and possible follow-up questions to be asked of the H&S witness during his deposition. (Yes, all the H&S team were men, which was not unusual at the big CPA firms at that time.) For each question, an arsenal of documents would likely be used to flesh out the details of why H&S did what it did and to hopefully help prove that the closing entries violated the Purchase Contract.

A few days before John was to take the H&S deposition, he called me while I was working on the fifteenth floor of PMM's office at 601 California Street. Clark was excited and asked me to come down to the building's Kearney side for a surprise.

When I walked out of the building, John called out to me from his new red Ferrari 246 GTS, parked at the bottom of the steps. I got in, and we were off. Clark headed north for six blocks, then turned left onto Broadway for four blocks until we reached the Broadway Tunnel.

Although the Broadway Tunnel's speed limit is 40 mph, and only slightly more than a quarter of a mile, John punched his new Ferrari up to 120 mph in that short span before applying the brakes hard just before he reached the light at Hyde Street.

I had never been in a car driven by Clark before. Imagine my kind of quiet hysteria…and euphoria.

My future rides with John were on the aggressive side, just like his lawyering, but never as crazy as the screaming red blur in the Broadway Tunnel.

However, the red 246 GTS Ferrari was not John's only surprise. He drove a few blocks further to the Ferrari of San Francisco dealership and stopped. He and I walked inside, and he introduced me to several people in the dealership. It turned out that John was not just the owner of a new Ferrari; he was the new owner of the Ferrari of San Francisco dealership!

This ownership had led Clark to a friendship with Enzo Ferrari, (founder of Ferrari S.p.A. in Maranello, Italy). In future years, he was Enzo's frequent guest in his box at races in Europe, including the famous Monaco Grand Prix in late May of each year.

I tell this story to demonstrate several of John's wonderful traits. He was filled with a joy for life. He was also aggressive, indulgent, willing to take risks, and he readily acted on this willingness to be bold and to enjoy what he loved.

CHAPTER 16

EXTREMELY UNCOOPERATIVE WITNESS

"Opposition is true friendship."

—*WILLIAM BLAKE*

PRENTISS BLOCK WAS a tall, blond senior on the Haskins and Sells team while it was doing its "due diligence" work on Air West's December 31, 1969, financial statements, the Deposit Agreement dispute, and the closing of the Purchase Contract. His role was to supervise the work done by approximately ten staff accountants on the H&S team at Air West.

H&S had designated Mr. Block under Rule 30(b)(6) of the Federal Rules of Civil Procedure. Since H&S was not a person that can be deposed, someone can be designated by an entity as its Rule 30(b)(6) witness. This means that this person can testify under oath, on behalf of that entity. Legally, this meant that H&S determined that Prentiss Block was the "Person Most Knowledgeable" about H&S's work in connection with these matters for Hughes and his testimony would be treated as the testimony of H&S.

Block was to be deposed by John Clark in the Spring of 1973. He was a bright, friendly young man in his late twenties. He was a CPA who had graduated with honors from Brigham Young University with a degree in accounting.

The deposition was in H&S's offices at 44 Montgomery Street in San Francisco. John and I arrived a few minutes before 9:00 am. Earlier that morning, a clerk from the Pettit firm had brought five banker's boxes of documents to be used during the deposition. These boxes contained six copies of each document expected to be used during the deposition. One copy was for the court reporter to mark as an exhibit and used by the witness. The other five were for the witness' counsel, Brad Elgin, as well as two lawyers from Davis & Cox, while John and I used the other two copies.

John began the deposition going over Block's education, work history, and experience in connection with the H&S work at Air West. This portion of the deposition was friendly and went as well as expected. However, when the questions got into the details of the accounting issues, Block became irritable and tense. It became clear that his counsel had schooled him in how to not "volunteer" information, or "know" anything, if possible.

An example of how witnesses are coached into both not volunteering and not knowing information is seen in the following coaching session between an attorney and her witness before the witness' scheduled deposition:

The Scene: An attorney is sitting with her back to a wall. On the wall is a large clock. The witness is seated at a conference table, looking at the attorney with the clock clearly in view.

Attorney: Do you know what time it is?

Witness: Sure, it's 2:20.

Attorney: (Coaching the witness) I just told you not to volunteer information or answer more than you were asked in the question. The question that I asked you was, do you know what time it is, and you jumped the gun and told me it was 2:20. Now I am going to ask you again. (Question) Do you know what time it is?

Witness: Yes.

Attorney: (Coaching the witness) You listened to my question and you answered the question that I asked you, but you went too far. Let's drill into this further.

Attorney: Do you know what time it is now?

Witness: Yes.

Attorney: What time is it now?

Witness: It's 2:22.

Attorney: (Coaching the witness) Okay, I asked you if you know what time it is, and you told me yes. That was an improvement from your prior answer. Then I asked you what time it is now, and you said 2:22. But you don't know what time it is. You only looked at the clock over my head and assumed it was 2:22. Because this is my office, I set that clock five minutes fast, so you looked at the clock and assumed that you knew it was 2:22 but you were wrong. In your deposition, I don't want you to assume you know something unless you are certain you know the answer. I can tell you that there is very little in this world that any of us actually know. Usually, we only have some reasonable estimate of what the answer to a question is, and I don't want you to guess. If you wanted to be helpful, and I don't advise that you be helpful, your answer could have been, "I'm not sure what time it is, but the clock on the wall behind you shows the time to be 2:22."

These examples show that witnesses are often coached in ways that getting helpful answers in a deposition is like pulling teeth. And if the attorney asking the questions does not have relevant documents supporting the questions, the likely answer is often, "I don't recall" or "I don't know." Witnesses at trial are generally coached to be more forthright than during a deposition to avoid looking evasive and causing the judge and or jury to not trust their testimony or conclude that the witness is not helping them in their search for the truth. But depositions are different than trials. Depositions are generally more contentious and combative, and witnesses are coached to respond much more defensively than at trial where a judge and jury may be offended by unhelpful behavior.

Prentiss Block had been coached by Brad Elgin to be an extremely uncooperative witness. Like a smart and good accountant testifying for one of his firm's most important clients, he not only learned well, but he put his learning into action. Consider the following exchange:

The Scene: A large conference room in H&S's offices in San Francisco. It was unusually dark, with no outside windows. The table was very large with Block, his counsel, and the court reporter on the west side of the table, several attorneys representing defendants sat along the north side. John and I sat on the east side, with the five boxes of documents surrounding me for ease of access. On the south side was a long credenza covered with provisions of water, coffee, tea, soft drinks, orange juice, and various snacks available for the participants.

John: During your due diligence work on Air West's financial statements as of December 31, 1969, did you analyze or review, in any way, the airlines prepaid landing fees?

Block: I don't recall.

John: I am handing you a document that is headed Air West, Inc., Prepaid Landing Fees, San Francisco International Airport, as of December 31, 1969. I am going to ask the reporter to mark this document as Exhibit 175. Have you seen this document before?

Block: I don't recall.

John: In the top right corner in the second box down from the top of the page there is a

place for the preparer of this document to write his or her name. This part of Exhibit 175

shows the handwritten name of P. Block. Did you write that name in that box?

Block: I don't recall.

John: Do you have any reason, as you sit here today, to expect that you did not write the name P. Block in that box on Exhibit 175?

Block: No.

John: Did you prepare any portion of Exhibit 175?

Block: Parts of this Exhibit appear to be in my handwriting, and other parts are not.

John: Okay, on the far-left side of this document, there are numbered rows. Please identify which rows do you have a reasonable basis to expect that the handwriting is not yours?

The deposition went on and on like this all day long.

John tried to be patient and thorough, but he was not happy that Prentiss's extreme lack of cooperation caused the pace of the deposition to be extremely slow, tedious, and unproductive. But by plodding through the key documents that were made Exhibits to the deposition, John coaxed Prentiss Block to testify about his understanding of the various assets and liabilities of Air West and how H&S's work was the basis for the closing adjustments that reduced the amount paid by Hughes for Air West.

Then late in the afternoon of Block's testimony, John began to examine him about a Memorandum, a typed summary of possible closing adjustments dated March 15, 1970. The lengthy Memorandum provided a detailed discussion of assets that the author considered as candidates to be written off and liabilities that could be increased or created as of the closing. This Memorandum epitomized a roadmap to the closing adjustments, which would later save Hughes millions when these adjustments were recorded "as of" the date the Purchase Contract was consummated.

John: I am handing you a document that is titled Memorandum to File, dated March 15, 1970. I am going to ask the reporter to mark this document as Exhibit 215. Mr. Block, have you seen this document before?

Block: I might have.

John: Did you prepare this document?

Block: No.

John: Do you have a reasonable expectation of who prepared this document?

Block: Yes.

John: Who is that person?

Block: Her name is Cathy Ames.

John: Is Cathy Ames an accountant?

Block: No.

John: Since you testified that Cathy Ames is not an accountant and Exhibit 215 is a memorandum devoted to discussing accounting issues relating to various assets and liabilities, how did Cathy Ames know what to write in preparing Exhibit 215?

Block: She typed this Memorandum based on a handwritten memorandum.

John: Do you know who wrote the handwritten Memorandum?

Block: Yes.

John: Who wrote the handwritten Memorandum that was used by Cathy Ames to type

the words appearing on Exhibit 215?

Block: I did.

John: Has that handwritten Memorandum been produced as a result of the subpoena that was issued to the custodian of records of H&S in connection with this litigation?

Block: No.

John: Do you know why this handwritten Memorandum was not produced?

Block: The practice at H&S is that when a handwritten memorandum is used to produce a typed document, the handwritten memorandum is destroyed at that time.

John: Why did you prepare the handwritten memorandum, which became Exhibit 215?

Block: I was asked to.

John: Who asked you to prepare the handwritten memorandum?

Block: Rob McComb.

John: Who is Rob McComb?

Block: Mr. McComb was the engagement partner on this assignment.

John: What is your understanding of why this Memorandum was prepared?

Block: The client asked H&S to prepare a detailed memorandum discussing Air West's assets, other than cash and accounts receivable, as well as its liabilities, that were recorded, or unrecorded contingent liabilities that were in place, as of the date of the closing of the Purchase Contract.

John: Exhibit 215 is titled Memorandum to File. To your knowledge, who has seen this document?

Block: Several of my assistants at H&S that assisted me in preparing the handwritten memorandum, also Mr. McComb and Chester Davis.

John: Did you understand why this document was given to Chester Davis?

Block: Mr. Davis is Mr. Hughes's attorney and the attorney for Hughes Airwest and Hughes Tool Company. He asked H&S to prepare this document.

No: Do you know why Mr. Davis asked for this document to be prepared by H&S?

Elgin: Objection. This line of inquiry is an effort to penetrate the attorney-client privilege and I instruct the witness not to answer this question or any questions about Mr. Block's communications with Mr. Davis, or any communications from Mr. Davis.

John: Mr. Block, within Exhibit 215, are there suggestions that Air West's assets be reduced, or its liabilities increased using accounting principles and methods that were inconsistent with those principles used by Air West when it prepared its July 31, 1968, financial statement?

Block: Yes.

John: Doesn't the Purchase Contract call for Air West's closing balance sheet to be prepared using accounting principles and methods consistent with those used by Air West in its July 31, 1968 financial statements?

Block: That's my understanding.

Clark: Then why does Exhibit 215 ignore this requirement?

Mr. Elgin: Objection. This line of inquiry is improper as it seeks to invade the attorney-client privilege, and I instruct the witness not to answer.

At the end of the deposition, John struggled to contain his fury. We returned to the war room at Pettit's office in the Transamerica Building. Ted Russell soon joined them to discuss how the deposition had gone. John let off steam by recounting the obstructive tactics used by Brad Elgin and how Prentiss Block had followed his coaching to be an extremely uncooperative witness.

I mentioned to John and Russell that H&S had a very long and trusted history with Hughes. Starting in 1925, when Hughes searched to find someone to act as his surrogate at Toolco so that he could leave Texas and move to Hollywood, he had hired the 36-year-old Dietrich from H&S. After that, the H&S firm became his trusted advisor, auditor, and consultant, not only with Toolco but also for Hughes Aircraft Company, Hughes Medical Institute, Summa Corporation, and many others.

John focused on the Memorandum to File, now known as Exhibit 215. The group brainstormed about who asked for it to be prepared and why it was prepared. They considered the timing, March 15, two weeks before the closing and its broad attack on the assets and liabilities of Air West, and the millions that it saved Howard Hughes at the Closing.

The group concluded that the Memorandum itself, and its end-use in guiding the closing adjustments was not something dreamed up by H&S acting alone. It had to be at Chester Davis's direction. And since the Memorandum violated the terms of the Purchase Contract, John Clark was convinced that Exhibit 215 originated at the request of Howard Hughes. Then, Davis used the Memorandum to guide H&S to which closing adjustments were to be recorded as of the closing, and in what amounts.

At the end of the meeting, John decided that H&S would be added to the federal complaint as having aided and abetted in the fraud against Air West's shareholders.

When the case was filed, the news spread throughout the financial press and the entire nation's business community. It was not common for auditors and members of the Big 8 to be sued for aiding and abetting in securities fraud. However, in this case, making for an even greater reaction was H&S's association with Howard Hughes.

In 1973, a story connected to Hughes attracted worldwide attention. This was a "double-header" with a white shoe Big 8 accounting firm involved with a massive securities fraud connected to Howard Hughes. Although there is a common view that any publicity is good publicity, this is not the view of "independent auditors" who strive to stay clear of accusations of aiding and abetting in a fraud for the benefit of a client's interest.

CHAPTER 17

THE DEPARTMENT OF JUSTICE'S CRIMINAL LAWSUIT

"Crimes sometimes shock us too much;
vices almost always too little."

—*AUGUSTUS HARE*

ON A MORNING in July of 1973, William C. Hanks called me in my office at PMM. He identified himself as a special assistant U.S. attorney for the District of Nevada. Hanks asked if I was able to discuss some questions that he had about Howard Hughes and Air West. I politely replied that I would like to be helpful, but because my work was confidential, I needed to check with my client's counsel before discussing my work with a third party. He stated that he understood, and we agreed that I would get back to him as soon as possible.

I immediately consulted with John, whose first thought was that it would be difficult and probably unwise not to cooperate with Hanks, but he wanted to discuss this with one of his partners, Stan Orr, who had been an assistant U.S. attorney for the

Department of Justice in San Francisco, for his input. In the end, John gave me the go-ahead to answer Hanks' questions to the best of my ability. I also had gotten Hanks's direct line at the Department of Justice in Las Vegas from John's partner so that I would be confident that I was speaking to William Hanks at the Department of Justice.

I called Hanks's direct line and told him that I had the okay to move forward with a meeting. Hanks said that he would be in San Francisco during the following week and suggested that we meet at 2:00 pm on Tuesday at the FBI office. Hanks was meeting there with an FBI agent in the morning on the Air West matter, and they would then meet with me that afternoon.

The Federal Building was a ten-minute drive from PMM's office, situated on the edge of the Tenderloin District, a seedy part of San Francisco with the dubious distinction of having 70 percent of the San Francisco's violent crimes. One of the more infamous strip clubs in the city is across the street from the Federal Building, but at this hour, not a stripper stirred. I drove to the meeting and parked in a garage across the street from the rear entrance of the building.

I arrived on the twelfth floor and entered the waiting area of the FBI office. Hanging on the wall were pictures of President Richard Nixon and Vice President Spiro Agnew (who resigned a few months later after being investigated for taking kickbacks from contractors in Maryland and pleading guilty to a felony charge of tax evasion), as well as the American and California flags.

I told the woman behind the bulletproof glass my name and that I had an appointment with William Hanks. After a brief wait, Hanks greeted me, and we went to an interior conference room decorated in the usual government style of a stark wooden conference table, surrounded by well-used wooden chairs. There were no decorations in this room, just an old table and old chairs.

No coffee or drinks were offered. This was a government office, not an office of a well-heeled law firm.

As it turned out, Hanks had been investigating Hughes's acquisition of Air West since the beginning of the year. He had an excellent grasp of the key players, the timing, and the facts at issue. I asked Hanks how he found out about my work on the Air West litigation against Hughes. Hanks responded that he had a recent discussion with Ed Converse, chairman of the board of the liquidating company and past CEO of Air West. Ed bragged about me doing an impressive job of analyzing Hughes's FUD activities and the closing adjustments that had violated the Purchase Contract. Ed also mentioned that I worked for PMM in its San Francisco office.

Hanks' questions focused mostly on my timeline of the trading activity of Air West's stock and the FUD activities, which correlated to those stock trades. The FBI agent showed me several charts and asked if I had any suggestions or modifications. My eyes and brain scanned the worthwhile info. I had a few suggested revisions and brought up possible additions for the agent to analyze and consider. It was clear that the Department of Justice had spoken with many people and had been doing a thorough investigation. After discussing these details for about three hours, the conversation ended cordially. Hanks thanked me for my help and cooperation.

Near the end of their meeting, I exchanged business cards with my unexpected new alliance and suggested that Hanks contact me if he had any further questions. I also mentioned that if Hanks came across any information about the closing adjustments, that I would appreciate it if Hanks could let me know since that was a significant part of my work in the civil lawsuit against Hughes.

CHAPTER 18

OPENING FORENSIC FILES

*"Take chances, make mistakes. That's how you
grow. Pain nourishes your courage. You have
to fail in order to practice being brave."*

—MARY TYLER MOORE

SHORTLY AFTER THE news of H&S being sued in federal court for aiding and abetting Howard Hughes in the Air West securities fraud litigation, Alice Saint appeared at the doorway of my office in San Francisco. Alice was Jim Perk's administrative assistant. Perk was the partner-in-charge of PMM's San Francisco Bay Area practice. Getting called into his office was generally not good news. This time was no exception.

In late August 1973, I entered Jim Perk's corner office on the fifteenth floor of the International Building that looked down California Street deeper into San Francisco's Financial District. Perk invited me to sit down in one of the visitor's chairs facing his desk and introduced Vic Count, PMM's General Counsel, who was on the conference phone.

From PMM's headquarters office in New York, Count began

the meeting by stating firmly: "I just got off the phone with Bob Harrison, H&S's general counsel. He tells me that some guy named 'Paul Regan' in our San Francisco office has been instrumental in getting H&S named in a securities fraud suit involving one of its longest and best clients, Howard Hughes. Bob says that this is causing H&S a lot of trouble, not just in California but also throughout the country. Then Harrison promised me that unless PMM backs off on this matter that he would bring upon PMM twice as much trouble as suffered by H&S on the Air West matter. He told me that he would do this by leaking to the press many terrible accounting issues that PMM had 'looked the other way on' that enabled Penn Central to get away with while PMM was the railroad's auditor. He then demanded that PMM stop helping the Pettit firm on this litigation against H&S."

Count then told us that PMM needed to stop assisting Pettit immediately. Stating that I was Paul Regan and hearing dead silence, I responded that PMM had billed a massive amount in fees for its work in assisting Air West's shareholders, and that its work was essential to their recovery of the millions of dollars that those shareholders had been deprived of as a result of the Hughes driven securities fraud, with the strong assistance from H&S.

Perk suggested that PMM back off any assistance to Pettit in its case against H&S but continue helping the case against Hughes. He also suggested that any future communication that I would have with lead counsel, John Clark, or anyone else at Pettit, would be sent to Vic Count for approval and modification, if needed, before I communicated it to anyone at Pettit.

I argued that during litigation, while in depositions or assisting in the interrogatory process or any part of the discovery process, communication with counsel generally needs to be immediate and responsive to quickly changing circumstances. For my assistance to be passed through Count in New York for his approval before I communicated to the attorneys at Pettit would fail to meet the litigation's needs on a timely basis. Besides, Count was a busy guy in the Eastern time zone and would generally not be available to respond for hours or days.

But Count insisted that this approach was needed to get H&S to back away from its whistleblowing threats over the Penn Central issues. Count and Perk concurred and demanded that this was the way forward. When the conversation ended, I knew that this process was designed to cause the case against Hughes to fail and would let down a client that needed continued accounting help in its litigation against Hughes.

I returned to my office and immediately called John to meet with him and Ted Russell.

Why was Vic Count so concerned about H&S's threat to expose PMM's wrongdoing on its audits of the railroad? I needed to do research on this mystery involving Penn Central.

I called Arnold Scott, a friend of mine in PMM's New York office. Arnold had recently been my roommate during a two-week training session that was presented by PMM at the Watergate Hotel in Washington DC.

During these two weeks, we had become good friends and had long discussions about many topics. Long discussions with Scott were easy because he was a fountain of information, a grand talker. He was the type of fellow that when you asked him what time it is, he would first tell you about his watch, how it was made and why it was so accurate.

True to form, it turned out that Scott was full of information and eager to unload. He explained that during the 1960s, the United States railroads were suffering from stiff competition from trucks and airlines. The Interstate Commerce Commission regulated the railroads, and it resisted efforts by the railroads to raise rates or allow them to abandon their unprofitable branch lines. On top of these handicaps, the US Post Office moved its contracts for delivering mail from railroads to airlines and trucking companies. To offset these adversities, railroads attempted to reduce costs, often through mergers in hope of eliminating duplicate services and jobs, while gaining operating efficiencies.

Then Scott gave me a history lesson about The Norfolk & Western railroad being purchased by the Virginian Railway in 1959. In 1960, the Erie Railroad merged with the Delaware, Lackawanna & Western Railroad. The Chesapeake & Ohio acquired the Baltimore & Ohio in 1963, and the Atlantic Coast Line Railroad merged with the Seaboard Air Line Railroad in 1967. The Pennsylvania Railroad and the New York Central Railroad had several "dates" but could never make it to the chapel. But after years of trying, the Interstate Commerce Commission finally approved their merger (along with the New York, New Haven and Hartford Railroad, a very troubled railroad, which joined the newlyweds as part of the government's approval); the merger was consummated in February of 1968. This complex merger was the birth of the Penn Central Transportation Company, known as the Penn Central: the largest railroad in the country and the sixth-largest company in the United States.

But Scott explained that Penn Central's start was inauspicious (I thought to myself that this was like Air West's poor start). Connecting carriers opposed its attempts to consolidate routes that were served by both railroads. Traffic was misrouted, and other railroads were slow to update their routing, causing many delays and railroad cars that were routinely lost, along with their cargo. Attempts to integrate operations, personnel and equipment failed due to clashing corporate cultures, incompatible computer systems, and union contracts. Meanwhile, labor unions resisted workforce reductions, and the Pennsylvania Railroad's investments in pipelines, real estate, amusement parks, and a small airline were also draining Penn Central of resources.

Scott finally got to the part relevant to my concern. He said that Penn Central managed to conceal its financial distress by deferring costs, avoiding write-offs of its bad investments, and avoiding the recognition of significant liabilities and more losses. It was alleged that PMM knew that these accounting shenanigans were improper, but it looked the other way.

There was $200 million ($3.9 billion in today's dollars) in bank debt due at the end of 1970, and the banks stopped providing relief. Penn Central pleaded for a government-guaranteed loan and was rejected by the Nixon Administration.

Two days after that rejection, Penn Central filed for reorganization under the bankruptcy laws on June 21, 1970. At that time, it was the largest bankruptcy in U.S. history. The Penn Central bankruptcy was a devastating event both to the railroad industry and to the nation's business community and naturally plummeted by massive press, television, and radio coverage.

Penn Central filed for reorganization under Section 77 of the Bankruptcy Law, which provided railroads the ability to retain possession of and continue operation of the railroad system and to conduct other normal business, pending appointment of trustees by the court. As a result, its 94,000 employees were instructed to continue their work. The railroad continued to carry thousands of passengers and millions of tons of freight on routes stretching from New York to St. Louis, north to the border with Canada and south through Virginia.

Scott told me that New York's Governor Rockefeller declared: "The bankruptcy of the Pennsylvania Railroad is a most regrettable development, but I can assure commuters in the New York metropolitan area that the state's emergency program to improve the Penn Central equipment and service will continue without interruption."

The court appointed trustees selected a different auditing firm. PMM had audited Penn Central's December 31, 1968, and 1969 financial statements, but H&S was appointed to become the bankrupt company's new auditor.

It was clear from my conversation with Arnold Scott that H&S could easily become a devastating whistleblower (or leaker) about possible audit failure issues that lead to a massive economic thorn in the nation's side. Clearly, Vic Count's threat was not going vanish. I needed to act quickly and decisively.

It was a troubling dilemma.

I had just been promoted into PMM's management group as of July 1, 1973, which came with a nice raise. Plus, my wife and I had recently purchased a home with the accompanying large California mortgage. We also just had our first child, Greg, a few months earlier in March. I greatly appreciated my work at PMM. It offered diverse and challenging work experiences with bright, hardworking young professionals that I admired and enjoyed being with, both at work and socially. It had been a great experience, and I looked forward to a future that continued those experiences.

However, I had devoted enormous energy to the Air West litigation. I derived great satisfaction in making a difference through my work with the attorneys at Pettit, particularly John Clark. He was educating me about the process of digging through documents, organizing them, teaching the attorneys what those documents meant, and pushing the ball over the goal line. John not only did that, but achieved this while building a dedicated team that were committed, like him to hard work, honesty, and integrity.

The next day, Ted Russell sat in one of John's large leather winged chairs as John eyed him from behind his massive wooden desk with its green and gold leather top. His office had hardwood floors covered with antique rugs.

I was waved into John's office and sat in the matching winged chair next to Russell. I then walked them through my conference call with Perk and Count, explaining its details and the threat by H&S, backed up by my conversation with Arnold Scott. After a long pause, I could feel the thermometer in the room hit the boiling point. You can't ignore anger radiating from two powerful men. To think that the case for Air West's shareholders against Hughes was going to be sabotaged by PMM, because of threats by H&S to expose PMM's failures during its audits of Penn Central, disgusted them no end.

Vic Count's ultimatum also fueled John's exasperation, not just at H&S, but now at PMM. I was torn and hesitant but suggested that I would consider leaving PMM, forming my own firm and continuing to work on the Air West cases with Pettit. I told them to give me a few days to assess whether this alternative was feasible and that I would alert them of my decision as soon as possible.

My best friend and colleague at PMM at the time was John Skelton. When Tom Adler left PMM to attend law school, and Mary Kay Griffin chose to return to Utah, John Skelton started at PMM the next week. He was a lateral transfer from a large regional CPA firm in Southern California. He and his wife, Lynette, had moved to Sausalito, a small, picturesque community that blossomed into a popular tourist destination on San Francisco Bay, just north of the Golden Gate Bridge. To get John Skelton started on his career at PMM, he was assigned as my assistant on PMM's Marine World Africa USA audit in Redwood City, California.

John was a smart, careful, and thoughtful man, with a wife and baby daughter. We quickly hit it off during our work together on the Marine World audit, where I was in charge of the field work (planning and performing the audit at the client's offices), assisted by Skelton. During our breaks on days when the Park was not open to the public, the two of us walked the Marine World Park and enjoyed playing with Big Lou, the elephant seal, poking him through the cyclone fence so that he would let out a great toot. Then we would say "hi" to Ella, the elephant (she was a water skier) and watch the dolphins play with their toys in their pools. We would also play catch with them, using under-sized footballs that fit in their mouths that were full of teeth to help them catch the ball.

After that audit was complete, we traveled to San Francisco to work together on PMM's largest audit client, measured by fees, in its San Francisco office. I was also in charge of that audit's field work, while John Skelton supervised the tax work for that client and other engagements that PMM handled for their many tax needs. This client was a publicly traded company, headquartered in San Francisco with over 100 subsidiaries operating throughout the world. From my perspective, it had the added benefit of being in the Embarcadero Center, which was only a five-minute walk to Pettit's office. This short walk was convenient for me to pop over for important meetings with Clark and Russell.

On returning from my meeting with Russell and Clark, about the conversation with Count and Perk, I met with John Skelton. We took a walk to the park on the eastern side of the Alcoa Building while I went over the two tumultuous meetings that had taken place earlier that day. As was his habit, Skelton listened intently and carefully. I proposed to him the consider-able risk of starting our own CPA firm together. I suggested that it was likely that I would be able to continue to work on the Air West litigation while Skelton, with his tax experience, could develop a tax practice. This was a considerable risk for John Skelton as he and his wife had recently moved from their apart-ment in Sausalito to a home in Belmont (just North of Redwood City). They, too, had a large California real estate mortgage and a young child named Sarah.

By this time in my career, I had met and worked with sev-eral attorneys, not just at Pettit, but at other large law firms like Heller, Ehrman, White & McAuliffe, and Farella, Braun + Martel. Heller's Chairman, Larry Popofsky, a Rhodes Scholar, had gotten me involved in assisting him and his gifted, young partner, Doug Schwab, in cases involving accounting issues at Wells Fargo Bank, Paramount Pictures and Universal Pictures, as well as Levi Strauss & Co. Heller Ehrman was a large national law firm headquartered in San Francisco. Then the highly esteemed San Francisco firm, Farella Braun + Martel, including its multiskilled and affable Randy Wulff, got me involved in other litigation matters that also involved accounting issues.

It was my dream to build a new practice area for CPA's beyond taxation and auditing. This practice area would assist attorneys by using the knowledge held by many CPAs of the disciplines provided by accounting (including its near universal structure and controls, the patterns of its processes, as well as its resulting document organization and record-keeping) that enabled the accounting function to become a company's history book of each of its transactions and activities.

I now had experience in educating attorneys that a company's accounting system represented an organized collection of documents that could be used to assist them in discovery, document organization, liability issues, and damage calculations. Then to present their cases to judges and juries using the companies own books and records to help the attorneys prosecute their cases successfully. I taught them that for every transaction entered into by a company, its accounting system created documents that reflected the nature and dollar impact of that transaction and who was involved. Drilling into those accounting systems was often a critical part of finding documents that led to the successful outcome of complex business-related litigation.

I called this process of drilling into a company's accounting organization (through subpoenas) and then organizing and analyzing that data into meaningful presentations, *forensic accounting.*

A few CPAs were dabbling in this type of work on occasion,

but it was mostly in divorce matters for high-profile, high-wealth litigation. I envisioned expanding this practice area to large-scale complex business disputes and believed that forensic accounting could become a significant public accounting practice area beyond just audit and tax work.

John and I decided that if we went forward with this idea, we could open an office in San Mateo, a location close to both San Francisco and the exploding businesses and law firms of Silicon Valley. It would also be close to our homes.

We decided to meet the next day, which was a Saturday, to pencil out a forecast of revenues and expenses and put together a plan for organizing a firm, then the two couples would go out to dinner to either celebrate starting a business together or continuing our successful careers with PMM.

That morning, John and I took over the dining room table at my home. The dining room had a large picture window that looked out to a large, serene backyard where Barby played with Greg. We built a model that estimated how many hours we would bill clients during each month, then assumed a rate per hour that we would charge for each hour worked. This provided a forecast of revenues by month. We then estimated the costs of office rent, telephone, postage, staffing, insurance, and other operating expenses.

All this led to the furious punching of keys on our old mechanical adding machines with paper tapes pouring out that needed to be checked and checked again.

The forecasting of revenues and expenses, along with their monthly timing, led us to a determination of how much we needed to invest of our own capital. Finally, we calculated when and how much we would likely be able to pay ourselves from the firm. Our capital investment was needed to fund initial costs, as well as the time it would take to find clients, complete the client's needed work, bill for that work, and finally collect the amounts billed. Each step in that process would take time, and our capital would be needed to pay the firm's expenses in the meantime.

By 6:00 that evening, we finished the cash flow model and a timeline of tasks to be accomplished, by date. It was time for a group discussion by John and Lynette Skelton and Barbara and I regarding whether and how to move forward with a new CPA firm. Since all of us were going to be called upon to take risks and invest our energy and capital, each of us needed to take ownership of the eventual decision.

The financial models looked good, but there were significant uncertainties and risks.

Barby and Lynnette's questions were not about clients, revenues, and expenses but more related to quality-of-life issues such as John and I being able to make our own decisions about where we lived and not being transferred to other cities around the globe or the country, while being able to coach soccer or little league.

By 7:30 pm, we decided to go to dinner and finalize our decision.

We had a wonderful dinner at the Iron Gate restaurant in Belmont, a traditional Italian restaurant with waiters in formal dress and bow ties, tablecloths, candles, and a warm fireplace. By the end of the meal, the firm of Regan & Skelton CPAs ("R&S") was born. Now it was time for us to meet with Jim Perk at PMM to announce the breaking news.

We decided to tell Jim Perk our decision early in the following week. As soon after that as possible, I would meet with John. The meeting with Jim Perk was hard. He was a good man, and, over the years, he had treated both John and I well. Perk asked both of us to take time to reconsider our decision and to let him know immediately if we changed our minds. Skelton returned to his office and returned to his work. I left the PMM office to meet with John.

John's enthusiasm was infectious. He told me that he would move the Air West forensic work to R&S, and he wanted to begin that process as soon as R&S had obtained a license to operate as a CPA firm, insurance, a partnership agreement, and a bank account so that he and I could work on interrogatories, depositions and other Air West matters.

I returned to PMM to share the big news with Skelton. We were both excited by our new journey but concerned about its considerable risks.

A few days later, we told Jim Perk that our decision to leave PMM was final. I also mentioned that I intended to take the Air West forensic work to R&S. That way, Vic Count could drop the bomb to H&S that PMM was no longer associated with the Hughes litigation and the related case against H&S.

However, Perk had prepared for this and responded that PMM would keep all the work papers that had been created by PMM over the past five years and that R&S could bill PMM for my time. That bill would then be marked up appropriately, then sent to Pettit, Evers & Martin for payment to PMM. In addition, Perk stated that all communications on the work's substance would go through him. Then he would communicate what was appropriate to the lawyers at Pettit. I listened but knew what was being proposed was designed to protect PMM and to implement Vic Count's goal to be sure that H&S would not blow the whistle on PMM's faulty audits of Penn Central. I also knew that this plan would squash the Hughes litigation and was not workable.

I immediately told John about Perk's plan. John also instantly saw through this scheme and knew that it was not viable. He immediately prepared his assault. He arranged a lunch later that same week at Jack's restaurant, located mid-way between the Pettit office in the Transamerica building and PMM's office in International Building at 601 California Street. Jack's opened in 1863 as a bar and restaurant downstairs with a brothel upstairs.

The tiny brothel rooms had been converted long ago into a series of small dining rooms, with walls and doors for privacy. John, Perk, and I met for lunch in one of the upstairs dining rooms.

The pre-lunch and lunch portion of the meeting was pleasant with plenty of conversation, and fresh and tasty seafood and San Francisco sourdough bread. After lunch, John summarized the plan that Perk had dictated to me two days earlier, and ripped it to shreds, attacking it as unworkable, unethical, and a complete abandonment of PMM's client, Air West, and its needs.

John reminded Jim Perk how much Air West had paid PMM for its work and demanded that any work papers prepared in connection with the Hughes's related forensic work be turned over to R&S as soon as they had established their office and that PMM have no further involvement in the matter. If Perk did not agree to these terms, A.W. Liquidating Company and Pettit would sue PMM and expose H&S's scheme to shut down PMM's forensic work for Air West in order to protect itself from embarrassment for its allegedly faulty work on its audits of Penn Central's financial statements.

To his credit, Jim Perk saw the merits of John's arguments, the weakness of PMM's proposition and its dangers. He agreed to comply with John's demands, but, from Perk's perspective, he was comforted that PMM would no longer be aiding the litigation against H&S, and PMM's exposure to leaks of its faulty audits on Penn Central were now much less likely.

In early September 1973, John and I packed up our offices at PMM, including the precious Air West work papers, and moved into a small office suite in San Mateo. The two of us, both under thirty years of age, were embarking on our own journey. Our success was now dependent on going up against one of the wealthiest and most powerful men in the world and his herculean defense backed by unlimited resources. We no longer had a mighty Big 8 international accounting firm backing us up. PMM was known as advisors to the Queen of England, auditors of the world's largest banks such as Chase Manhattan, and Wells Fargo bank, and technology companies like Xerox. Without that formidable reputation and resource behind us, we would be essentially alone, except for the considerable support of John Clark.

The R&S office was 1.4 miles from my new home, accentuated by one stop light between the office and my home. Some days this short commute was almost too short. There were many days that I remember getting in my car to return home from the office while thinking about the complexities of the Air West litigation, then suddenly I was home greeting Barby and Greg. The transition period between the office and life at home had disappeared and some nights I felt like I needed a bit more transition time to quiet the tension of the litigation before becoming husband and dad. On balance though, not having a commute to and from San Francisco every day and working close to home was a wonderful change.

Later, I would become a soccer and little league coach, as well as elected to the school board, town council and mayor.

CHAPTER 19

SOMETIMES YOU CAN'T
HIDE BEHIND EXOTIC,
PRIVATE DOORS

"Privacy is paradise."

—*HOLLY HUNTER*

A PPARENTLY, AT LEAST one of the many people Hanks had spoken to about his investigation warned Chester Davis about the Department of Justice's work and its status in early December of 1973. Davis learned what I had learned: Department of Justice was doing a serious investigation of the Hughes stock manipulation schemes, including stock trading and related FUD activities, which were orchestrated in connection with Hughes's acquisition of Air West.

Davis suspected that Hughes's criminal indictment was imminent and concluded that he needed to quickly get him to a country where his extradition to the United States would be as difficult as possible. At that time, Hughes was in London in his ninth-floor suite at the Inn on the Park. Although he was not going to attend personally, he was in high spirits because that month, he would be inducted into the National Aviation Hall of Fame, at its "Oscar Night of Aviation."

During that event, Hughes, along with the famous test pilot, Chuck Yeager, were joining fifty-two others, including Orville and Wilbur Wright, Eddie Rickenbacker, and Charles Lindbergh as members of the National Aviation Hall of Fame.

Incredibly, Davis had just read a December 8, 1973 article in the *New York Times* about financier Robert Vesco's fight to stave off extradition to the United States. After several years of risky investments and dubious dealings, Vesco allegedly committed securities fraud. The U.S. Securities and Exchange Commission's investigation resulted in its accusation that Vesco had embezzled $220 million from four different funds of the Investors Overseas Services complex of funds.

Because of Vesco's embezzlement and subsequent escape from the United States, he became known as "the undisputed king of the fugitive financiers." He fled to the Bahamas to avoid the SEC. Later, a court in the Bahamas ruled that the fraud charge on which the financier had been indicted in New York was not an extraditable offense.

Magistrate Emanuel Osadebay threw out the case brought by the United States for Vesco's extradition without even calling on Mr. Vesco to produce a defense. Further, the United States had no right to appeal the decision. Since Davis was informed that Hughes was soon to be indicted for securities fraud by the SEC, he ascertained that Hughes needed to move to the Bahamas as soon as possible.

On Thursday, December 20, 1973, Howard Hughes left London on a jet owned by Adnan Khashoggi, the Middle East arms dealer who had made hundreds of millions serving as a middleman between American manufacturers of military goods and

Arab countries, particularly Saudi Arabia. He had been a frequent high-roller visitor at the Sands Hotel and Casino. The Sands was Adnan's favorite casino, and he had a long and favorable association with the Hughes organization.

The aircraft took off from London, carrying Howard, six of his aides and two of his doctors. It landed at Freeport on Grand Bahama Island, and Hughes was escorted into the Xanadu Princess Hotel's penthouse. Hughes and his entourage took the top two floors of the twelve-story hotel tower. The Bahamian government welcomed the group and guaranteed their privacy.

The Xanadu was owned by Daniel Ludwig, Hughes's chief rival as the richest man in America at the time. Hughes was impressed with the security of the *Xanadu* (meaning an idyllic, exotic, luxurious place). It had a reputation for attracting the rich and famous because of its luxury and the privacy provided to its guests. Hughes felt that his relationship with the government in the Bahamas would be enhanced if he were to simply buy the hotel outright. He instructed Davis to begin negotiations with the Ludwig organization to purchase Xanadu. (Davis closed the deal in March of 1974.)

On December 28, 1973, Howard R. Hughes, Chester Davis, Robert Maheu, David Charnay, president of Four Star International, a television and motion picture production company in Los Angeles, and James Nail, who was now in charge of land acquisition for Hughes's Nevada operations, were named as defendants in a nine-count criminal indictment by a Federal grand jury. George Crockett, a long-time friend of Hughes's, and Hank Greenspun of the *Las Vegas Sun* were named as unindicted co-conspirators. Four of the five defendants were accused of stock manipulation, conspiracy, and wire fraud in connection with the acquisition by Hughes of Air West. The fifth defendant was accused of failing to report his knowledge of a felony and being an accessory to the felony.

A conviction for conspiracy carried a maximum penalty of five years in prison and a $10,000 fine. A conviction for stock manipulation could bring two years in prison and a $10,000 fine. Judge Roger D. Foley of the Federal District Court set January 11 for the arraignment of the defendants.

The first count of the indictment accused the defendants and co-conspirators of conspiring between June 1968 and April 1970 to depress the market price of Air West stock. The indictment described sales by Charnay, Greenspun, and Crockett of large blocks of Air West stock in two days in December 1968. These sales were alleged to have caused a significant decline in Air West's stock price by flooding the market with sales orders. These stock sales were at a time when the Air West board was deciding whether to approve the sale of the airline to Hughes or to consider offers from others.

Hughes, Maheu, and Davis were charged with bringing pressure through lawsuits against Air West directors who had voted against selling the airline to Hughes. This pressure was allegedly designed to cause them to change their votes. Hughes was also accused of directing Maheu and Davis, by handwritten memorandums and oral communications, to bring the suits and unlawfully manipulate Air West stock's market price to make the acquisition offer appear more attractive to stockholders.

It was reported in the press, at the time of the indictment, that Hughes's purchase of Air West was delayed until April of 1970 pending the approval by both the Civil Aeronautics Board and President Nixon. Presidential approval was required for changes in ownership of airlines when international routes were involved. In addition to regional service in eight western states, Air West flew to Canada and Mexico.

At the time of the indictment, the press also reported that the Senate Watergate Committee investigators were examining a possible connection between a $100,000 contribution by Hughes to President Nixon's election campaign and his approval of the purchase of the airline. Charles G. Rebozo, the President's close friend, had acknowledged taking the $100,000 from Hughes's agents delivered in two parts in 1969 and 1970. Each delivery contained $50,000 in $100 bills. He testified to the Senate Watergate committee that he held the $100,000 in a safe-deposit box in his Key Biscayne bank in Florida. Mr. Rebozo told the committee that the identical $100 bills had been returned to Davis.

The larger world savored a taste of Davis's style later in December 1973 when he was called before an executive session of Senator Sam Ervin's Watergate committee to explain what he knew about the mysterious $100,000 that Hughes had given Nixon in 1969 and 1970.

When it was time for Chester Davis to testify before the Senate Watergate committee, Davis burst into the hearing with a suitcase packed with the $100-dollar bills and announced, "You want the money, here's the goddamn money!" and dumped its contents on the table (current value: more than $1,500,000).

Another amazing coincidence associated with Chester Davis was that his powerful Manhattan and Los Angeles law firm at the time of the Air West acquisition by Hughes was named Davis & Cox. Maxwell Cox, his partner, was the brother of the special Watergate prosecutor, Archibald Cox, who was fired by Nixon in the famous Saturday Night Massacre on October 20, 1973, during the Watergate scandal.[8]

Counts 2 and 3 of the Department of Justice's indictments charged Hughes, Maheu, Davis, and Charnay with illegally using

---

8 On the evening of Saturday, October 20, 1973, President Nixon ordered Attorney Elliot Richardson to fire Special Watergate Prosecutor Archibald Cox. Richardson refused and resigned immediately. Nixon then ordered Deputy Attorney General William Ruckelshaus to fire Cox. Ruckelshaus refused and resigned. Nixon then ordered the next in line at the DOJ, Robert Bork to fire Cox, and he did.

the American Stock Exchange facilities to manipulate the price of Air West's stock. Count 4 charged the same four persons with the use of telephone lines to carry out their alleged scheme to depress the stock price.

This charge of wire fraud carried a maximum penalty of five years in prison and a $1,000 fine. Counts 5, 6, and 7 charged these same four individuals with violating the wire fraud statute in their take-over plan by sending telegrams to opposing Air West directors, urging them to change their vote. These counts also alleged that the four defendants telegraphed instructions to a brokerage firm to sell a large block of Air West stock owned by Crockett. Finally, these four defendants were also said to have caused a Nevada brokerage company to direct an American Stock Exchange representative to sell a large block of Air West stock owned by Greenspun.

Count 8 charged Nall with being an accessory in the unlawful manipulation of the Air West stock, and in Count 9, Nall was charged with failure to disclose his knowledge of an alleged felony. The maximum penalty for being accessory to a felony was half the prison terms and fines of the other defendants.

Although William Hanks headed the investigation, he turned over the lead on the case to the United States Attorney for Nevada, Dante Beaton. The key to the presentation of their case was the expected testimony of two confidential witnesses ("CW"). These witnesses were identified only as CW1 and CW2. It was speculated that they were insiders within the Hughes organization that had turned against the defendants. In January of 1974, these witnesses were to provide key testimony that directly linked the defendants to the charges included in the indictment and the events depicted in the related timelines. Their testimony was critical to the government's ability to present its case.

On the night before the testimony of CW1 was to be held, he was the last person to leave the office that night. The underground parking lot where he had parked his car was nearly dark. The only lighting in the parking garage was the emergency lights. As he approached his car, a large male with a ski mask lunged at CW1 from behind a large pillar with a fire ax in his right hand. CW1 was hit several times around the head and neck. He laid in the parking lot until the next morning when others arrived for work. He was taken to a nearby hospital in critical condition. He survived but sustained head injuries that impaired his speech and severely impacted his cognitive abilities.

When he failed to show up for his 9:00 testimony the next morning, Beaton called Hanks. Hanks checked CW1's office and learned that he had been taken to Sunrise Hospital and Medical Center, about two miles from the Desert Inn. Due to his mental impairments, he was never able to testify about the matters critical to the government's case. In fact, because he was a confidential witness, only a few people knew his connection to the Hughes litigation. However, CW2 did know about CW1's role and he was quick to learn about the attack.

Before the government could even try to convince him to participate in its a witness protection plan, CW2 disappeared. Despite a massive search effort to find CW2, the government's efforts were unsuccessful. CW1 was severely impaired and CW2 was gone, and so was Hanks' and Beaton's ability to continue the case against the defendants.

It was clear to the DOJ that the defendants would deny the charges and claim that the evidence against them was nothing more than speculation and circumstantial. Even the now sworn enemies, Howard Hughes and Robert Maheu, would not testify against each other in this case. To their great regret and disgust, Hanks and Beaton knew that their case would be dismissed in early 1974. The loss of CW1 and CW2 as witnesses in the governments' case was a bitter disappointment that was not to be forgotten.

John Clark heard about the dismissal of the DOJ's case from his partner, Stan Orr, who had been with the DOJ for several years before joining the Pettit firm. John asked Orr if he had any insight about CW1 and CW2. Orr told Clark that his buddies at the DOJ were very tight-lipped about these confidential sources, but they did confirm that both worked within the Hughes organization and they were viewed as traitors by his "Mormon Mafia."

CW1 was attacked in a parking garage behind a Hughes office where he worked. As for CW2, the DOJ folks did not know if his disappearance was of his own accord or if it was "involuntary." In any case, he was not to be found in time before the case was dismissed and even if he returned sometime in the future, the damage to the DOJ's case had been done.

CHAPTER 20

LAST GENTLEMAN SPY

*"It takes tremendous discipline to control the influence,
the power you have over other people's lives."*

—CLINT EASTWOOD

ON APRIL 12, 1973, the Hughes Glomar Explorer
("HGE") left the Sun Shipyard in Chester,
Pennsylvania. It headed south down the Delaware
River at low tide to pass under two bridges and one power line.
However, the clearance under the Delaware Memorial Bridge at
Wilmington still presented a significant issue for the giant vessel.
To allow the ship to pass under this obstacle, the top twenty-
eight feet of the derrick on the HGE was removed and stored on
its main deck.

Once the HGE had passed under the bridge, a huge floating
crane picked up the twenty-eight-foot section and it was reat-
tached on top of the waiting 200-foot derrick.

After shallow-water tests off Delaware Bay, deep-water tests were
conducted eighty miles northwest of Bermuda. After these tests concluded, no other major structural modifications of the ship's design

were needed. The mining equipment had performed as designed, and while the A-frame, derrick, docking legs, and piping had some defects, these were scheduled to be corrected either during transit to Long Beach or on the West Coast during mobilization.

On August 11, 1973, the HGE began its 12,700-mile voyage to Long Beach. It could not use the Panama Canal because its 116-foot beam exceeded the canal's capacity. Instead, it was scheduled to cross from the Atlantic Ocean to the Pacific Ocean by going through the Strait of Magellan.

The HGE left with a crew of ninety-six, a combination of regular crew members plus forty-nine Global Marine engineers and technicians whose jobs were to work on the defect punch list during the voyage. Arrangements proceeded through Global Marine in Chile to have two Chilean pilots board the ship for its 320-mile transit through the Strait of Magellan. However, during late August, the ship picked up news reports from Chile about the government of Salvador Allende being in shambles as a result of labor strikes, food shortages, and clashes between the right and the left political factions. Even of an impending military coup.

The U.S. Government and its Central Intelligence Agency had worked against Allende since before he became president in November 1970. It had been the U.S. Government and the CIA's long-established goal to foment a coup against the Marxist Allende. President Nixon had instructed CIA Director Helms to unseat him, because Allende threatened to nationalize U.S. owned industries, and Nixon did not want another Fidel Castro in the American hemisphere during his watch.

William Colby, known as the "last gentleman spy," was promoted to director of the CIA on September 4, 1973. Prior to his promotion, his role at the CIA was the head of its clandestine branch. Since Colby had been leading the CIA's political action and counter-insurgency activities, his September promotion provided a smooth transaction for the CIA's activities in Chile.

In late August, the CIA had stepped up its campaign of bribes, coercion, and blackmailing of political and military leaders to accelerate its push to remove Allende from the presidency. This background contributed to a concern that the Chilean pilots might not be allowed to board the HGE. In other words, the HGE would have to go around the tip of South America using the Drake Passage, which would take at least two days longer to move from the Atlantic Ocean to the Pacific and would expose the vessel and the crew to freezing temperatures, storms with massive forty-foot waves and treacherous currents where the forces of these two oceans meet.

On September 5, 1973, the two pilots boarded the HGE while it waited in Possession Bay on the southeastern portion of the border between Argentina and Chile. The ship left the Bay at 11:00 a.m. on the 5th of September and passed through the Strait without incident. It arrived in the Pacific Ocean at 3:00 pm the next day. At this point, the journey deteriorated further as the HGE passed through twenty-five-foot seas (which were better than the forty-foot waves of Drake's Passage) and sixty-knot winds.

But the ship handled well, and its performance was superb.

The ship and equipment remained intact. It was now time for a 1,700-mile journey to the Port of Valparaiso, Chile, which is seventy miles northeast of Chile's capital, Santiago. In Valparaiso, the two pilots would depart the ship, and parts for repairs and supplies were to be loaded on to the HGE, along with seven additional technicians needed for the repairs.

During the journey to Valparaiso, Captain Kingma monitored the radio for any news relevant to the voyage. As the HGE proceeded north along the coast of Chile, Kingma learned of increasing political tensions in Santiago, as well as Valparaiso. These tensions culminated in a military coup on September 11. The HGE anchored in Valparaiso's outer harbor at 9:00 p.m. on

September 12, and waited for word from Tom Williams, a Global Marine representative.

Williams arrived from California with another Global Marine employee in Santiago on September 7 and seven technicians who were to board the vessel in Valparaiso as part of the repair efforts to be made during the voyage from Chile to Long Beach. The two Global Marine representatives were to make the arrangements needed to move supplies to the HGE, bring mail to its crew, and work with customs to transfer the seven technicians to the vessel.

The Global Marine entourage from California traveled from Santiago to Valparaiso on September 10. There, the technicians checked into the Hotel O'Higgins, in the center of the city, and waited for the arrival of the HGE. However, on September 11, 1973, at 6:00 a.m., the revolution began. Tanks, soldiers, and other military vehicles surrounded the hotel. Guests were confined to the hotel, and, initially, communications were cut off. It was soon reported that Salvador Allende had been shot and killed. (It was later said that he had taken his own life.)

The Global Marine representatives did a remarkable job of overcoming this massive confusion and in getting the seven technicians, supplies, and parts loaded onto the HGE, in the middle of a revolution. It was an extraordinary coincidence that a key component of one of the CIA's largest and most elaborate covert operations, Project AZORIAN, was right in the middle of a military coup, which was sponsored, in part, by the CIA (with 200 agents in Chile for the purpose of ousting Allende), and neither group knew about the activities of the other.

The HGE began its lengthy journey for Long Beach at 3:00 p.m. on September 13. The trip was uneventful, and again, the ship performed without any significant issues. It arrived in Long Beach Harbor quietly on Sunday evening on September 30. Now, the vessel and crew were to be converted from a ship with no evidence of its intelligence objectives or the nature of what it was designed to recover, to one fitted for its covert operations. Its 178 crew members were to be trained, equipment was to be tested, operations fine-tuned, then tested, and retested.

However, these mobilization efforts were delayed by labor-management problems between the Marine Engineers Benevolent Association and Global Marine. The union set up picket lines; the ship's crew and shipboard workers were harassed, and delivery trucks were stopped. It was important for the sea trials to be completed because weather only allowed for the mission to occur within the July to mid-September timeframe, and it was anticipated that the mission needed fourteen to twenty-one days to be completed. If the HGE did not leave Long Beach by the middle of June, the recovery attempt would have to be delayed for one whole year.

Assembly of the Clementine, which took place while inside the HMB-1, and away from spying eyes, was complete. The HMB-1 departed from Redwood City, California, and waited not far from Catalina Island for the Glomar Explorer to continue its sea trials. During the last two weeks of February, the tests focused on the pipe-handling system to be sure that it could rapidly and reliably lower and raise the doubles of pipe (two 30-foot pieces attached to make one 60-foot-long section).

Although there were issues, the pipe-handling system passed its tests, and the HGE and the HMB-1 swiftly headed 65 miles southwest of Catalina Island into international waters. This move was necessary because the state of California had an inventory tax on all commercial vessels in its waters on March 1.

To avoid disclosing that the U.S. government owned the HMB-1 and the HGE, these vessels had to unquestionably be in international waters on March 1.

CHAPTER 21

Project Azorian Passes its Finals

*"In battle it is the cowards who run the most
risk; bravery is a rampart of defense."*

—Sallust

O N MARCH 2, 1974, the HGE returned to Pier E in
Long Beach. Time for its final preparations and tests
before starting its mission. The focus now was on its
Integrated Systems preparation and testing those systems: the
pipe string itself, thread compound, gimbal platform (which
allowed the piping to remain steady with respect to the horizon
despite the ship's pitching and rolling), the A-frame supporting the piping system, yokes (feeding and steering of the piping
system), hydraulic pumps and controls, and docking legs.

These preparation activities called for an around-the-clock
effort to meet their scheduled completion date of March 27.
Then testing would begin the next day. The HGE left Pier E early
on the morning of March 28 for a mooring eight miles east of

Catalina Island. The HMB-1 had also been towed near this site with the Clementine safely inside of it and invisible to observers. Now it was time to submerge the HMB-1. This process took almost three days.

Once submerged[9], in fifty-five feet of water, the roof of the barge opened.

During the night, the HGE was positioned directly over the HMB-1. The gates under its Moon Pool opened and its two docking legs lowered into the barge and attached to the Clementine. Now the docking legs were raised, and the Clementine was brought into the HGE's Moon Pool and secured in place. The HGE's gates were closed. It returned to Long Beach with the Clementine safely tucked away inside its Moon Pool.

Having completed its purpose, the HMB-1 returned to Redwood City.

Although there were fits and starts and some damage to the HGE's Integrated System components during April and the first part of May, the crew and the system passed all the challenges confronting them. On May 12, the Captain advised project headquarters that the scheduled tests were completed, and the HGE would return to Pier E for minor repairs.

During this time of final testing and repairs of the HGE's Integrated Systems, the ExCom met in April and May to review the testing results and the project's overall status.

Dr. Kissinger had also requested a final evaluation of the expected intelligence benefits of Project AZORIAN before seeking approval by the United States Intelligence Board ("USIB"). This process resulted in the following memorandum from the ExCom to Dr. Kissinger:

---

9 The HMB-1 was the largest submissible in the world.

The United States Intelligence Board has reviewed and updated its intelligence assessment of Project AZORIAN. On the basis of this review, the Board concludes that there have been no significant developments since the last Board assessment which would detract from the unique intelligence value of this target... acquisition of the nuclear warheads and the SS-N-5 missile system, together with related documents, would provide a much-improved baseline for estimates of the current and future Soviet strategic threat. The Board also expects that recovered documents would provide important insights into Soviet command and control and certain aspects of their strategic attack doctrine. In its evaluation, the board assumed a successful mission. On this basis the Board continues to believe that recovery of the AZORIAN submarine [the K-129] would provide information which can be obtained from no other source, on subjects of great importance to the national defense.

Dr. Kissinger prepared his own memorandum for President Nixon that covered the key points discussed by ExCom and the USIB. The President approved the mission on June 7, 1974, subject to the condition that the actual recovery must not be undertaken before his return from his trip to the Soviet Union, which was scheduled to take place from June 27 through July 3.

CHAPTER 22

INGENIOUS PLAN TO
INFILTRATE THE FORTRESS

"Plans are nothing; planning is everything."

—DWIGHT D. EISENHOWER

IKE JEFFERSON WAS a security guard at the block-long Hughes Operations and Records Center at 7000 Romaine in West Hollywood, California. He had been working for Hughes for less than two years starting in 1972. He was struggling financially to support his wife and their six children by working as a car salesman for a Chevrolet dealership in North Hollywood, and as a security guard in the Romaine building at night.

During shift changes, and from others working late in the building, he overheard that certain sensitive documents relating to a CIA operation in the Pacific and a securities case involving Air West were being gathered in one of the building's conference rooms. The documents were being carefully catalogued for Chester Davis, before being shipped out of the country to the

Xanadu Hotel in the Bahamas. Their delivery was to be scheduled soon after the closing of the hotel's purchase by Hughes from Daniel Ludwig was final. Apparently, Chester Davis wanted these documents to be out of the reach of the U.S. Government and Air West's attorneys.

Robert Maheu's very contentious libel suit against Hughes had also been a hot topic around the building and in the press. The trial was scheduled to begin in June 1974 and was expected to last for several months. Based on comments that Jefferson overheard, along with widespread media, Maheu had grown into Enemy No. 1 to Davis and Hughes.

Jefferson decided that these circumstances might be an opportunity to gain some financial security. Besides, he was not happy with the way he had been treated by several of the Hughes's people, particularly Chester Davis, so he felt no loyalty to the Hughes organization.

During his nightly rounds he began to look at records that would provide him with Maheu's telephone number. That turned out to be easy. It was in the Rolodex on Bill Gay's desk. In mid-March of 1974, Jefferson called Robert Maheu from the Chevy dealership to inform him of his rare discovery of sensitive documents relating to a CIA operation in the Pacific Ocean *and* documents relating to an Air West lawsuit. Before the docs made their way to the Bahamas, perhaps the desperate security guard could sell them to Maheu for the right amount.

Intrigue and revenge made his mind a seesaw of exciting thoughts. Maheu vowed to call the stranger with an offer back soon. Jefferson certainly hoped so, now that he had voiced this dangerous information and risked it all.

This conversation was music to Maheu's ears. The building where Jefferson was the security guard was also where Nadine Henley maintained an office. She had been Howard Hughes's private secretary for 34 years and likely held documents that would be useful in Maheu's libel suit against Hughes. If he could get the CIA to sponsor a burglary of 7000 Romaine, it would be a great cover to gather helpful documents from Henley's office for his case.

7000 ROMAIN STREET. SOURCE: BARRY KING / ALAMY STOCK PHOTO.

Robert Maheu had known Colby for many years. He first met him when he was doing cut-out work for the CIA. Colby had joined the CIA right after World War II as a real man's spy. As head of the CIA's covert operations and now as Director of the CIA, he was undoubtedly knowledgeable about the CIA's efforts to retrieve the K-129 and Hughes's role in the venture.

Maheu called Colby's office. He was not available, but Maheu left a subtle message with Colby's secretary, telling her that he had important information about Howard Hughes's "mining project" in the Pacific.

Colby called Maheu back about two hours later. After a few minutes chatting about old times, Colby mentioned that Helms had kept him up to speed on Project AZORIAN. Now that Maheu knew that Colby had connected his message about

Hughes's mining project with Project AZORIAN, he felt comfortable telling Colby about his telephone call from Jefferson. When Maheu mentioned the memorandum between Helms and Davis, Colby jumped into the conversation. Between the memo and the box of Air West documents that the Department of Justice would surely love to get their hands on, this could feasibly be enough explosive material to set Howard Hughes and Chester Davis ablaze.

Would a break-in involving a common security guard suffice? What about an extended plan for a cut-out, as directed by Maheu, resulting in taking these documents from Hughes before they left the country? What would the budget be for these clandestine endeavors?

The two men bantered back and forth for some time before Maheu lost the wind to talk and ended the phone call. He was a man of action. This project was like his old spy days and would likely help him slay his enemies, Hughes and Davis, if he could retrieve some delectable information from Nadine Henley's files.

He made a list of key elements of the plan, fully knowing 7000 Romaine was like a fortress. Nobody just walked into that building without permission. He decided that it needed to look like a burglary, without inside help. He needed to give Jefferson a good cover, and he did not want to just take documents from Henley's office, or just the Project AZORIAN memo and the Air West box as that would lead back to the CIA or the Department of Justice. There needed to be a much broader theft of documents.

Maheu decided that they would take other items to support the burglary motive, like Nadine Henley's butterfly collection and her Wedgwood bowls. Some of the Hughes movie memorabilia that had value should also be taken to support the burglary scheme. And of course, piles of cash that he had seen in the various safes and other files relating to contracts with starlets and movie scripts that might have value.

Although he had been in the Romaine building many times, he wanted Jefferson to give him a current layout of the building. He needed to know the location of the safes and security vaults. He also had to be sure that Jefferson knew how to disarm the closed-circuit TV cameras, any laser tripwires, telephone links to the police headquarters, and any alarm bells. He also needed to tell Maheu the make and model of the safes, if possible. With that information, he could hire team members that knew to bring the right equipment and how to flawlessly open the safes.

After his own research and helpful discoveries, Maheu called the Chevrolet dealership, where Jefferson worked, with his polished deal. After confirming that Jefferson had privacy and a pencil, he proceeded to give Jefferson a detailed list of items and tasks that would enable the break-in to be successful: a layout of both the first and second floors of the building, showing where the safes are located and their description (make and model, if available), where key filing cabinets are located and whether any of their drawers have safes. Of course, the layout needed to show the conference room's location where the Air West box was and the other documents that are being catalogued to be sent to the Xanadu Hotel. Then onto the location of Nadine Henley's office.

Maheu proceeded to tell him that since the previous night was a full moon, which provided good visibility, he went to LA and rented a car. He drove down North Orange Drive and turned into the parking lot behind 7000 Romaine at around 10:00 pm. He waited there until the first folks started coming to work at around 8:00 am. At around 1:00 a.m., Maheu noticed that someone came out of the back door of the building and walked toward North Sycamore Avenue, circled the building and went back in using the same back door.

Jefferson couldn't believe his ears. In no time, this bloodthirsty man had developed and actually tested his own break-in plan. Sure enough, he had gone out of the backdoor and circled the building as usual to look for anything unusual happening, but it also gave him some fresh air and kept him alert every night. The backdoor was very secure, requiring both a key and a combination that was changed every month. He also confirmed that the first folks showed up to work at around 8:00 in the morning.

Maheu almost found himself wetting his pants with excitement. Jefferson had confirmed all of his assertions about the location in question. The plan would be for his guys to meet Jefferson at the backdoor on the scheduled night at 1:00 a.m., then go in the building with him. This would give them a little over five hours before they needed to leave. They would need to tie up Jefferson and then, after around thirty minutes, he could try to escape to get to a phone and communicate with the police or wait until someone arrived for work that morning to untie him.

Other people's usual whereabouts needed to be identified on the layout. Closed-circuit TVs, any laser tripwires, and links to the police, needed to be disabled without anyone's knowledge.

Finally, according to Maheu, the big payoff to Jefferson would be a fake California driver's license, a fake military ID, a fake social security number, and a real PO box. The IDs would include his actual features. The driver's license and fake military ID would enable Maheu to obtain a PO Box and a real bank account for money movement: $5,000 upon acceptance of the assignment, the building layout and answers to his questions; $10,000 the day after a successful job, and a final $10,000 three months after that, assuming everything still flowed smoothly.

After this long list of needs and instructions, Maheu wanted to know if Jefferson was ready to accept this project—with the alias on these fake documents as Howard Davis, which he had selected as a middle finger to his enemies.

With Jefferson's calm and collected acceptance, Maheu gave him a PO box address to mail the information to him. He would then send him a checkbook for the new bank account and an ATM card, which were fairly new at the time. With this new-fangled instrument, Jefferson could instantly withdraw cash over an extended period, in $200 to $400 increments.

Jefferson was ecstatic, not to mention the fact that $25,000 was more than he would earn in a year. He would get out of debt and still have money to spend. Plus, he would be helping his country and getting back at that bastard, Chester Davis, who had treated him badly on several occasions.

CHAPTER 23

GOING FOR THE HEART

*"Pursue one great decisive aim with
force and determination."*

—CARL VON CLAUSEWITZ

THE DISMISSAL OF the Department of Justice's criminal case against Hughes and the other defendants because of the government's inability to provide the testimony and related exhibits that were to be sponsored by CW1 and CW2 was of great concern to Ted Russell, John Clark, and me.

We met in John's plush office to discuss our next steps in the civil suit against Howard Hughes, Hughes Air West, Summa Corporation, Chester Davis, and Haskins & Sells. Surely, some of the witnesses, in our civil case would now have concerns about their safety and welfare. We rationalized that our case was a civil matter, not a criminal case like the DOJ's. If Hughes was found liable, he would only lose money, not spend any time in jail. However, the bottom line was than the average witness would want nothing to do with this case, if it meant testifying against Hughes.

We had already deposed the designated corporate witnesses from H&S, Prentiss Block, and Marty Rollins, Air West's assistant controller, and a few other witnesses from Summa Corporation. However, those depositions were contentious and so obstructed by defense counsel that they were of limited use. Now, given the fate of CW1 and CW2, any other potentially cooperative witnesses were likely to become adversarial, evasive, or worse.

After going over various alternatives, John shouted, "Dammit! I say we go right for their heart. We depose Hughes himself." His rationale was that it was Hughes's tightfisted drive to squeeze money from the shareholders that set the FUD in motion, and the accounting shenanigans all flowed from him. Marty Rollins was only trying to keep his job, and H&S and Davis were trying to keep their long-time golden goose client happy so that he would keep laying golden eggs in their bank accounts.

Emboldened by his decision, John announced, "Yes, we need to hit Hughes with a deposition notice and a subpoena duces tecum. If he complies, we will take him apart. If he fails to show up, we will move for a default judgment. Either way, we come out on top."

"What the heck is a *subpoena duces tecum*?" I asked.

Russell responded that it means we serve a subpoena on Howard Hughes, which demands that he appear for his deposition and that he bring relevant documents with him. I thought this was a great idea, then I asked, "How are you going to subpoena Hughes?" Russell responded that it would be difficult but that they had folks in their Washington DC office who were wizards at getting that done, and he and John would make sure that they do their magic on this part of the case.

So, Russell and I prepared the subpoena duces tecum. I focused on the document request with Russell reviewing and editing my request. My efforts zeroed in on the accounting issues, particularly any documents evidencing Hughes's knowledge of those closing adjustments. In addition, I focused on his knowledge about who suggested that such adjustments be recorded, why they were suggested, whether the adjustments were consistent with the Purchase Contract, and to whom were the closing adjustments communicated to. We were hoping that this subpoena would produce memorandum, notes of meetings taken or to be taken, agendas, and any evidence of correspondence.

The subpoena was sent to Pettit's Washington DC office in early April of 1974. It called for Hughes to appear for his deposition on May 29, 1974. This gave the wizards enough time to do their magic in time for Hughes to produce the requested documents and appear for his deposition at Pettit & Martin's office. The relevant documents were to be provided by his counsel, Davis, three days before the deposition. Although these documents had been requested from him six months earlier, Davis had produced only a pathetically few innocent and meaningless documents of absolutely no value in response to that subpoena.

John and I prepared diligently for Hughes's deposition. Although we realized that Hughes might not appear, we would not be like the author Clifford Irving, who had expected that Hughes would not show up to expose his book fraud. If Hughes did appear and Clark was not well-prepared with meaningful questions and relevant documents at the ready, it would be malpractice and Chester Davis would surely file, and win, a motion for significant sanctions to be awarded to his client.

A key document was the log that I had prepared while I was at Air West's San Mateo offices. This log was a listing of those PMM work papers that H&S had borrowed as part of their due diligence review. The log showed the work paper letter and number (for example, A-1, B-9, or G-7), a brief description of the working paper, the date the working paper was provided to H&S, and the date it was returned PMM. Most entries showed that the date a particular work paper was provided to H&S and the date it was returned to PMM were the same day. This indicated that, generally, the work papers were photocopied and returned to PMM shortly after being provided. The photocopying of the documents gave the H&S accountants as much time as they wanted to analyze, discuss, and communicate the contents of these work papers among themselves and with their client.

For the Hughes deposition, we focused our preparation on those work papers that I could link to the closing adjustments. The expectation was that Hughes became aware of the assets and liabilities addressed in the work papers and established a process for how they became part of the closing adjustments. John wanted to prepare detailed questions about Hughes's knowledge of these assets and liabilities, and the chain of actions, and people, that enabled Air West's assets to be reduced, and its liabilities increased by the closing adjustments.

Nine days before Hughes was scheduled to appear to testify, Chester Davis filed a motion that Hughes be relieved from appearing for his deposition. Federal Judge Alfonso J. Zirpoli denied that motion and the court ordered Hughes to appear as scheduled. May 26 came and went without any new documents. Davis did send a letter saying that all relevant documents had been provided in response to the earlier subpoena.

On May 29, 1974, Ted Russell had Pettit & Martin's main conference set up for coffee, cream and sugar, orange juice, water, sweet rolls, and various types of soft drinks. The videographer, who was to videotape the deposition, arrived around 8:00 a.m. to set up the camera and a microphone for the witness, and microphones for two attorneys for each defendant, as well as for John Clark and Ted. I only intended to whisper to John or write notes. The court reporter arrived at 8:30. Her set-up was much less complicated than the videographer, only the unpacking and setting up of her stenograph machine.

A few minutes before 9:00, John, Russell and I entered the

main conference room and joined the videographer and the court reporter. After retrieving our drink of choice, we engaged in small talk while waiting to meet the world-famous Howard Hughes. To our disappointment, by 9:15 am, none of the expected defense counsel had arrived, and neither had Hughes. John suspected that each of the defendants' counsel had been told that Hughes was not going to attend his deposition and therefore, there was no point in their attending. It was not going to happen.

John called Davis to confirm that Hughes was not going to attend. Typically, Davis barked, "John, your deposition is a joke, its only purpose is to harass my very important and busy client about matters that he clearly has no knowledge, and we are not going to dignify your circus with his presence."

John smiled as he recapped Davis' comments. Although we were all disappointed that Hughes was not appearing (as were the videographer and the court reporter), Clark explained that this shenanigans by Davis would cost Davis and Hughes. John was going to move for a default judgment and sanctions.

CHAPTER 24

SCANDALOUS PAY PHONE CHAT

*"Inaction breeds doubt and fear. Action breeds confidence
and courage. If you want to conquer fear, do not sit
home and think about it. Go out and get busy."*

—*DALE CARNEGIE*

ON MONDAY, APRIL 15, 1974, Robert Maheu went
to the post office to mail his first estimated tax payment
for 1974, and to separately mail a request for an extension to file his 1973 income tax return. While he was there, he
checked his PO Box and found a letter from Mike Jefferson. It
contained the following information:

- A hand-drawn layout of the first and second floors of
  7000 Romaine. The layout showed:

- A walk-in-vault which also contained a Mosler safe.

- Kay Glenn's office (assistant to Bill Gay) had a four-
  drawer filing cabinet with a Mosler safe in the top
  drawer.

- Lee Murrin's office contained a Mosler safe. Murrin oversaw Hughes's personal financial affairs.

- Carol Snodgrass, an accounting clerk, had a combination filing cabinet with one drawer containing a Mosler safe.

- Two filing cabinets in Nadine Henley's office with Mosler safes in both top drawers.

- Mike noted that when he leaves the back door around 1:00 am for his exterior walk, he disarms the alarm system, leaves the building, then rearms it. When he re-enters the building, he has 10 seconds to enter a code that disarms the system, otherwise, the alarm will sound, and the police will be notified.

- There is a closed-circuit TV system that records from cameras located throughout the building. However, these can be turned off from locations at the back and front doors and at his security station. Therefore, when he returns from his walk around 1:15 am, he, and anyone with him, will be filmed and recorded. To maintain the appearance of a burglary, he needs to appear to be struggling with his captors who need to be in disguise, until he is forced to disarm the closed-circuit TV system.

- The only other person in the building from 1:00 a.m. until 7:45 a.m. is Harry Watson. Harry operates the telephones during the night if someone calls for anyone within the control of the operations center. Harry then either takes messages which are relayed to the appropriate person(s) in the morning or wakes them up if the call is an emergency. There are no documents in Harry's room and no offices near him that are important, so you must avoid Harry's area of the building, which is at the west end of the second floor. Most of the time

Harry reads books or takes a snooze so he should not be a problem.

- Mike enclosed a photograph that could be used for his new California driver's license and military ID. He also included his height, weight, and the color of his eyes to be used on his new driver's license.

Jefferson had done a fine job providing everything except the model numbers of the safes, but Maheu could work around that issue. Importantly, he needed to go through his records of people with the skill sets required to make this burglary work. His focus was on finding a person with the talents to open the Mosler safes. This would mean someone skilled with cutting torch kits and working with oxygen tanks and acetylene.

The options came down to three persons, but one was in jail, which left only two possibilities. Maheu decided to call his first choice and hope that he was available. The fewer people that knew about this project, the better. He decided on a fellow he had used on several projects involving the cracking of safes for the FBI, the CIA, and Hughes. This man was very skilled, worked quickly, had a good team, and kept his mouth shut. Lucky O'Leary of St. Louis.

Maheu drove to his "go-to" pay phone near the Desert Inn, which was in a quiet location and was seldom in use and called O'Leary. He informed him of the epic project that needed a man of his aptitude for a vault, two Mosler safes, and four Mosler filing cabinets with top drawer safes, requiring the use of cutting torch kits, oxygen tanks and acetylene, welding goggles, and necessary eyewear.

O'Leary's answer to this cut-out? A resounding yes for his old pal.

They agreed that the job must end before 7:30 a.m. and O'Leary would need to bring about fifteen empty boxes to fill with the goods, put in a van and drive to a warehouse in Las

Vegas. The payoff for O'Leary could conceivably be more than $200,000 from the safe in Kay Glenn's office. If he found less than that, the CIA would bring his fee to a total of $100,000. If he found more than $100,000, finders keepers! It was up to him whether he wanted to share it with his crew or not. The documents of high importance were the Project AZORIAN memo for the CIA, plus all of the other documents in the conference room on the second floor about Project AZORIAN, and the box with the Air West documents. Finally, Maheu ordered O'Leary to go through Nadine Henley's office for any information about Project AZORIAN, Air West and as a personal favor, *any* documents she had about him to go into a separate box labeled "Maheu."

O'Leary chuckled at Maheu's instructions to tie up the guard by his ankles, tie his hands around his back and tape his mouth shut. No extreme force. Another paramount step was to be aware that once they entered the building around 1:00 am, the closed-circuit TV system would record him tying up the guard, so it had to appear as if he were being forced to disarm the closed-circuit TV and alarm system by his biggest and strongest guy. Until these systems were off, he and his crew would have to wear masks or disguises. When the truck was fully loaded with the boxes, Lucky was to tell the guard to give them thirty minutes before trying to get help to give them plenty of time to be on the freeway to make their getaway.

Lucky O'Leary wasted no time figuring out that he needed to bring three guys to handle the oxygen tanks, find the memo, load the documents, and rent the equipment and the van. Maheu gave him two weeks to finalize the plan and gather the equipment. The thought of those documents being sent to the Bahamas was too much to bear.

Maheu vowed to O'Leary that the minute he received approval from Colby at the CIA, he would Federal Express ("if you haven't heard of this company, it's an overnight delivery system started last year that is fast and very reliable") a copy of the building layout, details about the key document that Colby wanted retrieved with Helms' signature on it, and other useful details.

O'Leary called Maheu at his home the next afternoon. Maheu had been relaxing by his family room when the telephone rang. O'Leary recited a list of budgeted expenses that demonstrated to Maheu he had given the project serious thought. He also had a detailed timeline by office and by safe. O'Leary was confident that he would be out of the building by around 4:00 a.m. His budget was reasonable, and Maheu was now ready to call William Colby. He traveled to his go-to pay phone near the Desert Inn and made the call.

Colby recognized Lucky O'Leary as the guy they had used to break into Egyptian President Nasser's Defense Minister's office just before the Six-Day War in 1967 to get intelligence on their air defenses. The Israeli folks had been so excited to see the documents that Lucky was able to photograph of the Egyptian air defense systems, and they sure paid off big time when the Israeli air force wiped out those systems at the outset of that war.

Maheu broke down the break-in budget:

- $25,000 for Mike (who would probably be fired after this and needed to support his wife and six kids)
- Lucky's equipment, tools and truck rentals, $7,500
- His three guys, $30,000
- Travel expenses for the trek from St. Louis to LA
- The usual fee for the forger of Jefferson's fake documents, $5,000

With Colby's rhapsodic agreement, Maheu hung up the phone and immediately contacted the forger that he had used many times over the years. The forger worked out of his home in Henderson, a twenty-five-minute drive from Maheu's home. Maheu hand delivered Jefferson's photograph and gave the forger a note with Jefferson's height and weight and the color of his eyes.

The home was a mess, but the forger's work was always done on time and flawless. Only a few days later, "Howard Davis" had a California driver's license and a military ID to use to open a PO Box. Then Jefferson could open a bank account and obtain an ATM card. Jefferson then telephoned Maheu with the bank's routing number and the account number. The $5,000 was wired by Maheu to Jefferson on May 29, 1974.

Maheu called O'Leary with the final details circulated by Colby about the six-page document, dated November 1, 1972, signed by Helms on November 3. This would likely be in the second-floor conference room in the stacks of documents on the conference room table. The crew also needed to be on the lookout for copies of this document. He reiterated the absolute need for the memo and documents on the second-floor conference table tied to the CIA's Project AZORIAN and the box of Air West documents. How many times would he emphasize these damned documents? O'Leary wondered, knowing burglars wouldn't forget the stash they were risking their lives for. Nevertheless, O'Leary chewed on his gum more voraciously, eager to get started.

From the freeway to Las Vegas, O'Leary would call him just after he passed the state line between California and Nevada. In that small community, at a gas station, he would call Maheu for a location to meet up in Las Vegas and then proceed to the warehouse, where they could sort through the boxes.

CHAPTER 25

TOO BUSY TO ABIDE BY LAWS

"Pretend inferiority and encourage his arrogance."

—*SUN TZU*

SHORTLY AFTER HOWARD Hughes failed to appear for his deposition, the trustees of A.W. Liquidating Company filed a motion for summary judgment against him. Since, by this time, Hughes owned 100 percent of Hughes Air and Summa's outstanding stock, they were also named in the motion. If successful, the Air West shareholders would get an award equal to the agreed purchase price called for in the Purchase Contract, less than the amount they received from Hughes. Since the agreed price was $22 per share times the number of shares, it was $89,398,091, less the amount paid by Hughes (after the FUD losses and the improper closing adjustments) of $41,398,091. The trustees also argued for interest, which would bring the total award to more than $70 million ($1.1 billion in 2020 dollars).

In response, Chester Davis filed his own counter-motion for summary judgment as well as a cross-complaint against the trustees. Davis based his argument on the premise that the notice of Howard Hughes's deposition was a fraud on the court.

The cross-complaint claimed that the deposition was a circus intended to harass Mr. Hughes by calling for his deposition relating to matters of which he had absolutely no knowledge. He further argued that Howard Hughes was a very busy man, and the issues in dispute were so beneath him that the plaintiffs knew that the deposition was not a legitimate effort, but rather part of an obnoxious campaign of harassment. In support of his motion, he attached as an exhibit, a letter to him from Hughes that stated:

> This is to confirm, and I hereby undertake, that if, after hearing and final determination of said motions for summary judgment, it is found that there are any genuine issues of material fact as to which I have any relevant knowledge, I will then answer appropriate questions under oath concerning the same to the extent of my knowledge...

The court denied the motions for summary judgment and ordered Howard Hughes to appear for his deposition on October 31, 1974.

CHAPTER 26

BREAKING OUT THE BUTTERFLIES

"Society as a whole benefits immeasurably from a climate in which all persons, regardless of race or gender, may have the opportunity to earn respect, responsibility, advancement and remuneration based on ability."

—SANDRA DAY O'CONNOR

O'LEARY'S TWO-VAN TEAM stopped in Kingman, Arizona, on the afternoon of Tuesday, June 4 to rent a covered 17-foot truck. Kingman was on the way from St. Louis to Los Angeles and less than 2 hours Southeast of Las Vegas. It would not be too far out of their way when they headed back to St. Louis. O'Leary would return the truck after delivering the boxes to Maheu.

It was a bright full moon on June 5, 1974, and the sky was clear. To be on the safe side, O'Leary had one of his cohorts make six fake California license plates that he planned to place on the front and back of the two vans and the truck. This was just in case someone, or a surveillance camera, picked up any of the vehicles while they were in the Romaine building's parking lot or entering or exiting that lot.

After O'Leary's three-vehicle caravan exited Santa Monica Boulevard, taking a left onto North Orange Drive, they pulled over. He quickly applied the fake license plates. It was only another block when they took a right turn into the Romaine building's parking lot.

The time was 12:30 a.m.

At 12:50 a.m., Mike Jefferson disarmed the building's alarm system. Then he left the building and reset the alarm system. Now the alarm and the closed-circuit TV system would automatically turn back on. Just as he did on the night Maheu watched him, he turned towards North Sycamore Avenue. As he walked along the building, he checked for anything unusual on the street or around the building itself. He turned right when he reached Romaine Street, admiring the building's Art Deco architecture with its beautiful plantings and ivy-decorated entrance. He turned right when he reached North Orange Drive. As he walked toward the rear of 7000 Romain, he noticed the truck and two vans. As he got closer to the rear door, four men rapidly approached him. Clockwork!

One of the four men was named Tiny, a 6-foot, 4-inch, 320-pound giant of a man. He grabbed Jefferson from behind, put an unloaded pistol to his head, and demanded that he open the door and immediately disarm the alarm and closed-circuit TV systems. From the view of the camera, Jefferson appeared to be struggling courageously, but Tiny was too big and too skilled. He overwhelmed Jefferson and forced him to disarm the security systems.

Now, O'Leary and the other two men in his team, Dave, and Charlie, carried in the cutting torch kits, oxygen tanks and acety-lene, welding goggles and needed eyewear, and the fifteen empty bankers boxes ready to be filled with documents to bring to Las Vegas.

Holding the layout of the building, O'Leary greeted Jefferson, and told him to lead the way to the walk-in vault outside of Kay Glenn's office. The team set up the equipment and easily penetrated the vault, then grabbed some of the contents that looked valuable. This helped to create the appearance of a burglary, with many targets of opportunity.

O'Leary then instructed Jefferson to show Dave and Charlie to Kay Glenn's office so they could begin their search for more documents. At this point, O'Leary spotted the Mosler safe in the back of the vault. Jefferson told O'Leary that this Mosler safe was like all the others. They had a single door, four shelves and were approximately five feet tall and three feet wide. O'Leary and Tiny, carrying their safe-cracking tools, efficiently made their way into the Mosler. Again, documents were briefly reviewed, and some were put into a box. It was now 1:30—time to move on.

Tiny and O'Leary joined Jefferson and the team in Kay Glenn's office and immediately went to the filing cabinet with the safe in the top drawer. O'Leary directed Dave and Charlie to review the other filing cabinets and desk drawers for any important documents. According to Maheu, the safe in this filing cabinet contained the cash. O'Leary had Tiny mark a banker's box with the word "Bills" on the top and all four sides. Once again, they set up the equipment and began working on the safe.

Click! The safe opened, and they pulled out multiple bundles of bills, as well as separate unbundled stacks of $100s, $50s and $20s. O'Leary estimated the haul to be around $290,000. *Yes, thank you, Mr. Maheu.* The cash was placed into the box labeled "Bills," and he grabbed some documents from the drawer to fill the box before putting on the top, taping the box closed. He told Tiny to put the box near the back door and to put it in the truck first, before any other boxes. It was now 1:50.

The team next split into two groups heading west. They searched the various offices, opening drawers and filing cabinets, taking selected documents, and putting them in boxes. They turned at the end of the hallway and reached the stairway to the second floor. Suddenly, the team heard someone walking down the hardwood floor of the second floor. Everyone froze. Jefferson whispered to O'Leary that it was Watson. He was likely walking from his office to the kitchen in the middle of the second floor to get a soda from the fridge. They listened to the footfalls, which stopped with Watson in the kitchen. The footfalls resumed as he returned to his office at the end of the hall, slamming the door to his office as he returned to his desk. The team took off their shoes and as quietly as possible, resumed their work.

The team carried the empty boxes and their equipment to the second floor. It was now 2:15.

There was another Mosler safe in Lee Murrin's office. Murrin oversaw Hughes's personal financial affairs and had many interesting documents, but none were relevant to what Maheu was interested in taking. The group moved on to Carol Snodgrass's office, where they cracked another combination filing cabinet and safe. Again, some interesting documents were taken, but none particularly relevant. Now it was time to rummage through Nadine Henley's office at 2:35.

Nadine Henley was the SVP president of Summa Corporation and a member of its board. This vibrant woman had been married five times and was known as the "First Lady of Summa." Her long career with Hughes began in 1940. She had multiple filing cabinets, two with safes in their top drawer. Tiny and O'Leary tackled the safes while Dave and Charlie scavenged the rest of the office. Several documents of interest were found, including memoranda from Hughes about Robert Maheu's good work for him. This was a keeper for Maheu.

In one of the safes, Lucky O'Leary found a copy of the

six-page memo dated November 1, 1972, that was signed by CIA Director Helms. Finding this key document triggered a short, but quiet, celebration.

As O'Leary was instructed by Maheu, he put the documents related to Robert Maheu into the box marked "Maheu" on each of its sides. O'Leary saved the six-page Helms' memorandum for the boxes of Project AZORIAN documents to be collected from the conference room. Before the group moved on, they boxed the Wedgewood bowls and the butterfly collection and other potentially interesting documents. It was now 3:05.

The conference room was down the hall, but away from Watson's office. It had a large table in the middle of the room surrounded by twelve chairs and many piles of documents. At the far end of the table was the unfinished index listing of the documents gathered on the table. The index listed each document's date, subject(s), author(s), the addressee(s), and person(s) copied, if any, and key issues contained in the document. They were all documents related to Project AZORIAN. The sixth document listed on the index was the original of the memo that Helms wanted out of Chester Davis's hands.

The documents on the table seemed to be in date order, so finding the November 1, 1972 memo was easy. The team boxed the documents to be taken to the truck. The key memo and its copy from Henley's office were placed on top of a box labeled "Helms Doc" on its sides. The Air West box was also easy to locate. As Jefferson mentioned to Maheu, it was on the floor in the conference room's far corner. O'Leary took a brief look into the box. It was filled with copies of handwritten work papers; most were headed with the words "Air West." O'Leary carried this box down to the rear door on the first floor. He wrote the words "Air West" on each side of this box at 3:50.

The team loaded the truck with the boxes filled with documents, plus the unused boxes. Now it was time to put duct tape around Jefferson's ankles. O'Leary gave Jefferson a paper towel so that he could blow his nose. Now he would be able to breathe through his nose without struggling when they taped his mouth shut. Jefferson appreciated this careful gesture. They put his wrists behind his back and taped them together. The clock on the wall showed 4:02 am.

O'Leary reminded Jefferson to give him a thirty-minute head start. Then he could struggle to knock a telephone off the hook, try to press the intercom key, and alert Watson that he needed help.

The two vans and the truck exited the parking lot and headed toward North Highland Avenue. After a quick stop to remove the fake California license plates from the three vehicles, they were soon heading north on US-101, then the Ventura Freeway. In around four hours, they would cross the state line into Nevada, where the team planned to grab breakfast, and O'Leary would call Maheu for further directions.

At 4:30 a.m., Jefferson rolled himself down the hall and into Kay Glenn's office. He rolled over the telephone cord knocking the telephone to the ground. With his nose, he pressed the inter-com line to Harry Watson and mumbled "help" as best he could with the duct tape covering his mouth. When Watson heard his cry for help, he rushed from the second floor and found Jefferson lying on the floor of Glenn's office. He pulled off the duct tape from Jefferson's mouth and cut his hands and legs free. Watson then called the police at 4:40 to report a burglary. He then called Kay Glenn.

The police arrived at 4:50. They questioned Jefferson, getting a detailed account of his movements and observations, starting from when he left the building four hours prior. They verified the time by reviewing the alarm system's data. The recording on the closed-circuit TV system picked up his return to the building. It also validated his story about how he was forced to turn off the security systems by a very large man with a gun to his head and his arm around his neck, while Jefferson struggled unsuccessfully to free himself.

The large man had a mask that covered his face. The other three men that followed also had their faces covered with masks. They all wore gloves to avoid leaving any fingerprints behind. Jefferson told the police that he had never seen these men before and did not recognize them. Although the video was clear, there was no way to determine the identity of any of these four men.

O'Leary and his team crossed the California-Nevada state line and pulled into a café called State Line Bar & Slots. The group quietly congratulated themselves on a job well done. They were hungry and enjoyed a hearty breakfast. As they were finishing, O'Leary made his way to the payphone for further instructions from Maheu in Vegas.

They agreed to meet in the parking lot at the corner of Paradise Road and East Desert Inn Road. Maheu would be in a sleek dark blue Cadillac. The warehouse would only be a few blocks away.

Satisfied from the breakfast and lucrative break-in, O'Leary led the caravan to Las Vegas. They pulled into the parking lot and spotted Maheu's Cadillac. Maheu waived to O'Leary to follow him. In less than five minutes, they were at the warehouse. Maheu led the two vans and the truck into the warehouse. Maheu closed the overhead door and happily greeted the team and expressed his appreciation for their fine work. O'Leary's crew unloaded the boxes. He and Maheu opened the box labeled "Bills." Together, they counted the cash and agreed that the take was $288,760. Maheu shook O'Leary's hand and congratulated him on his nice payday. He also told him to be careful about how he spent the $100 bills. He suggested to O'Leary that he spend them out of numerical sequence and to give it a bit of time before spending large amounts in any one place. The money was put back in the box, taped shut, and transferred to O'Leary's van.

Next, Bob asked about the Helms' memo. Lucky led Bob to the box marked "Helms Doc." Lucky and Bob both put on gloves before touching the box and the documents inside of it and any of the other boxes now on the warehouse floor. The first document in the box was the original six-page Helms memo, and the next document was a copy of it found in Nadine Henley's office.

Maheu whistled in delight that his team had found these jewels for William Colby.

Maheu next asked O'Leary to locate the Air West box. He mentioned to O'Leary that he had heard that the Department of Justice might be trying to reopen their criminal case against him, and Maheu wanted to be sure that he was not giving up any documents that might help the DOJ prosecute their case against him. Maheu opened the box and reviewed the documents. They were photocopies of accounting work papers. Many of the photocopies had original handwritten notes on them. Maheu recognized the handwriting as Hughes's, and they appeared to be his instructions and guidance to Chester Davis.

When Maheu got to the bottom of the box, it was clear to him these documents related to the improper closing adjustments which Maheu had nothing to do with at any time. These closing adjustments were instigated by Hughes and Davis. Maheu smiled, knowing that these documents could be damaging to both of them, but not him. As far as he was concerned, documents in this box were likely to bring more pain to both Davis and Hughes. That was fine with him. He set that box aside for delivery to the Department of Justice.

Finally, Maheu asked about the Henley documents. O'Leary pointed to the box labeled "Maheu." Maheu put that box aside and told O'Leary that Nadine Henley would soon testify in his libel lawsuit against Hughes. He would review these documents to see if any of them would be helpful in that matter. O'Leary told him that several memoranda from Howard Hughes were very complimentary of Maheu's work. Another wide smile appeared on Maheu's face. Maheu put that box in the trunk of his Cadillac.

Maheu shook each of the team member's hands and again thanked them for their terrific work. He wished them well and sent them on their way back to Kingman, Arizona, to return the truck. Then they would head back to St. Louis. Maheu told O'Leary where to send his expense report so that he would be reimbursed for his expenses. He and his team left the warehouse at around 11:00 am.

Maheu used a pay phone near the Las Vegas Convention Center to call Bill Colby with this most impressive news that the break-in operated so smoothly just like the blue Cadillac he was driving. The grab: eleven boxes (Maheu left out the box relating to him from Henley's office) and all the cold cash waiting for Lucky, which meant that Colby didn't have to pay another dime except for job expenses.

Colby howled in delight and said that a guy named Chuck Briggs would call to arrange to pick up the nine boxes of Project AZORIAN documents ASAP to get them back to Langley on one of their planes. As for the Air West documents, Briggs would retrieve them directly from Maheu, then deliver that box to William Hanks at the Las Vegas office of the Department of Justice. Obviously, Maheu couldn't have any contact with the DOJ folks.

Audacious plan executed.

The press provided brief coverage of the break-in. The Hughes Romaine Building staff, and everyone else in the Hughes organization, were not forthcoming about what had been taken during the break-in. In fact, the police were surprised by their laid-back reaction. The staff were secretive and reluctant to provide any details about what documents were missing. This behavior was consistent, however, with the reclusive Howard Hughes and his organization. They did mention that several safes were broken into, filing cabinets were ransacked, documents were taken (although they were not identified), and they stated that some cash was taken. They also mentioned that Nadine Henley's sophisticated Wedgewood bowls and spectacular butterfly collection had been stolen. How odd. What a pity.

In the following weeks, the LA police and the FBI office in Los Angeles made no progress in determining who was involved in the burglary and what documents were taken. The Hughes staff were told by Davis that they could not mention the Air West documents because these had been subpoenaed by both the Department of Justice in its criminal action and by the attorneys for Air West's shareholders in the civil litigation. Since Davis had denied their existence in both cases, reporting their theft was out of the question. They also could not mention the Project AZORIAN documents because of their secrecy, and they did not want the CIA to know that these documents were no longer in their control.

The police administered polygraph tests to seventeen Summa employees. Jefferson refused to submit to a polygraph, objecting to them as being against his principles and his belief that they were unreliable. He was given a choice to take the test or be fired. He refused and was fired.

When William Colby received the nine boxes from Maheu, he sent the Project AZORIAN documents to John Parangosky, the mastermind of the project at the CIA, for safekeeping. Colby knew that the HGE was about to leave Long Beach on its recovery mission. Consequently, the CIA would have no fear that the Hughes-related Project AZORIAN documents would be "leaked" to the press should Chester Davis find it in Hughes's interest to deflect any political or operational blame away from Hughes and onto the CIA. These documents would have given Davis the ability to blow the CIA's cover on the Project AZORIAN if some disaster struck during the retrieval of the K-129.

Colby then had Chuck Briggs pick up the Air West box from Robert Maheu and deliver them to United States Attorney William Hanks of the Department of Justice in Las Vegas.

CHAPTER 27

CLEMENTINE'S SECRETS

*"The roots of true achievement lie in the will
to become the best that you can become."*

—*HAROLD TAYLOR*

THE HGE DEPARTED from Pier E in Long Beach Harbor on Thursday, June 20, 1974. This would allow it to reach the site after President Nixon had left from the Soviet Union on his scheduled trip and before the rough seas in the target area would impair its mission. Its initial destination was the international waters just beyond Catalina Island to mark the transfer of the ship from Global Marine to Summa. There were representatives of both companies to celebrate this event. Pictures were taken of the ceremony consistent with the deep-sea mining cover story. Shortly after the ceremony, company representatives left by helicopter to return to Long Beach. The HGE turned and left for its recovery mission 3,008 miles away. The crew was euphoric. One of the CIA crewmembers wrote in his journal:

The sky was leaden, yet the crew had spirits that were as bright as polished silver. Under way at last! Finally, we were really going to do it. The course was set west-northwest—a direct line to the target. If we could only be there tomorrow—but an eight-knot rate of advance meant a 13-day voyage. We would not arrive until the Fourth of July. Surely that would void any evil spirits lurking in a 13-day voyage... Mission impossible? Nonsense! "Impossible" was not in our vocabulary. Moments like this must contain the true meaning of team spirit, that extra ingredient that hardware will never possess. To experience it once is enough for a career.

Captain Thomas J. Gresham commanded the ship's crew. Captain Gresham and his crew stood bridge watch, navigated, and operated the engine rooms, the laundry, kitchen, bakery, serving meals, and other tasks that kept the ship operating. The CIA's mission director oversaw the recovery mission, including the operation of the ship's lift system, mission control, and all activities and equipment related to the recovery effort. His cover name was Dale Nagle.

Various drills were conducted throughout the course of the trip. These included preparedness drills in case of nuclear contamination. And in case classified documents and equipment had to be destroyed, the crew also drilled for that sorry occasion.

Several ships passed by without incident and none closer than two miles in the distance. As expected, on July 4, the HGE arrived at the recovery site. The crew deployed wave-rider buoys and then calibrated the automatic station-keeping system. This first-of-its-kind, satellite-based system would keep the ship in its precise location while deploying its massive piping string that would guide the Clementine, whose claw would eventually grab the K-129 and bring it into the ship's Moon Pool.

The high waves of typhoon Gilda delayed the recovery for several days.

Then, just as Gilda had passed, a British merchant ship, the Bel Hudson, radioed the HGE that one of its crew members was badly in need of medical assistance. Based on pre-established protocol, the CIA's Mission Director had the authority to decide whether to provide humanitarian relief during the mission. He determined that the risks of assistance were negligible and sent the HGE's surgeon, medical technician, and security officer, to examine the patient on the Bel Hudson. They decided to bring the patient back to the HGE for X-rays and appropriate treatment.

The treatment quickly improved the patient's condition. During the communications back and forth between the mission director and the captain of the Bel Hudson, they used an open radio circuit. At one point, the captain of the British ship asked what the HGE was doing in these waters. The HGE's mission director responded that it was engaged in deep-ocean mining using sophisticated prototype mining equipment—hoping that the Soviets were monitoring this communication.

On Friday, July 14, ten days after reaching the recovery site, the crew began the recovery effort. They soon discovered severe cracks in both docking legs that were forward and behind the derrick. The repair of these legs called for a problematic welding process under ordinary circumstances, but it was made much riskier by high waves and winds caused by tropical storm Harriet. The entire repair effort took three days.

Just as the welding repairs to the ship's docking legs were completed, the HGE's mission director was advised that a Soviet Missile Range Instrumentation ship, the Chazhma was on a course heading towards the recovery site. The Soviet ship had left its base in Petropavlovsk, which is only about 11 miles as the crow flies from the K-129's base in Rybachiy. The captain was informed that the Chazhma was a large vessel that was equipped to carry a helicopter.

This information was very concerning, particularly the part about the helicopter. If the Soviets landed their helicopter on the HGE's helicopter deck and found the Clementine and its giant claw for grabbing the K-129, they might determine the HGE's true mission. It would then potentially be the start of World War III.

As a precaution, the HGE's captain ordered that piles of materials be put on the HGE's helicopter pad to reduce the possibility that the Chazhma's captain might be tempted to have its helicopter land on the HGE's helicopter deck, which was located at its stern. In the early morning of July 18, the Chazhma came to within two miles of the HGE.

At 2:30 p.m., Soviet crew members on the Chazhma began taking pictures of the HGE using a large telephoto camera. Then they launched its helicopter. For the next hour, the helicopter made many aggressive approaches to the HGE while taking photographs. To discourage the lowering of sailors from the helicopter, the mission director of the HGE sent crew members to the bow of the ship. The helicopter made a few more passes, and then, fortunately, it returned to the Chazhma.

But this event made it clear to all on the HGE that it was a sitting duck, alone in the vast Pacific Ocean, far from any friendly protective forces. The helicopter encounter made it very clear that there was a real need to be prepared, as a last resort, to implement and execute the destruction of documents and equipment on the mission director's command.

At 6:47 p.m., the Chazhma transmitted a message that it was ready to receive word from the HGE.

The mission director of the HGE responded, "We have no message; do you have a message for us?"

Five minutes later, the Chazhma asked, "What are you doing here?"

"We are conducting ocean mining tests, deep ocean mining tests."

The Chazhma then asked, "What kind of vessel are you?"

"A deep ocean mining vessel with experimental deep ocean mining equipment onboard." This response led the Soviet vessel to ask, "How long will you be here?"

"About two to three weeks."

Finally, the Chazhma's last message was, "I wish you all the best." It sailed away at 9:00 pm on July 18.

On July 19, all operations on the HGE were tested and the crew readied to lower the Clementine (the "Capture Vehicle"). The Moon Pool holding the Clementine with its grabber claws was flooded. Then its forward and aft floor gates were opened. At last, the Clementine could begin its three-mile descent in 60-foot (two 30-foot sections called "doubles") sections at a time as the piping system was constructed like a giant necklace hanging from the HGE's massive 228-foot-tall derrick. The lowering of the Clementine with its giant claw began its historic journey.

HUGHES GLOMAR EXPLORER. SOURCE: BETTMANN / CONTRIBUTOR VIA GETTY IMAGES.

ILLUSTRATION OF THE FOUR STAGES OF THE RECOVERY EFFORT. SOURCE: THE CIA LEGACY MUSEUM, THE EXPOSING OF PROJECT AZORIAN, MARCH 17, 2020.

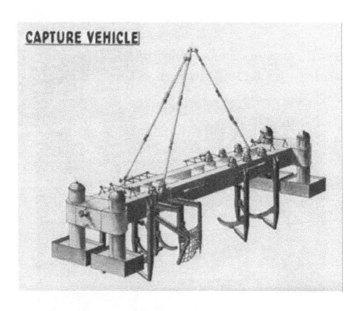

DETAILS OF THE CLEMENTINE (THE CLAW OR CAPTURE VEHICLE): SOURCE, THE CIA LEGACY MUSEUM, THE EXPOSING OF PROJECT AZORIAN, MARCH 17, 2020.

During the morning of Saturday, July 22, the SB-10, a Soviet ocean-going salvage tug, arrived on the scene. Initially, it kept a distance from the stationary HGE of three to four miles, as the lowering of the Clementine continued. Then, the SB-10 closed to within 200 yards. It passed on both sides of the HGE as its crew took photographs of the vessel.

At 11:00 p.m., it returned to its original distance of three to four miles. On July 23, as the claw's lowering continued, the SB-10 returned to its passing and photographing activities, sometimes as close as one hundred yards from the HGE.

These activities continued from July 24 through the 27th. During this period, there were repeated breakdowns of the piping system, but the recovery team overcame all obstacles. This cycle of breakdown, followed by successful repairs, gave the crew confidence in themselves and the system. By this time, the Clementine had reached 13,800 feet (of its 16,440-foot journey) below the HGE. All the while, the SB-10 circled, and its crew photographed the HGE.

On Friday, July 28, the piping system within the derrick jammed, causing a grinding noise with sparks flying and smoke pouring from the 228-foot-tall derrick. The crew was startled, and the system was immediately shut down. Key repair personnel inspected every aspect of the derrick and the piping doubles within it, and every part that demonstrated any wear or flaw was repaired or replaced. While these repairs were underway, high-resolution sonar on the Clementine was used to pinpoint the K-129. The crew of the Soviet SB-10 was still watching, but from a greater distance at this point.

At 7:52 p.m., Clementine's sonar detected the K-129, and its closed-circuit television cameras transmitted images to televisions onboard the HGE began to reveal an object. Everyone on board was caught up in anticipation of seeing the K-129 for the first time. All eyes in the control center also watched the display from the scanning sonars for any sign of the target. Then on one pass, an irregular hemispherical hump displaced the flat line on the screen. It was the submarine for sure. Word spread wildly throughout the ship. Clementine was on the target.

Within hours, the Clementine's television cameras picked up a clear picture of the submarine that was broadcast to television screens on board the HGE. All hands wanted to see the screen, and the mission director allowed the crew, in small groups, to file through the control center to see the submarine. The Mission Director recognized the entire crew's contribution to the project's success and decided to place several TV monitors around the ship so that the sailors, cooks, divers, drill crew, and all other hands could watch the historic mission proceed during essential moments of the recovery.

That evening the SB-10 continued to prowl around the ship. The HGE used its searchlight to illuminate the SB-10 as it closed to within 100 yards, then it backed off. But the piping system continued its journey toward the ocean floor and the K-129. Knowing that, at any time, the presence of the SB-10 could trigger termination of the mission, or worse, a major military confrontation, continued to fuel tension of the entire crew of the HGE. But their recovery work was their first concern. They pressed forward.

The crew was excited to see impressive details, including crabs crawling about the sub and rattail fish swimming around it. The towing eye in the bow was clearly visible. The missile tube was visible, as well as its warhead. Now the speed of descent dramatically slowed. From 1:02 p.m. on July 29 until 11:00 p.m., only two doubles (120 feet of pipe) were added to the pipe string, and the Clementine was now only 90 feet from the K-129. It was not until 1:00 am on July 31 that the last double was added to the pipe string.

On July 31, 1974, Clementine hovered directly over the

submarine. At 9:33 a.m., the crew in the control center positioned the claw so that its eight grabber beams and davit tips could dig beneath the submarine, with the help of water jets attached to the davits. The grabber beams and davits wrapped around the target portion of the K-129, digging into the ocean floor in the process. The target portion of the submarine was now firmly in the grip of Clementine's claws.

At 12:25 a.m. on August 1, 1974, it was time to put the so-called Brute Force Lift into action. Clementine had the K-129 in its grabber arms, 16,440 feet below the ocean's surface with its sailors inside the 136-foot length of the target portion and its 2,200,000-pound weight.

The piping string had descended more than three miles. Now it was time for the Clementine to come home to the HGE. Under tremendous strain, the derrick and the piping string exercised the Brute Force Lift. A few minutes before 3:00 am, the K-129 was completely free from the ocean floor. Progress was slow, but the lifting continued while the stubborn SB-10 circled the HGE.

Three days later, on August 4, with Clementine still 10,000 feet below the ocean's surface, the Clementine suddenly took a nose-down attitude as its grabber beam No. 6 lost all pressure. The sail of the K-129 rotated. On the HGE, the crew felt like they were back in California during an earthquake, and the ship rocked and rolled. They knew that something had gone terribly wrong. The ship's heave compensator indicated that a tremendous amount of weight had been lost. Two of Clementine's eight grabber arms had snapped and broken free. With the loss of these grabber arms, the claw lost nearly 100 feet of the target portion of the K-129. That portion of the submarine, along with many of its sailors, its nuclear missile and its fire control systems and some cryptographic equipment, returned to the ocean floor.

It was later surmised that those grabber arms were damaged during the process of gripping the submarine and digging into the ocean floor. The damage resulted from the combination of the hardness of that portion of the ocean floor encountered by those grabbers, and the use of maraging steel, which became brittle at the great depths in which the Clementine was operating.

The crew working the derrick and piping string realized that the Clementine, although still at a depth of 10,000, had suffered a sudden and significant weight loss.

Although the mission director was uncertain at the time of the reason for the weight loss, or its consequences, he determined that he needed to communicate with Summa headquarters in a way that was consistent with the cover plan. In an open commercial channel, he reported to Summa headquarters that its "nodule collector vehicle" might have collided with a hard outcrop, causing damage to the vehicle. It suggested that the HGE might need to seek permission from the U.S. Navy to berth for repairs at Midway Island or an anchorage off Maui known as Lahaina Road.

Even though the load was now lighter, the crew continued to struggle with serious heavy-lift system problems. The load was lighter, not only because of the loss of a portion of the K-129 but as the Clementine ascended, heavy piping sections were removed from the string. Since each 30-foot section of piping weighed 7.5 tons, the load was getting lighter and lighter as the Clementine returned to the HGE.

On August 6, the HGE received a message from the Summa Ocean Mining Division general manager. The message was sent to the senior Summa representative aboard the HGE. The instruction was that as soon as the Summa representative was able to assess the damage to the "nodule collector vehicle," he was to provide twice-daily reports on the need and recommended location for the repairs.

The SB-10 was still circling, but now it began to close periodically to within 75 feet. The HGE signaled to warn the SB-10 to keep clear because it was experiencing some unpredictability in its maneuvering, which might imperil the SB-10. The mission director was told that the SB-10 might have limited shallow water diver capability with depths limited to 30 feet. This 30-foot depth limitation would not expose the HGE's cover, unless the divers approached the Clementine just as it was about to enter the HGE's Moon Pool, with the sub in its grip.

Given that risk, the captain did all he could to persuade the captain of the SB-10 that any diving near the ship would expose its divers to danger.

Incredibly, crew members of the SB-10 waved goodbye after receiving this message, and, at 10:30 pm on August 6, the tug turned toward home, sounded three long blasts of its whistle, and left the recovery site, never to return. After spending almost 14 days at the recovery site, the SB-10 suddenly departed, just a few days before the Soviet submarine was to be brought to the surface inside the HGE's Moon Pool.

However, problems with the heavy-lift system continued. Seals were leaking on the bridle and yoke, troubles with the isolation valves were a constant, and blown hydraulic pump manifolds were plaguing the recovery. But knowing how much of the piping had been retrieved and stored on the HGE the crew sensed that the end was near, and the mission was soon to reach a significant milestone. As the lifting slowed, TV monitors on the ship revealed that the K-129 was in sight. Most of the crew were now watching intently.

The Soviet tug left.

We were going to be able to do the telltale pump down operation without surveillance. Our cover story had held. The Soviets had been fooled. Now we could anticipate seeing our prize without being concerned about sharing it with the owner.

Everyone wanted to get the first glimpse of the target. Those waiting anxiously on deck received a reward of a different type. Bobbing up to the surface (luckily in the well) was a brimming full Jerry-can of torpedo juice [torpedo fuel]. It had travelled over three miles to the bottom and back and been subjected to pressures of over 7,000 pounds per square inch without spilling a drop. The mission director and his team viewed the scene from a balcony-like portion of the ladder, which led down to the well gates. Radiation monitors had reported readings five times background even at this distance. We knew that we were in for a nasty time. Some of the earlier excitement of the mission returned to the exploration party.

As the Clementine slowly worked its way toward the ocean's surface and into the Moon Pool, the radioactive contamination team gathered with their tools and equipment. The recovered portion of the K-129 was now in the HGE's Moon Pool.

It was time to close the gates at the bottom of the ship. As the water was being pumped out of the Moon Pool, the recovered vessel became clear for all to see. Crewmen installed shoring to prevent the K-129 from rolling over. A team in protective suits with respirators checked the submarine for radiation. They quickly learned, from their Geiger counters, that the nuclear torpedoes were leaking plutonium from their warheads. Now the salvage workers needed to wear breathing devices to prevent inhalation of the plutonium particulates.

An examination of the Clementine revealed that of its eight grabbers, No. 4 and No. 5 were broken halfway up their length. No. 6 had its hydraulic cylinder torn away. This damage allowed the midships section of the K-129 to break out and fall through the gap caused by the broken No. 4 and No. 5 grabber sections. The falling portion of the K-129 then damaged grabber No. 6.

Immediately, exploration of the sub began. Mission specialists entered the sub like it was an archeological site where every inch was to be closely examined. There were sickening sights and smells. Several bodies and body parts were found. One sailor was found in his bunk, with a valuable manual of the submarine's torpedoes in his hands. While the sub was at the ocean's bottom, the bodies were preserved because of the near-freezing water temperature. Also, the intense pressure on the ocean floor inhibited decay.

Once brought to the surface and exposed to air, the bodies deteriorated. As for the recovered materials, the ship's facilities had special paper preservation substances and equipment designed to preserve the papers, documents, and manuals that were recovered. Ironically, several manganese nodules had also been scooped up during the recovery effort.

On August 9, 1974, the HGE sent a commercial message to "Summa headquarters," advising that it had completed "Event 36-A." This was a prearranged signal that the recovery phase had been completed and that the HGE would proceed to demobilize the site. Coincidentally, this was also the day Richard Nixon resigned as president because of the Watergate Hotel break-in of the Democratic National Headquarters and related cover-up, and Gerald Ford was sworn in as the 38th president of the United States.

The next day, Henry Kissinger, the secretary of state, and James Schlesinger, the secretary of defense, briefed President Ford on Project AZORIAN's status

On August 10, the HGE sent another message to headquarters stating that it was heading for Midway Island, but the next day, a new commercial message was sent stating that it needed guidance for a new site since the repairs to the "module collector vehicle" would take at least thirty days to complete. CIA headquarters responded with instructions for the ship to head to

Lahaina Road, a passage off the northwest coast of Lahaina on the island of Maui.

When the HGE was 665 miles from Lahaina, it came to a stop. All materials recovered from the K-129 with intelligence value were packaged for transfer to an undisclosed mainland location for more careful analysis. Any materials that were judged of no intelligence value were packaged and weighted for disposal to the ocean's bottom.

On August 17, the HGE anchored eight miles south of the Lahaina Road's buoy, approximately five miles offshore. There was a crew change with the new crew having specialized skills at examining the bounty that was now firmly in the hands of the CIA. The front page of the Honolulu Advisor featured a front-page article on the HGE's deep ocean mining exploits.

More than six years after the K-129 sank to the bottom of the ocean, it had been returned to the surface thanks to the efforts and skills to conceive, develop, build, fund and execute what has been described by many in the intelligence community as the greatest spy mission undertaken by any government—ever.

CHAPTER 28

ROSES ON THE OCEAN FLOOR

*"In nature there are neither rewards nor
punishments; there are consequences."*

—ROBERT GREEN INGERSOLL

W HEN THE HGE arrived at Lahaina Road, William
Colby, the last gentleman spy, determined how the
CIA would dispose of the remains of the Soviet sailors recovered during the Project. He decided a proper ceremony
was to be carried out with due respect and honors. The ceremony
itself took place during September 1974 at sunset.

The HGE traveled 104 miles southwest of the Big Island of
Hawaii and stopped at sea for the burial to take place. Because
of the Cold War, it was not until October 1992, that then-direc-
tor of the CIA Robert Gates presented a statement to Russian
President Boris Yeltsln in Moscow that stated:

> From the time of their recovery from the submarine's hulk
> until the burial ceremony, the remains were handled with the
> utmost care and respect. A heavy steel box, 8 x 8 x 4 feet
> in dimension, was chosen for the burial ceremony and six
> individual shelves were installed to support the bodies.

On the appointed day, on September 4, 1974, two rehears-
als were held to ensure that the actual ceremony would
proceed smoothly and with the appropriate dignity. A
six-person Honor Guard was selected from among the
volunteers. Immediately prior to the ceremony, the Honor
Guard transported each body to the burial vault individually. During transportation, a Soviet Naval Ensign, carried for
this purpose by the Glomar Explorer, was draped over each
body. The same ensign shrouded each body...

After all bodies were placed in the burial vault, with a representative portion of the vessel on which they served and perished,
the ensign was mounted alongside the US national flag behind
the vault.

The ceremony, attended by some seventy-five of the ship's
company, began with the "National Anthem" of the United States
and of the Soviet Union. It continued with what was thought
to be the closest ceremony approaching the actual Soviet Navy
burial at sea ceremony. In addition, the US Navy ceremony for
the burial of the dead at sea followed. An interpreter translated
the Soviet service and the US Navy Service into Russian.

After the vault doors had been bolted shut, the vault was
slowly hoisted over the side while the Committal and Benediction
were read, and the US Navy Hymn was played. At 19:21 local
time, during the final light of the evening twilight, the vault, now
completely flooded, was released into a calm sea, and fell free to
the ocean floor.

President Yeltsin was also presented with a film of this burial
ceremony. This meeting between Robert Gates and Boris Yeltsin
was possible because the Cold War had recently ended with the
collapse of the Soviet Union and with it the nuclear confrontation between the United States and the Soviet Union.

CHAPTER 29

EVIDENCE BOX

*"Diligence is the mother of good fortune, and
idleness, its opposite, never brought a man
to the goal of any of his best wishes."*

—MIGUEL DE CERVANTES

AS COLBY HAD promised, the CIA's Chuck Briggs
showed up at the warehouse on Thursday afternoon of
June 6 to meet Robert Maheu. It was a simple assignment. Briggs picked up the Banker's box marked "Air West" on
each of its sides. He then called William Hanks at the Las Vegas
Department of Justice to discuss the delivery. Briggs kept the
conversation straightforward; that he didn't know how the documents were obtained or what they revealed, but that he would
drop them off at his office.

The timing of this revelation could not be more impeccable.

William Hanks and Dante Beaton had been working on an
amended indictment since their previous case had been dismissed
over the permanent brain damage suffered by Confidential
Witness No. 1 and the disappearance, which continued, of

Confidential Witness No. 2. But now they were considering adding additional criminal charges involving Hughes's election contributions of hundreds of thousands of dollars to Richard Nixon, as well as loans to the President's brother, F. Donald Nixon, and the $100,000 transmitted in $100 bills from Hughes to the President's friend, Charles "Alvarado" Rebozo.

They had made considerable progress in finalizing their new indictment. They had determined not to include the accounting issues being pursued as civil actions in federal court in San Francisco. They would confine their case to the criminal issues charged in the first indictment and any criminal charges arising from Hughes's cash transactions involving President Nixon, his brother, and his friend Mr. Rebozo.

Later in the afternoon following their call, Briggs delivered the Air West box to Hanks. The two briefly exchanged pleasantries, and Briggs gave Hanks his business card. Hanks reminded him that if he and Beaton decided that this box's contents were not relevant to their new indictment, that Briggs would return to the Department of Justice's office to retrieve the box. Briggs again agreed to that arrangement.

The next day, Hanks opened the box. The documents were copies of accounting work papers. Many had original handwritten notes on the copies. These clearly related to detailed accounting analyses of various account balances of Air West on December 31, 1969. Hanks walked to Beaton's office to discuss his evaluation of the contents of the box, but after completing his evaluation of the materials, Beaton determined that they could not use them in their criminal case. They were well-aware that Air West shareholders had been robbed by the same villains. Hanks noticed my name on many of the imposing documents, and he remembered that I had politely offered to help Hanks if DOJ needed any workups on the accounting issues.

On Tuesday, June 11, 1974, I was working in my office of

R&S and received a telephone call from Linda Sills, the firm's receptionist. Linda told me that the mail had just been delivered, and it included a large box addressed to me. She said that the box was heavy and asked me to come to the reception area when I had a chance since it was too heavy for her to carry it to my office. Linda had a bad back, and she did not want to risk more trouble by carrying heavy boxes around the office.

I had a lunch meeting at noon but was curious about this mystery box. I went to the reception, carried it to my office and put it on my conference table. It didn't seem particularly threatening, but weird things were known to be packaged up in obscure brown packaging.

I noticed that it had no return address on it or any other markings other than the post office mark over the stamps, which indicated that it was mailed from Las Vegas. I was tempted to open the box, but I was worried about being late for my lunch meeting. I decided that the contents of the box would wait until I could fully give it my attention. Was I a bit apprehensive? Probably.

Nevertheless, when I returned from lunch, I meticulously removed the brown wrapping paper from the mysterious box in my office. My mother always carefully removed wrapping paper from gifts and saved the paper for reuse. I routinely kept up this family tradition!

The sender of this box did not want to be identified. Not only was there no return address, but it was unusual in business mailings for stamps to be used rather than a postage machine. Postage machines, however, usually have links to the sender, such as a license number, slogans, and other identifying marks. When the wrapping paper was removed, I noticed the words "Air West" in black marking pencil on each side of the box. *Could it be?*

My interest intensified. I removed the top of the banker's box and was shocked to see photocopies of work papers that my staff and I had prepared while at PMM during our audit of Air West's December 31, 1969, financial statements.

These documents were copies of work papers given to H&S as part of their due diligence while working for Hughes. The copies were primarily "comment paper" used for handwriting text to describe the contents of accounts, accounting methods, or accounting procedures used by Air West. In the bottom, left-hand corners in a small font, the label read "Form-WP-61 Ralph PRTG. & LITHO. CO. – Omaha," which was the form number and name of the vendor that supplied PMM its blank work papers. There were also four-column, ten-column and 16-column ledger work papers with the same small legend on the bottom left, except the FORM – WP numbers were 71, 81 and 91, respectively.

Each work paper in the box had its specific reference number (E-1, G-1-1, G-1-2, etc.) given to it by the PMM preparer, and the name of the accountant who prepared it (for example, Mary Kay Griffin, Tom Adler, Mike Cook, or Peter Meeks), and the reviewer, who was primarily me. All the work paper forms had horizontal lines, and the accountants who prepared them universally wrote or prepared analysis obeying the document's lines. Yes, accountants tended to write within the lines on these forms.

But on many of these documents, there now was original handwriting in blue pen. The new handwriting had not obeyed the lines on the documents. The blue handwritten comments tended to be written diagonally across and down the page. Often with arrows pointing to portions of the original text or amounts. Of great importance, the blue comments were generally addressed to "Chester" and ended with the initials HRH. The HRH letters were encircled starting from the bottom right portion on the last "H," then a line that circled the three letters that returned to a position under the last H. These comments were extremely telling. For example, on a working paper analyzing the balance of unamortized JT8D engine overhauls was the following comment with an arrow pointing at the unamortized balance of the over-haul cost for one engine, among a long list:

Chester:

I am not buying these so-called assets. Not only do I want you to make sure these get written off, I want you to see to it that there is an accrual for future required overhauls. For example, this accountant's work paper shows a JT8D engine for a DC-9 aircraft had an overhaul that cost $1.8 million. That overhaul brought its TBO [time-between-overhaul] down to zero hours. According to this accountant's work papers, it now has 4,000 hours on it, so it has used up 40 percent of that overhaul until it must have its next overhaul when it reaches 10,000 TBO. So, this leaves an unamortized overhaul cost for this engine on Air West's balance sheet of $1.08 million [60 percent of $1.8 million] as an asset. I am not going to pay for that $1.08 million unamortized overhaul cost. And, since that engine will need an overhaul at 10,000 hours at a cost of probably $2 million at that time, I want a liability set-up for 40 percent of that $2 million overhaul for the hours that Air West has put on that engine since its last overhaul. I want H&S to do a calculation like this for Air West's unamortized overhaul costs for each of its engines and airframes. These accounting adjustments will save me many millions when this transaction closes.

HRH

I was astounded to read this note and many others like it. I also determined that Hughes's comments revealed several vital factors that were critical to the civil litigation against him:

1. The notes were written after December 31, 1969, but before the closing of the Purchase Contract on April 1, 1970.

2. The box of PMM work papers, on which Hughes had written his comments to Chester were photocopies of the work papers that H&S had received from me during their due diligence work.

3. The content of what was photocopied and then written on by Howard Hughes agreed to the original PMM audit work papers.

4. The notes to Chester from HRH could be traced to the closing adjustments that violated the Purchase Contract.

5. The notes demonstrated that Howard was extremely knowledgeable about sophisticated accounting concepts, including those peculiar to an airline (TBO and the related overhaul accounting methods) which Howard likely became familiar with during his ownership of Trans World Airline.

6. The assets being targeted for write-off in these notes and the liabilities to be established before the closing cost the Air West shareholders many millions of dollars.

I could hardly believe my eyes! Armed with this information, a spectacular gold mine of evidence, I called John. I was estatic. It was almost 5:00 and the firm's softball team had a game starting in thirty minutes. I had almost forgotten that I was scheduled to pitch that night. As much as I wanted to meet John, who was practically panting over the details of this box of evidence, the big reveal would need to wait until morning.

That night when I left my office in San Mateo, I returned the documents into the Air West box and the brown wrapping paper that it came in through the mail. I brought my large brief-case that contained many of the tax work papers I had used to summarize the closing adjustments I had identified as being in violation of the Purchase Contract. I also packed the log, which listed the work papers that I had lent to H&S so they could make copies, if they chose, as part of their due diligence work.

I put the box and the briefcase onto a folding hand truck and wheeled this precious cargo to my car's trunk. The Air West mate-rials were nestled among multiple baseball bats, baseballs, gloves, a catcher's mask, and other gear for the firm's softball team, the "Padres." After the game, I told Barby about receiving the box. We both celebrated this amazing turn of events and its impor-tance to my work on this case over the last four years.

Sweet dreams? I had a great night's sleep!

The next morning, I pulled into the downstairs parking lot of the Transamerica building on Montgomery Street in San Francisco. I chose the self-park option so that only I had to deal with the audit bag, the Air West box, and the hand truck. I unfolded the hand truck and loaded the box and my briefcase onto it for the walk to the elevators. Once I arrived on the twenty-first floor, I went directly to the conference room to unload my briefcase, the Air West box and the wrapping paper used by who-ever mailed the box to me. I then walked north toward John's office, popped my head in the doorway and, with excitement in my voice, announced to John and Russell that I was ready for the "show" to begin.

I took them through the contents of the box from the begin-ning. I showed them the brown wrapping paper pointing out that there was no writing or markings on the paper other than my name and address and the stamps with a postmark indicating that the box had been mailed in Las Vegas, Nevada, after noon on June 7, 1974. They speculated that someone from one of the Hughes entities in Las Vegas was acting as a good Samaritan, but they had no real idea who would do something like this.

Then we poured through the contents of the box. I showed them how each work paper number containing Hughes's comments was on the original log that I had maintained while I was participating in the audit of Air West's 1969 financial statements. Then I showed them a few of the original work papers and compared them to the photocopied portions of those documents that were in the box. Everything was the same except for Hughes's notes and comments to Davis. I also reviewed some of the notes with them, including the one about the engine overhaul costs.

They agreed that these documents showed that Davis' cross-complaint against the Trustees which claimed that their notice of Hughes's deposition was a circus intended only to harass Hughes about something about which he had absolutely no knowledge, was a blatantly self-serving and false statement to the court. Further, Davis's exhibit that he attached to his cross-complaint where Howard Hughes, under oath, stated that if,

...it is found that there are any genuine issues of material fact as to which I have any relevant knowledge, I will then answer appropriate questions under oath concerning the same to the extent of my knowledge...

provided the court with a gold-plated invitation to order a default judgment against Howard Hughes and put Chester Davis' motion for summary judgment in the trash.

However, there was one big problem. I had no idea how I got the box and its compelling documents. Davis would likely argue that the blue notes penned by HRH were a complete fabrication, made up to frame Hughes. We needed a handwriting expert to testify that these notes were written by Howard Hughes. John remembered a *Life* magazine's issue from a few years earlier that had examples of Howard's handwriting in one of its articles.

Russell had a new assignment, to go to the San Francisco Public Library and copy the cover of that *Life* magazine, and the article inside it with examples of Hughes's handwriting. John and I then poured over HRH's notes to Davis, identifying 20 that were most important to the case against Hughes.

Later that day, Russell returned from the library with a copy of the cover of the November 22, 1971, issue of *Life* magazine and an article with examples of Howard Hughes's handwritten letters. Tricia Nixon graced the cover of the magazine, which touted an article about her romance with Ed Cox, whom she had married in a White House Rose Garden ceremony on June 12, 1971. The cover's top right portion contained the headline, "The Elusive Howard Hughes As Revealed in His Letters." Congratulations were in order for John's sharp memory and for Russell finding the article. Now it was time to look over some of the HRH notes in the Air West box and compare them to the handwriting included in Life magazine article. Bingo! To the three non-handwriting experts John, Russell and me, there was a clear match.

Even assuming we had overcome our biased layman's handwriting analysis, John decided that it was time to hire a real expert. He told Russell to find a handwriting expert whose testimony would hold up in court about the authenticity of the HRH notes on the Air West documents.

CHAPTER 30

BRAZEN BLUE INK

"The real voyage of discovery consists not in seeking
new landscapes, but in having new eyes."

—MARCEL PROUST

THE NEXT DAY, John again asked Russell to go back to the library and this time, look for news about documents stolen from a Hughes office or the office of Chester Davis. John thought that perhaps the Air West box had been taken by someone during a break-in, and, if so, perhaps he and Russell would be able to use that information to their benefit.

Russell did find an article in the June 6, 1974 issue of *The New York Times*, which included the following information under the headline, "Hughes's Office Ransacked on Coast":

- "On June 5, a security guard in Howard Hughes Hollywood message center and office building was bound and gagged by a group of men who ransacked private papers…"

- "Mr. Hughes, who lives in seclusion in a hotel on Grand Bahama Island in the Bahamas, is involved in several legal disputes and is the target of a continuing investigation by the Securities and Exchange Commission."

- The security guard, "was making his rounds about 12:30 am Pacific daylight time when a gun was shoved against his back. He said he had a glimpse of two men before he was bound, gagged and blind-folded. He told the police that he thought there were four or five men in the burglary group."

- "The burglars left about 4:45 am after examining files that interested them. Hughes's staff members would not say what papers were missing."

Russell also spoke with several of his partners in Pettit's Los Angeles office about the burglary. The scuttlebutt that he picked up from those conversations was that the L.A. Police Department was not getting much cooperation from the Hughes folks, and there were also rumors that the Feds were not enthusiastic about digging too deep into the burglary, for reasons that no one could figure out.

John, Russell, and I discussed Ted's findings. We were puzzled. Not surprisingly, many people had strong motivations to burglarize 7000 Romaine. This group included the SEC, the Department of Justice, the FBI, Robert Maheu, and anyone else in the world that wanted to profit or gain advantages by stealing documents from the mystery man about whom so many people around the world were curious. I almost felt sorry for a man who had racked up so many powerful enemies. The looming question was, why would any of these people or organizations send the Air West documents to me?

Still, the bottom line of this conversation was that we were unlikely to find out who sent the documents to me. Even if we did, it was unlikely we would get their agreement to discuss why they sent the box to me, or to admit that they had stolen the documents from Hughes. Because of these issues and concerns, John concluded that the case against Hughes might be better off if the three of us never found out who sent the box to me.

Next up, Clark and Russell needed to find a handwriting expert to determine if the HRH notes were, in fact, written by Howard Hughes. Russell interviewed several experts that had frequently testified in various state and federal courts in cases involving contested wills and other cases where handwritten documents were important to the litigation. After speaking with three, he selected one that had an impressive resume that included teaching classes and writing books on forensic handwriting analysis. This expert also had significant courtroom experience in which his testimony had been accepted by the judge and by juries.

When Russell met with the handwriting expert, he brought with him Hughes's letters that had appeared in the January 1971 issue of *Life* magazine, along with copies of several HRH notes from the Air West box. The expert also brought copies of handwritten documents submitted by Hughes to the Nevada State Gaming Control Board when he applied for licenses to operate casinos in 1968 and 1969. It did not take long for the expert to describe the similarities in pen lifts, letter spacing, connecting strokes, unusual letter formations (including the way Hughes presented the letter "P"), and other flourishes between the various documents.

Unfortunately, the letters in *Life* magazine and the license applications were formal documents and only used Hughes's full signature rather than the moniker HRH, so that portion of the notes could not be verified. In any case, the expert assured Russell that he was confident that Hughes wrote the HRH notes.

In the federal civil case, the judge had now ordered Hughes to appear for his deposition on October 31, 1974, a little more than four months away. This new deposition date, with the assumption that Hughes would appear, meant that Clark had to go back over the key accounting and FUD documents to know those issues cold again. The complex facts and their interrelationships were easy to lose track of, so John and I again spent many hours reviewing the details to prepare for the possible deposition, again.

This time, however, John also needed a grand strategy about how to deal with the HRH notes. John, Russell and I debated at length two approaches to take with Howard Hughes during his deposition concerning these notes. The first approach was to find the very best ten notes and copy them in color, so the HRH notes, written in blue, stood out from the black text of the photocopied handwritten portions of the original documents. John would then mark the color copies as exhibits to the deposition. He would confront Hughes with them directly at the start of the deposition, before he had a chance to settle in, and ask him questions such as:

- Mr. Hughes, please read what the Court Reporter has marked as Exhibit X then tell me whether you have seen that document before today?

- I want you to carefully read the note written in blue ink that starts with the word Chester. Did you write that note on Exhibit X?

- If Hughes denies that these are his notes, ask if he had a practice of signing notes or documents with the initials HRH with a line at the end of the last H that circles the three letters before it?

- Is he aware of any other person that signs his or her notes with the moniker HRH with a line at the end of the last H that circles the three letters before it? If yes, he would ask him the name of that person.

- These notes are directed to Chester, is that Chester Davis? If his answer is vague, ask him if it is likely that this is Chester Davis or if he has any reason to believe that it was not Chester Davis?

- When did he write these notes?

- Clark would show him notes where it is clear Hughes is instructing Chester to write certain Air West assets off or establish or increase certain of its liabilities prior to closing the Air West Purchase Contract. Then ask him what closing he was addressing in the notes.

- In the note to Chester about the unamortized overhaul costs on Air West's JT8D engines on its DC-9 and Boeing 727 aircraft, he would ask about his use of the term TBO, asking him if he knows what that acronym means. If he claims not to know that term, ask him if it is likely to represent Time Between Overhaul?

- Then Clark would continue, when did you learn about the term TBO?

- Did you learn that acronym while you held a majority interest in the stock of TWA?

- How did you get these documents?

- Who sent you these documents?

- Mr. Hughes, why were you sent these documents?

- What was your objective when writing these notes to Chester?

- Mr. Hughes, are you aware that these documents are copies of PMM audit work papers of its audit of Air West's December 31, 1969, financial statements?

- Did you or Chester Davis ask or instruct H&S to copy hundreds of PMM's audit work papers?

- Did you ask or instruct Mr. Davis to send you copies of these PMM audit work papers so that you could review them?

- Why did you want to review these work papers of PMM's audit of Air West's December 31, 1969, financial statements?

- Did you believe at the time you reviewed these audit work papers that you understood the nature of the assets and liabilities addressed in these work papers? If he says no or is vague in his answer, take him through other work papers that have notes written by HRH that demonstrate a strong knowledge of accounting (such as deferred route costs and prepaid landing fees).

- Did you believe that you were competent to understand the accounting principles used by Air West in recording the assets and liabilities analyzed by these audit work papers?

- Mr. Hughes, I have had the court reporter mark as Exhibit XX a document that your attorney Mr. Chester Davis has represented is a letter from you to the court with jurisdiction in this matter, which states, in part:

    This is to confirm, and I hereby undertake, that if, after hearing and final determination of said motions for summary judgment, it is found that there are any genuine issues of material fact as to which I have any relevant knowledge, I will then answer appropriate questions under oath concerning the same to the extent of my knowledge…

- Mr. Hughes, did you write, or dictate, or approve in any way the words contained in this Exhibit? If he denies writing this, ask him if someone wrote it for him, or if he suggested to someone language similar to that used in this letter?
- Did you sign this letter?
- Mr. Hughes, did you read the letter before you signed it?

The other deposition strategy was to start with the letter in which he denies knowing of any genuine issues of material fact. Then John would walk him through various closing adjustments where millions of Air West's assets were written off and liabilities established or increased and ask him to describe his knowledge and involvement in these adjustments.

We expected that this second approach would lead to Hughes recognizing the importance of the notes and his need to strongly deny that he had any knowledge whatsoever of any of these closing adjustments, that he was not an accountant, and that, when it came to accounting issues, he hired accountants and/or H&S to deal with those types of issues.

We debated the merits of the two deposition strategies.

The second strategy could lead to great success. However, Hughes's answers leading up to the disclosure of his notes would make it almost certain that Hughes and his counsel would do everything possible to deny that the notes were his. They would then move toward a strategy that would preclude them from ever being permitted to be used in court.

John decided that he would use the first strategy that would not telegraph the notes' importance until their significance was in place. Then Davis would not be able to dig Hughes out of the trouble his own statements had gotten him into by that point in the deposition. The first strategy was an enthusiastic GO.

During July, August, September, and October, John, Russell, and I studied the more than 100 HRH notes to Chester David. Once again, I coached John about what the notes meant, what accounting issues were involved, tracing them into the resulting closing adjustments, and why they violated the Purchase Contract.

As usual, John was a quick learner and was ready to deal with the evasive tactics likely to be used by Hughes and his counsel's obstructions. We knew that the first deposition question asked about a topic or document is usually avoided by the witness. Therefore, it is the follow-on questions that penetrate the evasion tactics that are key to getting meaningful answers. Then, as the deposition progresses, the witnesses often realizes that his or her evasive attempts are not working and, instead, are harming their credibility. This process and that realization would then lead to more truthful answers to future questions.

Russell and I reviewed the April 24, 1974 subpoena duces tecum sent to Chester Davis for Howard Hughes's May 29, 1974 deposition. My efforts focused on the accounting issues much the same as the previous subpoena duces tecum sent to Chester Davis on April 24, 1974. But this time, I made sure to include a request for any notes that Hughes had made directly to Chester Davis that would demonstrate his knowledge about the makeup of Air West's assets and liabilities on December 31, 1969. Although I now had these documents, Hughes might have kept copies of those PMM work papers and made notes on them or one of his aides might have made copies of these documents with his notes on them. If they did make such copies, this subpoena would also call for their production.

The new subpoena was sent on Monday, September 22,

1974, to Chester Davis acting on behalf of his client. It gave Hughes, his staff, and his counsel a month to gather any responsive documents to be provided to Pettit & Martin three days before Hughes's rescheduled deposition on Tuesday, October 28. It also allowed him time to study those documents for his appearance at his deposition, as ordered by the judge, at Pettit & Martin's office on October 31, 1974.

Once again, a key document was the log that I had prepared while I was at Air West's San Mateo offices. It contained those PMM work papers that H&S had borrowed as part of their due diligence review. This log showed the work paper letter and number, the subject matter, the date the working paper was provided to H&S, and the date that it was returned to PMM.

Now, I updated the log to show a column for whether a copy of the document was in the Air West box and another column indicating whether it had an HRH note on it. Finally, there was a column indicating whether the HRH note could be linked to a closing adjustment and if so, how much that adjustment totaled. These additions would be useful to John as a glaring reference to know how many dollars of damage any HRH note caused to the Air West shareholders.

We had spent thousands of hours building this case and the strategy for pursuing it.

Receiving the Hughes notes was an extraordinary and unexpected gift. We needed to do everything that was proper and possible to harvest the benefits of that gift.

CHAPTER 31

PHOTOS OF THE
K-129 GRAVESITE

*"When words become unclear, I shall focus
with photographs. When images become
inadequate, I shall be content with silence."*

—ANSEL ADAMS

A FTER THE BURIAL of the Soviet sailors, the HGE returned to Long Beach. Containers were lowered into the Moon Pool and loaded with portions of the recovered submarine that had been set aside for further study and analysis. These materials were transferred onto trucks headed for a CIA warehouse within Area 51 in Nevada, 80 miles northwest of Las Vegas.

While these activities were taking place, William Colby and Carl Duckett met to strategize about the status of Project AZORIAN. They understood that the project had recovered the forward portion of the K-129 and its two nuclear-tipped torpedoes and related cryptologic materials, but the missile section and its coding materials had slipped through the vehicle's broken claws. The project was close to a complete success, but unfortunately, it was not a total triumph. They now discussed another project that the CIA called Project Matador. This Project was to try for a second bite of the K-129 apple.

They asked the Lockheed folks to refine the study of why the original claw failed and determine if improvements to the claw could be recommended, assuming the HGE returned to the scene to retrieve the lost missile section. This request seemed reasonable since that portion of the K-129 was smaller and lighter, and even with the original payload, it was able to lift it 10,000 feet toward the surface before grabbers 4, and 5 snapped and dropped the missile section. In contrast, Project Matador would only be tasked with retrieving the missile section, a much lighter payload.

Duckett and Colby also met with the U.S. Navy to request that they send a submarine to return to the new gravesite of the K-129 on another photographic mission.

This mission's goal would be to determine the missile section's new location and its condition for being lifted to the surface. In response, the U.S. Navy had the Seawolf, a nuclear-propelled submarine, equipped with an electronic "fish" to carry cameras down to the lost submarine's new gravesite with particular focus on photographing the sub's missile section and to determine its new landing position(s).

These photographs would be critical in determining whether Project Matador was a likely candidate to be successful. Their principal concern was that the fragile, and broken missile section had fallen 10,000 feet to a hard ocean floor. If it was no longer in one piece, how many pieces needed to be retrieved, and was their retrieval practical?

If the photographs from the Seawolf showed that the missile section of the K-129 was in one piece, or only in a few pieces, Duckett and Colby would then consider whether Lockheed could assure them that its claw could successfully retrieve the missile section of the K-129. If both of those factors came back with a positive response, they would consider the security concerns of returning the HGE to the site for a second retrieval mission. However, given the close and sustained observation of the Soviets by the Chazhma (the Soviet Missile Range Instrumentation ship) and their SB-10 (the ocean-going salvage tug), they knew those concerns would be difficult to overcome.

When the photographs taken by the Seawolf were ready for viewing, Duckett and Colby were called for a meeting at the Office of Naval Intelligence (ONI), located 15 miles southeast of the CIA's headquarters in McLean, Virginia. They arrived at the ONI and were led to an interior conference room, which was used to process sensitive and confidential information. It was clear from the many photographs taken by the Seawolf that the K-129's missile section had shattered when it hit the ocean's floor. It now was on the ocean's hard bottom in hundreds of small unidentifiable pieces scattered over many acres. Duckett and Colby knew there was no reasonable possibility of recovering any meaningful portion of the submarine's missile section. Project Matador was dead.

CHAPTER 32

CHOOSE VALET WHEN UNDER THREAT

*"People don't realize that now is all there
ever is; there is no past or future except as
memory or anticipation in your mind."*

—ECKHART TOLLE

CTOBER 28, 1974, came and went without any new
documents from the Hughes defendants or their counsel.
Chester Davis again sent a letter stating that all relevant
documents had been provided in response to earlier subpoenas.

Once again on October 31, Ted Russell had Pettit & Martin's
main conference room set up for coffee, cream and sugar, orange
juice, water, sweet rolls, and various types of soft drinks. The videographer arrived early to set up the camera and microphones for
the witness, and all the attorneys expected to attend. The court
reporter arrived with her stenograph machine. By 8:50, all preparations were in place, and John, Russell and I were ready for the
deposition to begin.

All we needed was for Hughes and his counsel to walk through the door. Once again, we were anxious to actually meet this extraordinary man that many around the world followed like a rock star. In fact, everyone in the office from the receptionist to the secretaries, associates and partners was anxious to catch a glimpse of the mysterious Howard Robard Hughes. Surely, this time he would appear!

Again, by 9:15, Hughes and Davis had not arrived, and none of the other counsel for defendants showed up. John called Davis to confirm that Hughes was again not going to appear for his deposition. Davis had expected the call and pounced. He launched an assault on John's efforts to depose his client. He spat that he was filing a motion to dismiss all further discovery and his intention to file another motion for summary judgment.

When John hung up the telephone, he was so angry that it was easy to imagine steam coming out of his ears. Russell and I listened to his rant and concurred with his disgust. Once again, Chester Davis proved he was undeterred by orders from a federal judge. He would never end his sword-waving belligerent aggression to protect his client and would strive to destroy all obstacles in his way.

True to his word, a messenger delivered Davis's new motion for both summary judgment and a motion to dismiss all further discovery. John and Russell immediately got to work on preparing their own motion for summary judgment, as well as sanctions against Hughes and Davis for his failure to appear for his deposition, once again.

Judge Alfonso J. Zirpoli scheduled a hearing in federal court for Thursday, November 14, 1974, at 9:30 am to hear the parties' various motions. We met in early November to plan the strategy and outline the opening argument.

After John and Davis's opening arguments, John and Russell agreed that I would testify about the Air West documents and

241

Hughes's handwritten notes. Depending on how my testimony went, John would decide whether the handwriting expert would be called next. He was deeply concerned about Judge Zirpoli's reaction to a handwriting expert and would avoid calling him if he was not needed. Everyone had confidence in John Clark's ability to think on his feet and make the right decision on the spot though.

After an extensive discussion, it was decided that the key points of his opening argument would focus on the following:

1. A sanctions demand to the court to award a reimbursement paid by Hughes of the costs incurred by A.W. Liquidating Company ("AWLC") to prepare for his two depositions since these costs were rendered of no value as a result of his failure to appear.

2. That on December 31, 1968, Air West and Hughes agreed to a Purchase Contract, where Hughes contracted to purchase, and Air West agreed to sell to Hughes, all the property and assets of Air West.

3. Air West performed all its obligations on its part pursuant to the Purchase Contract, and on April 1, 1970, Air West transferred to Hughes Air (now wholly owned by Howard Hughes) all of the property and assets of Air West.

4. The Purchase Contract obligated Hughes to pay Air West at least $89.4 million, in exchange for all its assets.

5. Howard Hughes, through his FUD campaign and his forcing Air West to record improper accounting adjustments as of the closing of the Purchase Contract, reduced Hughes's Purchase Contracts price to Air West's shareholders by $48 million.

6. Howard Hughes understood, participated in, and encouraged both the FUD campaign and the recording by Air West personnel of the closing adjustments, which violated the Purchase Contract.

7. Howard Hughes and Chester Davis had made statements that the Plaintiffs' efforts to take Hughes's deposition were a circus intended only to harass Hughes by calling for his deposition relating to matters of which he had absolutely no knowledge. They further stated that such issues were so beneath him that the plaintiffs knew that Hughes's deposition was not a legitimate effort but rather an obnoxious campaign of harassment against Howard. These statements are demonstrably false and will be shown as false through the expert testimony of Paul Regan.

8. Because of 1 through 7 above, the court should conclude that Howard Hughes's failure to appear for his depositions on May 29, 1974, and October 31, 1974, was due to his bad faith and willful disregard of the judicial process. As a result, AWLC is entitled to a default judgment of $48 million, plus interest. (More than $1 billion in 2020 dollars.)

John had to notify Davis and the court that I would be a witness at this hearing. He explained to me that the notice would only give a summary of my education and work experience, as well as my experience at Air West. The notice would also include a vague statement about the nature of my accounting related testimony including why the closing adjustments violated the Purchase Agreements. It would be sent to Chester Davis and the Court at the close of business three days before the hearing.

And what about CW1 and CW2?

Although John hoped that CW1 and 2 were singled out for horrible treatment because they were Hughes "insiders" who were about to betray Hughes, he informed me that he had hired a bodyguard named Li Qiang to be with me 24 hours a day starting at 5:00 p.m. the day after Davis received the notice. I admitted that I had been concerned ever since I heard about what happened to CW1 and CW2. I thanked my friend for his efforts to protect me, but it was still pretty surreal!

I certainly hoped that he was correct that what happened to the government's confidential witnesses was motivated by the so-called Mormon Mafia's desire to punish a "family member" that in their eyes had turned on their leader. I began to consider how to approach these issues with my wife, who would have to provide for a houseguest and deal with her own concerns about my safety.

Before prepping Barby for my having a bodyguard, John needed to go over a few ground rules and tips regarding my testimony at the hearing. I had to nail it.

"First, listen carefully to each question that I ask, think for a moment, and then answer the question. When Chester begins to ask you questions, same thing. Your delayed response not only gives you time to think, but it gives me time to object to the question, if necessary. If the Judge asks you a question, think about it, then answer it as honestly as possible. Even if that is obviously not the answer that he wants to hear. Many witnesses can't summon the courage to give an answer that contradicts a judge's rhetorical questions. Do not fall for that trap. Finally, remember testifying is easy, after you listen to the questions, always give a truthful answer. I will always live with the truth; that is my job."

Over the next forty years, I would hear John Clark give that same short sermon to all his witnesses. He lived with the truth. It was his job to work with it.

Li Qiang arrived at my office in San Mateo at 4:00 p.m.

on November 11. Li was somewhat shy, but I pried out of him that he was a Grandmaster in Jiu-Jitsu with a coral belt, one step higher than a 6th degree black belt. He also had a concealed weapon permit. Li suggested we leave the office at 5:00 while it was light outside and head to my car, which was parked in an open-air parking lot. Li joined Barby, Greg, and me for dinner and slept in our guest bedroom.

On Tuesday, Li stayed with me while I worked in my office and on Wednesday, we met with Russell and John at Pettit's office in San Francisco to rehearse for the hearing the next day. Li asked me where I parked when visiting Pettit's office. I told him in the basement of the Transamerica Pyramid. Li said to choose valet, not self-park, because it was more secure. He added in a joking manner, "Valet is better because when the attendant starts the car to bring it to us to go home, he is blown up not us."

CHAPTER 33

CHESTER DAVIS COMES FOR ME

"All confrontation is based on deception."

—*PAUL WATSON*

OHN CLARK, TED Russell, Li Qiang and I arrived at the Federal Courthouse at 450 Golden Gate Avenue in San Francisco in a town car at 9:00 a.m. on November 14, 1974, for the hearing before Judge Zirpoli. The hearing would determine the consequences of Hughes's failure to appear for his scheduled depositions in this matter. As usual, we arrived at the courtroom early so that Clark could review key documents and avoid the judge's wrath should we be stuck in traffic and arrive late for the hearing. Most judges strongly frown upon tardiness and may take it out on anyone that abuses the judicial process by being late.

Judge Zirpoli's courtroom was on the nineteenth floor. I thought it was ironic that this was the same building in which I had met with William Hanks more than a year earlier to discuss the Department of Justice's case against the Hughes defendants. Now I was about to confront, and be confronted by, the famous and pugnacious Chester Davis. The courtroom was at the far end of the west side of the Federal Building. It was a massive room with greenish marble walls on the sides and plenty of room for counsel, even with the entourage representing the defendants, and the curious spectators watching from the rear of the courtroom.

Judge Zirpoli sat high above the large gathering of attorneys and their associates, as well as an audience of press and interested observers. The sixty-nine-year-old judge was a man of the people. His undergraduate degree was from the University of California, Berkeley as was his law degree. He had served as an Assistant United States Attorney of the Northern District of California and on the San Francisco Board of Supervisors before being nominated to the District Court by President John F. Kennedy in 1961. He was a no-nonsense, imposing man, and straightforward in his confidence. He commanded and received great respect.

Chester Davis rose to present his opening argument. In his early sixties, this tall, overweight, boisterous New York lawyer, was dressed in a three-piece suit, white shirt, and red tie. He had a broad smile, but a serious and loud voice. By now, his points had become familiar. He paced back and forth, ranting about how "disrespectful" the whole process had been to Howard Hughes. He again blamed John Clark for treating the judicial process like a circus and apologized to the Court for having to impose on it once again to request that his client be granted summary judgment in this matter.

Davis reiterated that his client was a busy man, and these so-called FUD issues and accounting mumbo jumbo were certainly not something that Howard Hughes had anything to do with, at any time. At the conclusion, as he returned to his chair, he stared at John with contempt in his eyes, then sat his large body down onto his chair in a huff.

John Clark began his arguments requesting that Judge Zirpoli impose sanctions on Hughes for the costs wasted in preparing for the two depositions that Hughes ignored. He then masterfully went through his remaining seven points, emphasizing Hughes's involvement in both the FUD campaign and his intimate role in causing the improper closing adjustments to be recorded "as of" the date of his purchase of Air West.

When John finished, Chester Davis rose to his feet and walked to the podium to present his rebuttal to John's presentation. He went on a blistering attack of each of the eight-point opening arguments. As to each point, according to Davis, Hughes was completely innocent. Instead, Hughes was a victim of the ambulance-chasing of a wealthy man who happened to be very busy running many important businesses. He again referred to the FUD campaign and the accounting issues as a circus act invented by John Clark, in which Hughes played absolutely no part in and to suggest otherwise was a fraud on the Court. As Davis concluded his remarks, he boldly asked Judge Zirpoli to stop the harassment of Hughes and award the defendants' summary judgment and costs incurred to date.

Judge Zirpoli studied the courtroom and its audience. He looked at his notes for a few moments. Then he instructed John to proceed with his presentation of evidence relating to Howard Hughes's involvement in the accounting and FUD issues which was the basis for his demand for Hughes's deposition.

At this point, John called me to the witness stand. I had been seated "behind the bar," swinging half doors that separate the attorneys from those in the audience. The separation between the audience and the judge and counsel are part of a symbolic barrier separating those who have not "passed the bar" from those who have.

Hearing John Clark state "we now call Paul Regan as our witness" was a profound moment. Yes, I was nervous, but I tried hard not to show it. All the years of effort were truly now very much on my shoulders as I stood up from my seat among the audience. I had been sitting on the aisle in anticipation of this moment. Now, I needed to walk ten feet to the bar, then past the swinging half doors, then walk another forty feet down the middle aisle between John Clark, Ted Russell and two paralegals on one side and Chester Davis and his hoard of attorneys, and paralegals on the other side.

As I walked forward, my eyes moved from John Clark to the bailiff, to Judge Zirpoli then to the court reporter. I took two steps up to the witness stand. Standing, I looked straight at the court reporter, who asked me to state my full name and swear under oath to state, "the truth, the whole truth and nothing but the truth, so help me, God." Then prompted by John, I stated my educational background and work experience, and confirmed my role as a CPA, licensed by the State of California.

Then I was asked to describe my work assignments at Air West. I began by explaining my work in the summer of 1968 when I reviewed the three merged airlines' accounting practices: Pacific, West Coast, and Bonanza Airlines. This work allowed me to determine that those accounting practices were consistent with each other and that those practices were in accordance with generally accepted accounting principles. I then explained my work on both the 1968 and 1969 audits of Air West's financial statements, the Deposit Agreement dispute after the closing, and finally, the airline's tax returns for the three months ended March 31, 1970.

When John asked me approximately how many hours that I had personally spent working on these Air West engagements, I surprised myself by the number vocalized: approximately 3,000. Three thousand hours amidst starting my career, marrying the love of my life, becoming a father, buying a house. It was all kind of dizzying.

He continued:

Clark: While you were working on the audit of Air West's 1969 financial statements, did you lend portions of PMM's work papers to Howard Hughes's auditors, Haskins & Sells?

Regan: Yes, sir.

Clark: Did the Purchase Contract between Air West, Howard Hughes and Hughes Tool Company call for this lending of work papers by PMM to H&S?

Regan: Yes, it was part of the Purchase Contract that H&S would perform due diligence for Hughes, and, as part of that due diligence, H&S could review PMM's work papers, and that it could make copies of those documents.

Clark: Did you prepare a listing of documents reviewed by H&S as a result of this due diligence agreement?

Regan: Yes, sir, I did.

Clark: I would like to have the Court Reporter mark as Exhibit 1, a six-page document titled "PMM Work Papers Shared With H&S." Did you prepare Exhibit 1?

Regan: Yes, sir, I did. And you can see where I wrote my name in the box near the top right section of this working paper, where there is a space labeled "Preparer."

Clark: Please explain to the court what this document represents.

Regan: When I shared any work paper with H&S, I listed the work paper number, its title and subject, the H&S person requesting the document, the date that I provided the document, and the date the H&S person returned it to me.

Clark: Now, I am going to show you what I would like the Court Reporter to mark as Exhibit 2. This Exhibit is a three-page document titled "Unamortized Engine Overhaul Costs." Did you prepare this document?

Regan: Yes, sir, I did.

Clark: Is this document listed on Exhibit 1 as one of the documents that you provided H&S while it was doing its due diligence for Mr. Hughes?

Regan: Yes, sir, it is on page 1, at row 17 of Exhibit 1.

Clark: Please explain to the Court what Exhibit 2 represents.

Regan: This working paper lists Air West's JT8D engines used on its DC-9 and Boeing 727 aircraft. The three pages were given the number G-10.1, G-10.2, and G-10.3 by me when I prepared this document. Each engine has a unique number assigned to it by Pratt & Whitney, the manufacturer of these engines. That number is in the first column. The next column is the date of the last time each engine was overhauled. Then the next column shows the cost of that overhaul, which for the first engine listed was $1,783,593. Now since that overhaul brings the time between over-hauls on that engine to zero, the industry refers to that as zero time between overhaul, or TBO. This overhaul cost of $1,783,593, was accounted for by Air West as an asset, to be amortized over its next 10,000 flight hours that it provides Air West, at which point the Federal Aviation Administration, requires that this engine must be overhauled again. After that future overhaul, its TBO will be brought back down to zero.

Clark: So, let me interrupt you for a moment. Was this the same accounting method for engine overhauls used by Pacific, West Coast and Bonanza before their merger into Air West?

Regan: Yes, sir, each airline accounted for engine overhauls this way and Air West continued to account for the cost of its engine overhauls using this same method.

Clark: Now, why did Air West amortize that overhaul cost of $1,783,593 over the next 10,000 hours of flight time?

Regan: The government had determined that the overhaul provided 10,000 future flight hours until the airline needed to bring the TBO on that engine back to zero. Therefore, each future flight hour on that engine reduced this asset by $178.36 ($1,783,593/10,000), which was charged to Air West's costs for each hour flown on that engine before its next overhaul.

Clark: Now is that accounting methodology that you just described consistent with generally accepted accounting principles?

Regan: Yes, sir.

Clark: Please explain to the Court the next columns on Exhibit 2?

Regan: The fourth column from the left shows the number of hours of flight time on each engine since their last overhaul. Using the first engine as an example, it shows that on December 31, 1969 there have been 3,829 hours flown on this engine since its last TBO. Column five takes those 3,829 hours times the cost per hour for the overhaul ($178.36), this provides that $682,940 was required to be expensed for this engine, leaving an unamortized asset on Air West's balance sheet on December 31, 1969 of $1,100,653 ($1,783,593 less $682,940). This is the amount seen in the far-right column which, is titled "Unamortized Engine Overhaul costs."

Clark: Now, I am going to show you what I will ask the Court Reporter to mark as Exhibit 3, which is also a three-page document titled "Unamortized Engine Overhaul Costs." Did you prepare this document?

Regan: Yes, most of it. Exhibit 3 is the same document that has been marked as Exhibit 2, except it is a color photocopy, and it contains new handwritten comments that are in blue. These blue comments are written diagonally and down the rows on the first page. The blue handwritten comments were not on Exhibit 2 when it was given back to me by H&S on March 21, 1970. They were added after Exhibit 2 was returned to me.

At this point Chester Davis jumped to his feet and shouted:

Davis: Objection, your honor, Exhibit 3, was stolen from my client's office. Mr. Clark is attempting to introduce into the record a stolen document. This witness cannot testify about information on a document that Mr. Hughes wrote to me on a document that was stolen from his office. It is a confidential communication from my client to me. This information was not only stolen, it is privileged!

John Clark was poised to respond to Chester's argument, but Judge Zirpoli instructed both attorneys to sit down immediately and to be silent. The judge then turned to me and asked:

Mr. Regan, how did you get this document that has been marked as Exhibit 3?

Regan: Your honor, it was in a box that was delivered to my office by the U.S. mail. The box had the words "Air West" written in large letters by a marking pen on each of its sides. The box contained Exhibit 3, as well as hundreds of other copies of PMM work papers that had been shared with H&S by me during the audit of Air West's 1969 financial statements.

Judge Zirpoli: Was there a return address on the box when it arrived?

Regan: No, your honor.

Judge Zirpoli: Were there any other markings on this box.

Regan: Your honor, there was only my name, my firm's name and address, and stamps, which showed that they had been canceled in Las Vegas, the day before they were delivered to my office.

Judge Zirpoli: Ladies and gentlemen, we are going to take our morning break now. Please be back in this courtroom by 11:00 am.

After a brief restroom break, John, Russell, and I met in a small conference room just east of Judge Zirpoli's courtroom. John was ecstatic because of Davis' reckless and foolish admission that the blue handwriting on Exhibit 3 was Howard Hughes's and that these were notes to him, Chester Davis, as Hughes's attorney. John was confident that Judge Zirpoli had called the morning break so he could consider Davis's dual objections to Exhibit 3. The first objection being the admissibility of documents that were allegedly stolen from Hughes's office. The second being that Howard's notes to Davis were protected by the attorney-client privilege.

Russell and I were anxious and concerned that if either of these objections resulted in Exhibit 3 (and the many similar exhibits to follow) being inadmissible, the hearing, and the entire case, would be a disaster. However, John was not concerned for several reasons. He explained that Davis could not prove that the documents were stolen from Hughes's office. In fact, the accounts and the police report that Russell had located about the burglary, stated that the Hughes representatives could not determine what documents were stolen from 7000 Romaine. In addition, Hughes's comments to Chester on the documents in the Air West box did not fall within the attorney-client privilege doctrine. Those comments did not ask for legal advice; in fact, they were Hughes's instructions to Davis as his business agent about what accounting entries he wanted to be recorded prior to the closing of the Purchase Agreement.

John Clark leaned back in his chair, smiling from ear to ear. Hughes's handwritten notes were ticking time bombs for both Davis and Hughes. Exhibit 3 also demonstrated that Hughes had put himself knee-deep in Air West's so-called "accounting mumbo-jumbo." The accounting concepts presented in this exhibit were sophisticated, and Hughes displayed that he not only understood them—he knew how to manipulate them for his own benefit.

John continued that Judge Zirpoli would be furious that Davis had characterized the deposition of Hughes as a circus and that he had no knowledge of the accounting mumbo jumbo that was a central issue in this litigation. To top it off, Davis had perpetrated these misguided theories by submitting a written statement by Hughes to the Court to support these falsehoods. These circumstances would unleash the wrath of Judge Zirpoli on both Davis and Hughes. Although there was always uncertainty with a judge's expected rulings, John simply could not wait to get back in the courtroom. I imagined this is what most attorneys feel when they are on the road to taking down their foe.

Russell looked at his wristwatch and announced that we needed to hurry back. As he was about to leave the small conference room, John told Russell that he should inform the handwriting expert that his testimony would not be needed since

Davis had foolishly admitted that the blue comments on Exhibit 3 (and by logical extension the rest of the comments in the Air West box) were made by Hughes to Davis.

Judge Zirpoli announced:

> During the break, I considered Mr. Davis's objections to the introduction of Exhibit 3 into evidence. Mr. Davis alleged that it was stolen from his client's office. Mr. Davis also argued that Mr. Regan should be prohibited from testifying about Howard Hughes's handwritten comments to his attorney, who happens to be Chester Davis.
>
> As to the position taken by Mr. Davis that the documents in the Air West box were stolen from his office, Mr. Regan has testified under oath that this box and its documents were delivered to his office by the U.S. Postal Service. Mr. Davis' statement that these documents were stolen from Mr. Hughes's office is unsupported by any evidence presented by Mr. Davis and is therefore not relevant.
>
> Now I will address Mr. Davis' objection that Exhibit 3 contains privileged communications and should not be accepted into evidence in this case, which would preclude the testimony by Mr. Regan based on these comments. I have considered elements of the law which are needed for the privilege doctrine to be valid.
>
> To qualify as a privileged communication between a client and his attorney, the client must be communicating with an attorney to obtain the benefit of legal services. I have read Mr. Hughes's comment to Mr. Davis on Exhibit 3. In that comment, Mr. Hughes is not asking Mr. Davis for legal advice. Instead, he is giving Mr. Davis rather complex accounting instructions, demanding that certain assets of

Air West be written off and certain liabilities established in their place. Mr. Hughes is not seeking legal advice from Mr. Davis. Instead, Mr. Hughes is instructing Mr. Davis in his capacity as a business agent to reduce the amount that he would have to pay for Air West at the closing.

As a result of these findings, I am going to allow Exhibit 3 to be placed into evidence in this matter. I will also allow Mr. Clark to question Mr. Regan about this document and any similar documents with comments written by Mr. Hughes to Mr. Davis on any remaining relevant documents that were located within the so-called Air West box. Mr. Clark, you may continue with the examination of Mr. Regan.

Full of fire, John continued to ask me about HRH's' written instructions to Chester on Exhibit 3. For this exhibit and those that followed from documents taken from the Air West box, neither John nor I needed to assume that HRH was Howard Hughes or that Chester was Chester Davis. These facts were now in evidence thanks to Chester Davis's admission that such comments were indeed, from Howard Hughes to him, as his enforcer.

As my direct examination continued, it was made extremely clear that Howard Hughes had a deep knowledge of accounting and the accounting methods employed by Air West. It was also certain that he used that knowledge, through his demands to Chester Davis, to acquire Air West at a price reduced by millions of dollars. This clarity was accomplished, in part, by Davis's threats that if the accounting entries were not made "as of" the closing date, Air West would go bankrupt, and its accountants would be out of a job. However, if the accounting entries suggested by Hughes were made, the closing would take place. Once Hughes owned Air West, he would establish a powerful hub in

Las Vegas, and the jobs of Air West's accountants would be secure with the assistance of his deep pockets.

At the conclusion of John's direct examination of me, Judge Zirpoli asked Davis if he wished to cross-examine the witness. Davis replied with a devilish look. "Absolutely, your honor." I watched Davis stand and approach the podium and again, took a deep breath and tried to remain calm. He began his inquiry in a loud and demanding voice. He looked like he wanted to swallow me whole.

> Davis: Mr. Regan, how long after your graduation from the University of San Francisco did you start your work at PMM?
>
> Regan: It was two weeks after my graduation.
>
> Davis: And how long had you been at PMM before you started your work on the Air West engagement?
>
> Regan: It was approximately six weeks later.
>
> Davis: So, how old were you at that time?
>
> Regan: Sir, I was 21 years old.
>
> Davis: So, you were just a child when you were doing this work at Air West. How can you possibly have had the skills to understand these complex accounting issues and testify about them in this court?
>
> Clark: Objection your honor, Mr. Davis is preaching and stating a conclusion.
>
> Zirpoli: Sustained. Mr. Davis please ask the witness questions, and refrain from making your own conclusions.
>
> Davis: And how old are you now?
>
> Regan: My birthday is October 6, 1946, so I am 28 years old.

Davis: Now Mr. Regan, you described for the Court, a very successful career at PMM, a prestigious international accounting firm and you stated that you left that firm to start one that had no clients. Isn't it true that you were terminated by PMM?

Regan: No sir, I had just been promoted into the firm's management group and, when I resigned, the partners that I reported to each asked me to please reconsider, but I chose not to and left in the fall of 1973.

Davis: Now let's address this mystery box of Air West documents. I want to remind you that you are under oath. Isn't it true that you do know who or what organization sent you this box of documents to you?

Regan: No sir, I have no idea.

Davis continued his cross of me, but he was severely handicapped by the truth and his string of previous statements to the Judge Zirpoli about Hughes's lack of participation and knowledge about the closing adjustments, as well as his lack of knowledge of accounting in general both of which had now been exposed as blatantly untrue. This handicap was doubly difficult because of his evident participation in this charade and resulting conflict of interest.

After a relatively short cross-examination, Davis ended quietly with:

Davis: I have no further questions your honor.

By the end of my testimony, it was clearly established that the closing adjustments required by Hughes violated the purchase agreement's requirement that the closing assets and liabilities of Air West be established using accounting methods that were consistent with those used by the merged airlines at July 31, 1968, and that the assets and liabilities that were established at the closing violated the purchase agreement because they were no longer presented in accordance with generally accepted accounting principles that were consistent with those standards.

During my testimony, Ted Russell met with the handwriting expert who was in the audience portion of the courtroom and told him that his testimony would not be needed. However, rather than leave, he was excited to see how the arguments played out and how the judge would decide the issues. Neither attorney had further witnesses. I think my heart started racing at this time. Had my testimony been enough to secure justice?

Judge Zirpoli stated that he would announce his decision on the plaintiffs' demand for a default judgment against Summa, Hughes Air, and Howard R. Hughes on January 15, 1975. He stated that these findings and conclusions would be based, in large part, on the failure of Howard R. Hughes to appear for his deposition on both May 29, 1974, and October 31, 1974, after having been ordered to do so. He added that this decision would be based, in large measure, on the relevance of Hughes's likely testimony as to the facts and circumstances at issue in this litigation.

Judge Zirpoli then informed counsel for the shareholders' that they would submit written arguments supporting a default judgment and sanctions against the Defendants in this matter, Howard Hughes and his wholly owned companies, Hughes Air and Summa Corp. These arguments would be filed with the Court no later than Tuesday, December 31, 1974. The proposed findings should include the basis for such findings and, should the shareholders prevail, a determination of the amounts to be awarded from defendants. The Judge then instructed the defendants to submit a response brief to the Court no later than January 8.

Final arguments by counsel for the shareholders and the

Defendants would begin at 9:30 a.m. on Wednesday, January 15, 1975. The end…for now.

Together with two paralegals, Li Qiang, Clark, Russell, and I left the courtroom and proceeded to get into taxi cabs to return to the Transamerica building. We all then assembled in the firm's large conference room on the twenty-first floor. We were exhausted, relieved, and overjoyed. The day could not have gone better for the shareholders. The group collectively relived how Chester Davis lost it when he objected to Exhibit 3 and admitted that Howard Hughes wrote the blue comments. To add to that bombshell admission, Davis admitted that he was the Chester that Hughes was addressing in his notes. Finally, Judge Zirpoli had concluded that Davis was acting as Hughes's enforcer and "fix-it man," not as his attorney. This was all celebrated by the group with great joy.

We expressed our respect and admiration at the poise and skills with which John Clark orchestrated and executed the entire proceeding. The team also congratulated me on my multi-year effort to bring these accounting issues forward, starting in 1971 and continuing through the afternoon by presenting complex accounting issues clearly and convincingly. We all celebrated that this time, truth won, and justice prevailed.

CHAPTER 34

THE KREMLIN'S MESSAGE

"I eat death threats for breakfast!"

—*MIRIAM DEFENSOR-SANTIAGO*

IN DECEMBER OF 1974, one more reason to cancel Project Matador surfaced. Six months after the recovery mission was completed. The U.S. Navy held its annual holiday party for foreign naval attachés in Bethesda, Maryland. During the party, the Soviet naval attaché briefly met with the U.S. Navy liaison officer for foreign naval attachés. Once they were alone, the Soviet officer alerted the U.S. representative that the Kremlin knew that the U.S. had tried to raise the K-129. Then in no uncertain terms, he told the U.S. representative that he had a message from the Kremlin, "If you go back, it will mean war."

When Director Colby was informed of this conversation, he called Carl Duckett, deputy Director of the CIA, to his office, to reiterate these words and the underpinning message.

Colby informed Duckett that after the Soviets watched the US mission for more than two weeks, they returned not long after the HGE left the site. They brought in their equivalent of the Seawolf with its fish-like cameras and bang, they spotted that there were sections of the K-129 sitting on the bottom of the ocean, primarily the portion past the sail toward the stern. In addition, some of the photographs certainly picked up the bottom portion of the Clementine that we left behind. That clearly informed them of the retrieval mission *and* retrieval of the forward portion of the sub. It was logical for them to suspect a return to the site for the stern portion. That's why the Soviet naval attaché briefly met with the U.S. Navy liaison officer for foreign naval attachés and dropped the "if you go back it will mean war" warning.

Duckett assured Colby that the unrecovered portions of the K-129 may have been viewed, but the Kremlin still had incomplete data and information on what the mission did recover. Duckett and Colby decided not to return to the site for fear of signaling to the Soviets that there was more valuable information to recover, and of course, not to risk World War III.

The Soviets would conduct an intensive study to identify any vulnerabilities that might have been gained from the U.S. having recovered the forward portion of the sub.. This would force them to perform workarounds and major revisions to eliminate those vulnerabilities, costing them years of time and effort, and billions of dollars.

Duckett urged Colby to set up a meeting with Henry Kissinger and Secretary of Defense Schlesinger in order to deliver an update on both Project AZORIAN and Project MATADOR. They would also mention the threat from the Soviets and advice on where we go from here.

CHAPTER 35

CELEBRATING AT THE RESTAURANT ACROSS FROM THE MORGUE

"Where there is unity there is always victory."

—*PUBLILIUS SYRUS*

THE TEAM OF John Clark, Ted Russell and I were energized by the success we had achieved during the November 14 hearing. Now it was time to plead for a default judgment against Howard Hughes and his wholly owned defendants, Summa Corporation and Hughes Air.

Since Hughes owned one hundred percent of Summa Corporation and Hughes Air, John Clark's clients, the Trustees of A.W. Liquidating Company, only needed a full judgment from Hughes. Assuming the trustees were fully compensated for their losses by Howard Hughes, they did not care if he decided to take any portion of that award from either Summa or Hughes Air.

One of the key benefits of a party winning a default judgment against an opposing party is that the successful party is entitled to the benefit of all reasonable inferences from the evidence tendered. Also, the party against whom a default has been entered is barred from attacking the validity of the allegations deemed proven by the Court. In other words, the winner of a default judgment gets all reasonable inferences from the evidence presented and the defendant is essentially helpless. The logic behind this result is that a contrary rule would work to the benefit of the party who has obstructed the rightful prosecution of wrongdoing by refusing to cooperate with the judicial process (such as the willful failure to appear for a properly ordered deposition) would be repugnant to the American system of justice.

Based upon my testimony, related exhibits, and rulings by Judge Zirpoli at the November 14, 1974 hearing, we were armed with the belief that Judge Zirpoli now knew that Hughes and Davis had:

1. Wrongly failed to appear for his properly ordered depositions on May 29, 1974, and October 31, 1974, which were not a circus but rather a legitimate discovery effort by the shareholders' counsel.

2. Filed a blatantly false statement with the Court in connection with Hughes's summary judgment motion to persuade the Court that Hughes knew nothing of the accounting issues and other matters complained of in this ligation and falsely stated that the purpose of the depositions was merely to harass Hughes.

3. Falsely stated that Hughes had no knowledge of the closing accounting adjustments when, in fact, Hughes and Davis had orchestrated these adjustments which violated the Purchase Contract and enabled Hughes to pay Air West's shareholders millions less than the amount called for in the Purchase Contract.

Based upon these factors, John Clark and Ted Russell laid out the Finding of Facts, which firmly supported a default judgment to be rendered by Judge Zirpoli against Hughes. They argued that the resulting reasonable inferences to which A.W. Liquidating Company was now entitled, were the following:

1. On or about December 31, 1968, Air West and Hughes entered into a written agreement entitled and referred to as the "Purchase Contract."

2. Pursuant to the Purchase Contract, Hughes agreed to purchase, and Air West agreed to sell to Hughes or its designee, all the property and assets of Air West, except specific identified items, set forth in the Purchase Contract.

3. Except as prevented by defendants, Air West had performed all its obligations pursuant to the Purchase Contract and, transferred to Hughes all of the property and assets of Air West as called for by the Purchase Contract.

4. Under section 1.2(a) of the Purchase Contract, Hughes was obligated to pay to Air West in exchange for all its property and assets at least $89,398,091.20.

5. The net amount paid to and received by Air West in exchange for all of its property and assets was $41,398.091.20, and defendant Hughes has failed and refused to pay any part of the remaining $48 million due and payable to Air West under the terms of the Purchase Contract.

6. By reason of the foregoing, Air West was damaged in the amount of $48 million, plus interest.

Ted Russell finalized the Motion for Default Judgment and

resulting findings. This document was ready before Christmas Day, but he and John Clark chose to wait until the filing deadline on December 31 to submit it to Judge Zirpoli and Chester Davis.

On the evening of January 8, 1975, the Defendants' response was filed with the Court, with a copy to John Clark. It conceded nothing and continued to seek summary judgment on behalf of Hughes's interests against A. W. Liquidating Company. Chester Davis, consistent with his past and his reputation, never backed down and continued to attack his opponents. He renewed his arguments that the use of documents stolen from Hughes's office which led to the introduction of evidence against the Defendants, was inadmissible. Finally, he argued that such documents were inadmissible because the attorney-client privilege protected them from being introduced as evidence.

Wednesday, January 15, 1975 was a thrilling day for our team. Each of us dressed in our finest suits, ties and shirts, and polished shoes, eager to hear Judge Zirpoli's rulings.

John Clark's opening statement was short, well-structured, and well presented. He summarized the key Findings of Fact, then presented the resulting reasonable inferences flowing from a default judgment. In the end, he indicated that the Plaintiffs were entitled to an award from Mr. Hughes of $48 million, plus interest, which totaled more than $70 million.

When it came to Chester Davis's turn, he rose with a rumble and a fury. Claiming to have been insulted by John's presentation, he began preaching like an evangelist at the height of his sermon. In the end, he declared that all the findings presented were an abuse on the court, based on documents stolen from his client's office. He passionately argued stated, "These thieves should not be rewarded. Howard Hughes saved Air West and its shareholders. They should have gotten nothing for their worthless airline, and they should be thankful that Mr. Hughes gave them $48 million for their bankrupt airline."

Looking exhausted after his diatribe, he took his seat, wiping his sweaty brow with a handkerchief.

The courtroom sat silent and waited for Judge Zirpoli to respond to the two completely opposite presentations. Looking principally at Chester Davis, the judge unloaded. He had obviously done his homework, and he revealed his undergraduate and legal education at the University of California at Berkeley by stating:

I have never seen so many lawyers appearing on behalf of the defendant - I mean not only counsel appearing in court, but counsel on the briefs and writing on the briefs—as I have seen in this litigation. The Hughes interests, such as they are, are able to engage substantial numbers of attorneys to present innumerable objections and motions. In fact, you completely outflank the Plaintiffs in that respect. The Court has a very distinct feeling and reaction that there is a continuous effort to obstruct the procedures in this case, evidenced all the way through, starting with the depositions, the failure to appear for depositions, the excuses offered which the Court deems to be entirely without merit. Attempting to apply orderly judicial processes to Hughes is like twisting with a ghost.

Hughes's immunity from examination by governmental bodies and the judicial system is an American phenomenon. The presidents of great American corporations have been summoned before Congressional committees or required to give testimony in court, and Vice President Spiro Agnew was brought before the judicial bench. But Hughes has two potent inquiry-repellants working on his behalf.

One is his uniquely reclusive lifestyle. Not even the top executives of his enterprises see him face to face, and it is said that he has never attended a board meeting of any of his companies...

Government agencies, which can invoke sanctions against a recalcitrant witness, have shied from any such test of wills with Hughes. He has been a financial benefactor to many members of Congress and has ingratiated himself at the highest levels of the executive branch with open and hidden contributions. He has gained and diligently exploited "access" to the White House, to Cabinet officers, to powerful Congressional leaders. His objections to having the 1969 reform law applied to his private medical foundation were presented directly to the White House and immediately forwarded by President Nixon's counsel, John Dean, to the Under Secretary of the Treasury. Attorney General John Mitchell granted two private conferences to a Hughes emissary when the Justice Department blocked further Hughes purchases of Nevada casinos. Mitchell overruled his own antitrust division in Hughes's favor.

Such favorable responses by top Federal authorities send subliminal messages down the Federal structure. The messages do not have to be spelled out, and usually aren't. Bureaucracies being what they are, for any lower echelon official to insist upon punitive action against a man as well-connected as Hughes would require a rare excess of courage. Equality under the law is an American ideal, but some Americans are more equal than others. Particularly in the Nixon years, when the Federal agencies were intensely politicized, it is doubtful that there was any American citizen that was more equal than Howard Hughes.

Judge Zirpoli then laid down the hammer on Davis and Hughes.

It is time that Hughes pays the piper for his bad behavior. He and his counsel are going to be held to account for their shenanigans in my court. I have studied the Plaintiffs findings and their related motions. I conclude that a default judgment is clearly appropriate in this matter and that the inferences asked by Plaintiffs are reasonable based on the proposed Finding of Fact. As a result, I order that Mr. Hughes pay the Plaintiffs $48 million, plus interest at the legal rate of 7 percent, to be calculated from April 3, 1970 to the date payment is due which shall be January 31, 1975 [approximately $1.1 billion in 2020 dollars].

With that opinion, almost five years of extreme tension, hard work, frustration, and uncertainty had come to an end. The combined plaintiffs' and defendants' massive collection of attorneys, associates, paralegals, and other attendees packed up their files, charts, and boxes of documents. Once completed, they left the nineteenth floor of the Federal Building. The members of both sides ignored each other completely as if they became invisible.

Everyone on John Clark's team assembled in Pettit & Martin's large conference room in the Transamerica Pyramid. John got a count of those able to attend a late celebratory lunch at the Blue Fox, only a half a block west of the Pyramid and famously known as the "restaurant across from the morgue." It served wonderful French food (escargot, frog legs, duckling flambe with tasty sauces) and was regularly listed as one of the country's top restaurants by the Mobil guides. When Bing Crosby, Joe DiMaggio, and Marilyn Monroe lived in nearby Hillsborough, they became regulars at this posh and lively restaurant.

At the Blue Fox, the entire team was both relieved and ecstatic. We had all done our part. We knew that John respected us for our skills, effort, and integrity, and each of us respected him and were in awe of his skills and dedication to the effort to take on one of the richest and most powerful men in the world, who was defended by a pit bull, with unlimited funds and a willingness to flaunt justice. Through our tireless efforts and dedication to justice, we sank the shark. Hughes paid the judgment by check. When I had the chance to hold it in my hand, I smiled for having been so fortunate to have had such an unforgettable experience.

EPILOGUE

Howard R. Hughes

On the morning of April 5, 1976, an official of the Howard Hughes Medical Institute telephoned the chairman of the Methodist Hospital's department of internal medicine, Dr. Henry McIntosh. Dr. McIntosh was informed that Hughes was seriously ill in Acapulco and was to be flown to Houston that afternoon. Dr. McIntosh set aside a heavily guarded room for Hughes. Hughes never made it to that room. He died during the flight to Houston Intercontinental Airport of chronic kidney failure. He was 70 years old at the time of his death.

Project AZORIAN

Following the spread of rumors among the press, articles about Project AZORIAN began appearing in the *Los Angeles Times* on February 7, 1975, and the next day in the New York Times. Journalist Jack Anderson detailed the CIA's first reasonably accurate account of the effort to retrieve the Soviet ballistic missile submarine on his national radio show on March 18, 1975.

The Soviet ambassador to the United States, Antoly Dobrynin, on March 29, 1975, sent a communication to Secretary of State Dr. Henry Kissinger:

Moscow paid attention to the reports in foreign press, including the American press, regarding the fact that certain U.S. services have conducted for some time the work of raising the Soviet submarine that sunk in 1968 in the open sea in the area northwest of Hawaii. According to these reports, the operation had been carried out by a special U.S. ship, the Hughes Glomar Explorer. It was reported, in particular, that a part of the submarine has been recovered some time ago with the bodies of the crew members, that were thrown out into the sea."

It goes without saying that we cannot be indifferent to any operation of raising any parts and property of the submarine belonging to the USSR.

Special concern is caused by the fact that the bodies of the crew members of the sunken submarine, according to the press reports, were recovered and then thrown back into the sea. The matters related to the submarine and to the submarine and the dead seamen are the prerogatives of the Soviet Union alone.

We expect from the U.S. side explanations with regard to the above-mentioned reports, including complete information about the crew members of the sunken submarine and also information on the discontinuance of any operations connected with the submarine.

Dr. Kissinger sent a communique to President Gerald Ford on April 2 informing him of Dobrynin's communication telling President Ford that he intended to respond orally to the Soviet ambassador with the following statement:

The United States has issued no official comment on the matters related to the vessel Hughes Glomar Explorer. It is the policy of this government not to confirm, deny or otherwise comment on alleged intelligence activities. This is a practice followed by all governments, including the USSR. Regardless of press speculation, there will be no official position on this matter.

Despite this official position of the United States government, as the press reports detailed the exploits of Project AZORIAN and its extraordinary achievements, morale within the CIA soared and pride in those achievements filtered throughout the organization. This result had significant value since, at that time, morale and pride within the CIA had become known as a "time of troubles" with a dark cloud hanging over the agency from its other, less successful activities. These revelations provided the members of the agency a remarkable achievement that was worthy of praise, and for which they could be proud.

The Security Guard and the Burglary

Following Jack Anderson's broadcast on March 18, 1975 of details about project AZORIAN that were more compelling and accurate than previous reports there was a flurry of reports, from many sources. Reporters flocked to those involved with the burglary in their attempt to find another big scoop. They interviewed Mike Davis, the actual name of the security guard, which I changed to Jefferson so my references to him would not be confused with Chester Davis.

During this flurry of news Mike Davis reported that he had picked up a $100,000 certificate of deposit, and a copy of a top-secret memorandum between Hughes and the CIA. Davis was reported to have said that "the burglars must have dropped these documents, I picked them up and jammed them into my pocket and in all the excitement that followed with the arrival of the police and everything, I forgot that I had the documents. It was just an absent-minded thing."

He further reported that the memo gave the details of an arrangement in which Hughes, under contract with the CIA, lifted part of a sunken Soviet submarine from the ocean floor. He kept the certificate of deposit for a period but later gave it to the police. As for the Hughes/CIA memorandum, Davis stated that he "tore up the memo and flushed it down the toilet."

The Air West Box

In 1980, Ted Russell received an unsolicited telephone call from a person who stated he was with the CIA. He asked Ted if he was curious about the Air West box that Paul Regan had received at his office six years earlier. Ted responded that the whole Air West team working on the case, including Paul, had been curious about that fortuitous mystery for years. The caller filled Ted in about the whole story of the Air West box and the circuitous route that it took from the Romaine building to Paul Regan's office. He included that the CIA memo was returned to its headquarters in Langley, Virginia.

John B. Clark, Esq.

John continued a successful and expansive international career as an attorney, mediator, and arbitrator. I must reiterate that he was a friend and mentor until the day he died and will be remembered for his legacy of fairness and justice served.

Theodore Russell. Esq.

Ted became the chairman of Pettit & Martin and guided it through the aftermath of a tragic shooting at its offices in 1995 by a crazed ex-client who opened fire with automatic weapons killing nine people and wounding six. Russell was not at the Pettit office on the day of the shooting. He died after suffering a heart attack while skiing with his family near Truckee, California. He was 57. Walter Pettit, the firm's founder, called Ted, "a fortress of strength" and "an extraordinary leader in a time of great difficulty."

ABOUT THE AUTHOR

PAUL REGAN WORKED as an expert in forensic accounting-related litigation with John Clark over a span of 40 years. Their work took them to many states and federal jurisdictions throughout the United States. Often John and Paul worked simultaneously on several cases at the same time.

Paul Regan's career in public accounting started in 1968. He is a certified public accountant and is certified in financial forensics. He holds both undergraduate and graduate degrees in accounting. As an accounting expert and forensic consultant, he has testified in more than 125 trials and arbitrations and in more than 225 depositions. He has worked on more than 1,000 complex litigation matters. Many of these have required extensive analysis and determinations involving financial fraud. He has performed these analyses for companies in the private sector, as well as for various state and federal agencies (e.g., FDIC, the Department of Justice, and the SEC). These analyses have involved such companies as: Countrywide, Xerox, Parmalat, Sunbeam, Cisco, Enron, Bernard L. Madoff Investment Securities LLC, and Lehman Brothers.

Paul has been actively involved on many levels with the 40,000-member California Society of Certified Public Accountants (CalCPA) and the more than 450,000-member American Institute of Certified Public Accountants (AICPA). He is a past chair of CalCPA and its Forensic Services Committee. In 2009 he received the CalCPA's Distinguished Service Award for his lifelong contribution to the accounting profession. He is also a past member of AICPA's Governing Council and Forensic and Valuation Services Executive Committee, which is the standard-setting body for the practice of forensic and valuation services.

Paul has written numerous articles and contributed chapters to technical books on various forensic accounting issues. He has been a partner in Hemming Morse, LLC's forensic and financial consulting firm for more than 45 years and is one of its past presidents and chairman of its board.

In service to his community, Paul was elected to the Hillsborough City School District Board of Trustees, where he served for ten years. Then Paul was elected to the town of Hillsborough's City Council, where he served for 12 years, including as its Mayor. In 1995, Paul and his wife Barbara were named Citizens of the Year of the town of Hillsborough, California.

The Forensic is his debut as an author.

CPSIA information can be obtained
at www.ICGtesting.com
Printed in the USA
LVHW072127091121
702920LV00011B/48/J